BECOMING A LEADER IN PRODUCT DEVELOPMENT

AN EVIDENCE-BASED GUIDE TO THE ESSENTIALS

Ebenezer C. Ikonne

Apress®

Becoming a Leader in Product Development: An Evidence-Based Guide to the Essentials

Ebenezer C. Ikonne
Mableton, GA, USA

ISBN-13 (pbk): 978-1-4842-7297-8   ISBN-13 (electronic): 978-1-4842-7298-5
https://doi.org/10.1007/978-1-4842-7298-5

Managing Director: Welmoed Spahr
Acquisitions Editor: Shiva Ramachandran
Development Editor: Matthew Moodie
Coordinating Editors: Rita Fernando and Mark Powers

Cover image by Freepik (www.freepik.com)

Distributed to the book trade worldwide by Springer Science+Business Media New York, 1 New York Plaza, New York, NY 10004. Phone 1-800-SPRINGER, fax (201) 348-4505, e-mail orders-ny@springer-sbm.com, or visit www.springeronline.com. Apress Media, LLC is a California LLC and the sole member (owner) is Springer Science + Business Media Finance Inc (SSBM Finance Inc). SSBM Finance Inc is a **Delaware** corporation.

For information on translations, please e-mail booktranslations@springernature.com; for reprint, paperback, or audio rights, please e-mail bookpermissions@springernature.com.

Apress titles may be purchased in bulk for academic, corporate, or promotional use. eBook versions and licenses are also available for most titles. For more information, reference our Print and eBook Bulk Sales web page at http://www.apress.com/bulk-sales.

Any source code or other supplementary material referenced by the author in this book is available to readers on GitHub via the book's product page, located at www.apress.com/9781484272978. For more detailed information, please visit http://www.apress.com/source-code.

Printed on acid-free paper

For Ada, Odi, Osi, and Obi.
You fill my life with joy.

Contents

About the Author

Dr. Ebenezer C. Ikonne is a practitioner-academic (pracademic) with over 20 years in product development. He is currently a product and engineering leader at Cox Automotive. Ebenezer started his technology career as a network engineer and software developer. He later transitioned into product development leadership and management and has held middle- to senior-level leadership and management positions in large organizations, small corporations, and startups.

Ebenezer has extensive experience leading organizational change and understands the complex challenges leaders face in demanding product development contexts. His experience, coupled with his education, provides him with a unique perspective on how 21st-century product development leaders can become more effective.

Ebenezer is passionate about fostering a positive workplace where people thrive. He regularly speaks on issues relating to leadership, followership, organizational culture, business strategy, product management, and software development. He publishes content both on LinkedIn and at eikonne.wordpress.com. He has also written for the Cutter Consortium. Ebenezer's aptly named YouTube channel "Joy at Work" (http://www.youtube.com/c/JoyatWork) provides practical tips on how anyone can experience joy at work.

You can reach Ebenezer on LinkedIn (http://linkedin.com/in/ebenezer-ikonne) and Twitter (@eikonne).

Acknowledgments

Even though a book will only have a handful of authors on its cover, many people contribute to its creation. Directly and indirectly. It is no different in this case. Many people have contributed to this book.

I must thank my parents, Chiemela and Chinyere, who nurtured the love of learning in me and set me on this path. They taught me the importance of hard work, critical thinking, and challenging the status quo. Outstanding and accomplished educators and even better parents, I can proudly say I learned from the best. Thank you, Mom and Dad.

My grandfather, Alson Woma Ikonne, told me I would someday write books. Sadly, he is not here to see this book published, but his belief in me continues to inspire me. Rest in peace, Papa.

I looked forward to sending a copy of this book to my doctoral chair, Dr. Gary Oster. His research and writing suggestions, feedback, and encouragement during my doctoral program—where the idea for a book gained momentum—helped me immensely. Unfortunately, Dr. Oster passed away before the publication of this book. I remain forever grateful to him.

I am indebted to several people who gave me feedback on different parts of my manuscript. Amy Balog, Jim Kimball, Marcin Floryan, Astrid Claessen, Ruth Malan, Heidi Araya, and Dan Sloan generously gave their time to review a book draft by a first-time author when they could have spent that time doing other things. Their constructive criticism was invaluable as it pushed me to try and improve delivery and content. Any shortcomings in the book are solely mine. Their feedback provided me with new perspectives and caused me to deepen my commitment to particular perspectives. For their contributions, I will always remain grateful. To my brother and friend, Frederick Nwanganga, thanks for the advice and guidance throughout the book-writing process.

I have had the privilege of working with several excellent leaders throughout my career, and I have told some of their stories in this book. However, I specifically want to thank Sam Addeo and Michael Noel, who helped me at critical stages of my career. Sam was the first leader to show me that caring for people and achieving desired organizational outcomes did not have to be at odds with each other. Michael took a chance on me (twice) by giving me opportunities to lead in challenging contexts. I would not be the leader I am today without Sam as a role model and Michael as a sponsor. I owe much of whatever professional success I have achieved to them.

I am also grateful to the leaders who provided examples of leaders we need less of in organizations. Without their examples, I could not have distinguished between effective and ineffective leaders. When I was half-awake at 3 a.m. trying to write, but low on energy and desire, I would often remember my experiences with these leaders and then magically find the energy to stay the course. Hopefully, this book contributes to increasing the number of effective leaders in the workplace.

I have been privileged to lead and follow hundreds of people across several organizations in various domains and industries throughout my career. I have led in good times and bad times and yet I have always been blessed to work with great people. I want to thank the organizations that have provided me with the opportunity to lead. I am even more grateful to every individual who has been part of an organization I led who has given me feedback (constructive and not so constructive) that has aided my development. I am a better leader today because of all these experiences, and without these experiences, I would not have these stories to tell.

I also want to thank my Apress publishing team. Shiva, for working with me from the onset. Mark, for keeping me on top of the book project schedule. Matthew, for reviewing my manuscripts and giving me feedback. I truly appreciate everything you have all done to make sure this book is published.

Most importantly, I would like to thank my wife, Ada, for her support during this entire process. She read the manuscript multiple times and patiently gave me feedback. In addition, she made sure I had space and time to write. Without her loving support, words of encouragement, and belief in me, this book would not exist. Nwanyim, imela.

Introduction

Everything has been said before, but since nobody listens we have to keep going back and beginning all over again.

—Andre Gide[1]

I believe the pertinent leadership question of our time is not "are you a leader?" Instead, it is "what type of leader are you?" How you consistently lead others ultimately determines what kind of leader you are. Unfortunately, it does seem like there are too many ineffective leaders in the workplace. In one study that sought to understand what would make American employees happier at work, 65% of Americans preferred having a new manager over 35% who preferred receiving more money.[2] Jim Gallup suggests that a leading source of employee dissatisfaction and disengagement in the workplace is their manager.[3] Sadly, the statistics suggest it is more likely than not that you are not the effective leader you might think you are. Here is a question for you: If given a choice, would your team(s) follow your lead voluntarily? Regardless of how you answered the question, the fact is there is a shortage of effective leaders in the workplace. Unfortunately, many executives are so focused on immediate results that they pay little to no attention to how leaders throughout the organization lead. And as a result, tens, hundreds, and even thousands of demotivated and disengaged people show up to work every day. Organizations, including product development organizations, succeed "in spite of" mediocre leaders.

And yet, it does not have to be this way. Research shows that leader behaviors do impact team member engagement.[4] So, if you want to positively impact the people you lead and help your firm succeed, this book will help you do those things. Facilitating the leadership process is serious business, especially when an organization assigns you to a leader role (like a manager, director, vice president, etc.). The organization has given you one of its most critical and consequential jobs, regardless of where the role sits in the organization's

---

[1] Andre Gide, *Le Traité du Narcisse*, (1892).
[2] Lynn Munroe, "Two-Thirds of America Unhappy at Job," http://www.prweb.com/releases/2012/10/prweb10013402.htm
[3] Jim Clifton, "The World's Broken Workplace," https://news.gallup.com/opinion/chairman/212045/world-broken-workplace.aspx (last accessed 19 July 2020).
[4] Vivi Gusrini Rahmadani, Wilmar B. Schaufeli, Jeroen Stouten, "How Engaging Leaders Foster Employees' Work Engagement," *Leadership and Organization Development Journal* 41, no. 8 (2020): 1155-1169.

structure. By asking you to lead people and teams, the organization has placed the well-being of other employees and their families in your care. And by accepting this role, you commit to the well-being of these individuals, even as everyone works together to achieve organizational goals. Becoming an effective leader requires an ethical and moral commitment to the conscious and unconscious needs of the group(s) you lead.

You must understand your leadership context—the product development context and other contexts that you interact with. You need to understand your business and its objectives, the national cultures represented on your team(s), the different organizational cultures present, and a host of other leadership elements. For example, sometimes, you will need to mobilize organizational cultural change as part of the leadership process. At other times you will need to adapt your leader behaviors to flourish within the constraints of the cultures that comprise your firm. Understanding how to work within your context is essential if you want to maximize your impact on the organization. You would not entrust your health to a doctor who does not have a solid understanding of how the body works. Why would you lead without an understanding of how organizations function?

While many leadership theories—authentic, transformational, leader-member exchange—exist for you to choose from, servant leadership and adaptive leadership provide a set of leader behaviors I consider central to making a difference as a leader. These theories will help you become more effective and impactful regardless of the scope of your leadership position. Many leaders self-identify as servant leaders without understanding servant leadership's radical requirements. Servant leadership is a countercultural approach that requires you to focus on meeting people's needs and enabling them to address the organization's needs. It is a people-first approach to leading.

Leadership is not about maintaining the status quo. Instead, effective leaders facilitate the movement of their organization from its current position to a new (and hopefully) better position. Adaptation is inevitable if you intend for your organization to continue to thrive. If you have learned a new musical instrument, run a marathon, or even embarked on a healthier lifestyle program, you know that making meaningful changes is hard. In a product development setting, meaningful change can include adopting new "ways of working" during a pandemic, reorganizing teams, offering new products and services, overhauling hiring practices, and even going through a wholesale change in strategy or identity. These changes necessitate a change in team members' attitudes, beliefs, and behaviors. Practicing adaptive leadership will help you become more effective at leading your organization through change.

Effective leaders are also effective followers. They support the goals of the organization but are not afraid to appropriately challenge their leaders. As followers, they recognize that leadership depends on complementary followership. Unfortunately, leadership discourse does not pay as much attention to the importance of effective followership as it needs to. Many leaders do not recognize the importance of following their peers, partners, and followers. Understanding how to excel in the follower role is critical to effective leadership, and your leadership practice will benefit from adopting effective followership behaviors. By practicing good followership behaviors, you also show your team members how they can become more effective followers.

Practicing the leader behaviors outlined in this book will require that you pour yourself into the work of leading, and this will be stressful at times. Leading from a place of empathy and care is not a bed of roses. For example, you may need to "coach out" an individual from the organization because they cannot effectively perform their job after you have provided them with all the resources they need to succeed. In addition, negative stress can lead to poor health that hampers your effectiveness as a leader. Learning how to practice self-care will help you manage your stress. It is challenging to meet the needs of the people you serve when you have unmet needs.

Throughout this book, I share experiences that illustrate the negative and positive impacts of ineffective and effective leader behaviors. These stories draw from my experiences and the experiences of various product development leaders that I have observed.[5] I initially thought becoming a leader meant making sure my team achieved goals solely through commands and directives. However, after nearly two decades of hands-on practice leading teams in diverse contexts and spending years researching and studying leaders, leadership, and followership, my understanding of what it means to lead effectively has (and continues to) evolved. I have observed leaders that served as catalysts and leaders that served as inhibitors. My leadership practice changed as I learned through new experiences. Now I am sharing vital practices that will be game changers for you.

And yet, I see the challenges that might come with a book like this. First is that people might use the ideas in the book to promote the notion that organizational success depends solely on leaders and that effective leadership results solely from effective leaders. Nothing could be further from the truth. I am yet to see an organization that was successful solely because of its leaders. (I have, however, watched groups find ways to succeed despite ineffective leaders.) Each part—and the interactions between the parts—of the leadership system is vital to leadership effectiveness. Effective leaders are necessary for organizational excellence but not sufficient. You can either make the leadership process enjoyable or make it a burden. The choice is yours.

Another challenge is that you might conclude that I am attempting to create a perfect leader—a unicorn. The perfect leader does not exist because we are all imperfect. Every leader makes mistakes. I continue to make mistakes, and you will make mistakes as well. We will respond poorly in certain situations.

---

[5] The names in these stories have been changed to protect the innocent.

We will use our positional power when some other form of power would have been more effective. We will jump to conclusions when we needed to engage with curiosity. We will be slow to make a change because the change is uncomfortable for us. I am not in the business of creating perfect leaders; instead, I desire to provide leaders like you with knowledge and behaviors that can help you improve, learn from your mistakes, and become more effective. If you know the behaviors that lead to positive leadership outcomes, you can work at them. Leadership is a profession. It is a continual journey that we continually get better at.

Many other factors impact the leadership process. Factors such as organizational rewards and incentives, business climate, organizational structure, and even other people (including leaders) in your organization, to mention a few. Many of these factors may be outside of your control and influence depending on your role in your organization. These factors can even prevent the leadership process from achieving its desired goals. Leaders, at all levels, belong to systems that govern what they can (and cannot) do. For example, you might not be able to give someone a raise on a whim even though you know they deserve it. And yet, the one thing that is largely in your control is how you show up as a leader.

I am convinced that adopting the recommended practices in this book will help you become a better leader. But I must also warn you that these practices are not popular in many organizations (and that might include yours). Coercive and brute force methods yield results (albeit at the expense of the human spirit). Hence, do not be surprised if your superiors and peers consider you soft, slow, weak, and even overprotective—I know how it feels. However, I challenge you to have the courage to remain faithful to the leader you want to become—a leader positively impacting those you lead. It is the right thing to do, and you will experience fulfillment and satisfaction from doing so.

I recognize that I have given you a lot to take in, so I urge you to consider this book a leadership resource you frequently reference. After reading Chapters 1 and 2, you can read the book in any order that you choose. Commit to adopting one or two behaviors from each chapter. Deliberately practice these behaviors until they become part and parcel of your leadership approach and then identify new behaviors to adopt. Pay attention to the "Takeaways." Those you lead will acknowledge a change in how you show up as a leader if you adopt these recommendations. Good luck on your leadership journey. I hope you leave a lasting leadership legacy that people will not forget because of the positive difference you made in their lives. Fostering a product development environment where people experience joy sets the stage for excellent performance. Good luck fostering and experiencing "Joy at Work."

Why Assigned Leaders

He that thinketh he leadeth, and hath no one following, is only taking a walk.

—Benjamin L. Hooks

Leadership is familiar, but not well understood.

—Gerald Weinberg

I could not believe what my manager was saying to me while I sat in his office. I had not seen this coming. How could it be that I was doing such a terrible job leading my engineering team? What did he mean by this? I mean, I had been a stellar software engineer before being promoted into a managerial leadership position. Everyone had appreciated my work in my previous role and would ask for my help whenever they had problems. I had been the resident technical expert on several systems in our organization, and I had never received this amount of negative feedback from anyone in the organization. Never. But here I was in this strange position where everyone on my team was unhappy that I was the leader. They wanted me out of the role. The truth was that I did not understand how to lead effectively and

© Ebenezer C. Ikonne 2021

E. C. Ikonne, *Becoming a Leader in Product Development*,
https://doi.org/10.1007/978-1-4842-7298-5_1

ethically. Fortunately, I had a manager who was a seasoned leader, and that first feedback session set me on a different leadership path.

The Gerald Weinberg quote at the beginning of this chapter says it all. There is much talk about leadership, and yet leadership is not well understood. So many people find themselves in organizational leadership positions without being adequately equipped to lead others. We expect medical doctors and lawyers to receive robust training before they practice and we engage them in their services. Yet, we have no problem putting people in leadership positions without adequately preparing them and providing them with the resources for the job. If leadership were well and adequately understood and practiced, poor leadership would not be one of the top causes of employee dissatisfaction in the workplace. Unfortunately, our leadership approach lacks the focus and attention it deserves, and the results are often dire. Jim Clifton goes as far as to observe that "employees everywhere don't necessarily hate the company or organization they work for as much as they do their boss."[1] What a sad state of affairs!

My story shows that I was that leader, causing significant dissatisfaction for team members without even knowing it. Unfortunately, my story is not the exception—it is the rule. Maybe it is your story as well. Maybe, like me, you have leadership responsibility for product development teams but were not provided with adequate leadership knowledge and practices. Maybe you have only experienced and seen poor leadership for most of your career or muddled your way through leadership challenges to become a decent leader eventually. The good news is that it is possible to become a more effective leader, and this book will provide you the tools you need to do that.

But before we can talk about adopting new leadership approaches and becoming a more impactful product development leader, it is essential to revisit leadership and the leader's role in the leadership process. First, you need to understand aspects of leadership that you must grapple with, such as power, influence, and authority. Popular culture often positions management (and managers) as lesser than leadership (and leaders), but is this correct? Second, understanding the relationship between leadership and management is essential. Without a solid understanding of leadership, it is hard to lead others well. This chapter equips you with the foundational leadership constructs essential for a successful leadership career. Let us start by attempting to define leadership.

---

[1] Jim Clifton, "The World's Broken Workplace," https://news.gallup.com/opinion/chairman/212045/world-broken-workplace.aspx (last accessed July 19, 2020).

What Is Leadership?

Ask 15 different people, "what is leadership?" and you will most likely receive 15 different responses—everyone is a leadership expert. A Google search for "leadership" returns thousands of articles on the topic. Peter Northouse, who has written one of the more popular academic texts on leadership, notes that leadership is highly valued and extraordinarily complex.[2] Northouse accounts for over a dozen distinct leadership theories. One-liner definitions of leadership are, at best, a slice of the truth and, at worst, a gross simplification that does not take into consideration the moving parts of the leadership process. Leadership is a complex phenomenon occurring in complex settings. Simplistic definitions or conceptualizations can lead you to incorrectly adopt a single definition without appreciating the various contexts under which leadership occurs. Leadership scholars Bruce Winston and Kathleen Patterson identified 90 distinct dimensions for leadership.[3] Leadership is challenging to define and describe. Anyone who suggests otherwise would benefit from an in-depth study of leadership.

Before trying to establish what leadership might be, I must share assumptions about leadership that limit our understanding of the leader's role. D. Scott Rue does a fantastic job outlining four limiting assumptions that you should remember:[4]

1. Conflating leadership with hierarchical supervision: While this book focuses on leaders occupying hierarchical supervision positions, hierarchical supervision and leadership are not synonymous. Occupying a hierarchical supervisory role does not make you a leader.

2. Portraying leadership as one-directional influence: Many consider leadership a one-way process where a leader influences others, and that is it. However, leadership involves bi-directional influence.

3. Depicting leadership as a personal attribute: Treating leadership as a personal attribute might be the most limiting and pervasive assumption because it ties leadership back to an individual(s), the leader(s). The result is that people, who do not think they are leaders, do not appreciate and recognize how their actions can positively (or negatively) impact leadership.

---

[2] Peter G. Northouse, *Leadership: Theory and Practice*, 7th ed., (Thousand Oaks, CA: Sage Publications, 2016), 1.

[3] Bruce E. Winston and Kathleen Patterson, "An Integrative Definition of Leadership," *International Journal of Leadership Studies* 1, no. 2 (2006): 6–66.

[4] D. Scott Rue, "Adaptive Leadership Theory: Leading and Following as a Complex Adaptive Process," *Research in Organizational Behavior* 31, (2011): 127–131.

4. Treating the environment as exogenous to the leadership process: Many leadership theories suggest that leaders have to adapt to their environment, which is true. However, it is also true that leadership modifies the environment.

Leadership means different things to different scholars depending on their approach to studying leadership, and so leadership scholars disagree on a single definition of leadership. However, as mentioned above, many scholars now consider leadership more than a set of traits, skills, or behaviors an individual possesses. Instead, many scholars now see leadership as a relational process in which people engage in multidirectional influence.[5] The aspect of "leadership as a process" is vital because it means that leadership requires a two-way interaction between individuals in a group. Leadership is a complex adaptive process consisting of a leading-following dynamic that is socially constructed.[6] Leaders have an impact on the group they lead, and the group impacts their leaders. Effective leadership requires these two-way interactions that ultimately result in the achievement of a shared objective.

The Center for Creative Leadership (CCL) provides additional clarity on the social process aspect of leadership by defining leadership as "the process of producing direction, alignment, and commitment (DAC) in collectives."[7] Leadership occurs as a group agrees on what they intend to achieve, aligns on how they will work together, and commits to working with each other as they strive to achieve group goals. The CCL's definition positions leadership as a responsibility of the group and not just the leader's responsibility (s), i.e., while leaders play a vital role in making leadership happen, leader and leadership are not the same things. Everyone in your group has a part to play in producing direction, alignment, and commitment. Let us look at these aspects of the leadership process next.

Where Are We Going?

In leadership, direction refers to a shared understanding of where the group wants to go. It is an agreement on the objectives the group intends to achieve. Leadership often involves challenging the status quo and moving forward as a group. Direction answers the question of "where do we want to be in the future?" Examples of direction include bringing new products to a specific customer

---

[5] Dennis Tourish, "Is Complexity Leadership Theory Complex Enough?" *SAGE Publications*, (2019): 1.

[6] D. Scott DeRue, "Adaptive Leadership Theory," 131–140.

[7] Cynthia D. McCauley, Ellen Van Velsor, and Marian N. Ruderman, "Introduction: Our View of Leadership Development," in *The Center for Creative Leadership: Handbook of Leadership Development* 3rd ed., ed. Cynthia D. McCauley, Russ S. Moxley, and Ellen Van Velsor (USA: Jossey-Bass, 2010), 20.

segment or improving collaboration on the team to reduce unproductive conflict. Whatever your situation might be, you need to ensure that the collective understands the desired direction. Each team member needs to understand the goal and know that other team members know the goal.[8] Ensure that people appropriately participate in determining direction as this helps them understand the "what" and "why" of the desired direction. Make sure you frequently revisit the direction with your group to keep everyone on the same page.

Working Well Together

Effective leadership produces alignment and coherence. Alignment occurs through cooperation, coordination, and collaboration, and you need to make sure people understand when each interaction best suits the group's challenge. In some cases, individuals will need to work independently on goals specific to them; however, they will need to make sure that they do not inhibit others' progress—this is cooperation. Sometimes individuals have a shared goal but have independent tasks. In these cases, coordination might be the preferred interaction style. Finally, collaboration is often the more appropriate work approach when there is a shared goal and highly interdependent tasks. Coherence happens when all aspects of the work required to achieve the goal come together holistically. Everyone can see how their functions integrate with the functions of other people on the team. Senior Fellow at CCL, Cynthia McCauley, stresses the importance of all aspects of the work fitting together to serve the shared direction.[9]

The instruments in an orchestra or jazz band playing in harmony with one another provide an example of alignment and coherence. Businesses consist of multiple departments with different specializations; departments consist of multiple teams with different focus areas; teams consist of team members with different skill sets. You have alignment and coherence when team members, teams, and departments work together to achieve the shared goal(s). It is your responsibility to ensure that team members understand how their roles and responsibilities support each other. Help team members appreciate how their roles might overlap. Provide them with training opportunities that enhance their collaboration and conflict management skills.

The Collective over the Individual

Commitment emanates from the leadership process. Leadership happens when individuals place group goals above their personal goals because they

---

[8] Cynthia McCauley, "Making Leadership Happen," https://www.ccl.org/articles/ white-papers/making-leadership-happen-alignment/ (last accessed July 19, 2020).
[9] Ibid.

are committed to the group and what the group can achieve. There is commitment when team members go the extra mile to support the collectives' goal even if they have already achieved their personal goal, e.g., software developers help each other finish a task. You need to nurture a workplace that grows organizational commitment by removing demotivators. Providing people with opportunities where they can use their strengths in activities for which they have intrinsic motivation is another way of fostering commitment to the group and its goals.

Leaders often resort to charisma to foster commitment. We have empirical evidence showing that charismatic leaders can inspire employees to tackle lofty organizational goals found in startups and organizations facing an existential dilemma.[10] However, it is critical to remember that charismatic leadership can also have a dark side. Natasha Kaul notes that some charismatic leaders display psychopathic behavior and manipulate team members to their bidding using their charm and charisma.[11] While charisma is not inherently bad, do not focus your energy on developing charisma so you can foster commitment; instead, focus on nurturing an environment where individuals thrive. Have the work and workplace be the source of inspiration and commitment for your teams.

Leadership Through DAC

The goal of leadership is to produce the outcomes of direction, alignment, and commitment. The exciting aspect of viewing leadership this way is that it elevates the "how" of leadership. The definition does not narrow leadership to the actions of a single individual high up in the organization; instead, it recognizes that anyone (or group of individuals) within the collective can contribute to the leadership outcomes of direction, alignment, and commitment. It is your job to make sure that this process occurs and that leadership happens.

Leadership as a System

Because leadership has a purpose and aim, it would not be out of place to describe leadership as a system, and some leadership scholars do precisely that. Leadership scholar Barbara Kellerman described leadership as a system consisting of three different aspects: context, followers, and leaders.[12]

---

[10] Jane Whitney Gibson, John C. Hannon, Charles W. Blackwell, "Charismatic Leadership: The Hidden Controversy," *The Journal of Leadership Studies* 5, no. 4 (1998): 20.

[11] Natasha Kaul, "Charismatic Leadership: Blessing or Curse," *International Journal on Leadership* 1, no. 2 (2013): 12–18.

[12] Barbara Kellerman, *Professionalizing Leadership*, (New York, NY: Oxford University Press, 2018): 123–136.

A discussion on leadership that does not consider these three aspects is not holistic. Unfortunately, as previously stated, much of the leadership material focuses primarily on leader roles in organizations. They ignore the impact that context and followers have on leadership. Effective leaders understand the importance of context and followers within the leadership system. To nurture direction, alignment, and commitment requires understanding the leader role, the follower role, and the surrounding context in which leadership happens. Let us look at three leadership dimensions briefly, starting with context, followed by followers, and finally, leaders, as shown in Figure 1-1.

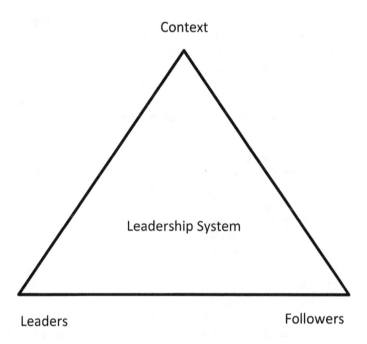

Figure 1-1. Kellerman's Leadership System. Source: from Barbara Kellerman, Professionalizing Leadership, (New York, NY: Oxford University Press, 2018), 123–136

Understanding the Context

Leadership does not happen in isolation. There is always a context in which leadership is occurring. For example, leadership in a church is different from leadership in a Fortune 100 organization. Political leadership differs from business leadership in certain areas. Leadership can even vary for different teams in the same organization. For example, the context for a team engaged in highly creative work (like a product development team) is quite different from that of a team engaged in routine and repetitive work (like an order fulfillment team). Leadership in tightly regulated industries will differ from leadership in loosely regulated industries. Leadership during times of crisis will differ from leadership in times of stability and peace. While upcoming chapters discuss national and organizational culture, it is essential to note that different cultures also impact the context. Thus, leadership will differ depending on national and organizational cultural contexts.

Unfortunately, it is not uncommon for leaders to ignore the various contexts in their organization and attempt to lead their entire organization in the same way. These leaders, for example, apply the same leadership approach to problem-solving departments as they do to production-oriented departments. Production-oriented departments have daily quotas or targets to meet for predominantly repetitive work. On the other hand, problem-solving-oriented departments must tackle new challenges by developing novel solutions. While both types of departments are crucial for organizational success, the nature of their work is different, and so they require different forms of leadership. Leading the entire organization in the same way and having the exact expectations for the departments results in one of the departments facing pressure to work in ways that are not compatible with what the department does. You need to understand your organizational context(s).

So, what might the context look like for you, a product development leader? First, the product development context primarily involves meeting the needs of people through software solutions. People with needs rarely know exactly how to satisfy their needs best; hence, the product development team aims to elicit needs and meet these needs through software. Second, your teams must also deal with an ever-changing technology landscape. Mainstream technologies from a few years ago are now obsolete. Product developers need to keep their skills up to date to remain current. Third, many of the solutions that product developers create are bespoke, i.e., people cannot buy these solutions in the marketplace. Because these solutions do not exist and the teams need to create them, there is always some uncertainty on how long it will take to develop new software. Fourth, the average tenure of a software developer with any organization is somewhere around three years.[13] You must deal with the reality that your organization will face a certain amount of attrition. These are examples of factors just within the product development context. You still need to understand the factors that exist within your broader business context to lead well.

---

[13] "How Long Do Tech Pros Stay in Their Jobs?" https://insights.dice.com/2016/07/08/how-long-do-tech-pros-stay-in-their-jobs/ (last accessed July 19, 2020).

The Importance of Followers

Little is accomplished without the active participation of those whom we do not formally identify as leaders, and yet with all the focus on leaders, you might be led to believe that leaders do all the work. Ask yourself the following questions:

- What percentage of your organization's developmental programs target team members in non-leadership roles?

- What percentage of your organization's developmental programs focus on team development?

It is probably not a high percentage of your organization if your organization is like many other organizations that I have studied. Most companies focus their developmental programs on people in the leader role. Leadership literature pays little attention to followers as it does to leaders.[14] And yet, every successful organization consists of committed team members working hard every day to nudge the organization closer to its objectives.[15] In fact, organizational success depends on the work that these team members do. They produce products that are either sold or used internally. Kellerman calls these team members followers because they have less authority, power, and influence than their superiors.[16] Followers may not be responsible for setting organizational direction. However, without followers, little is achieved.

Unfortunately, the term "follower" carries with it baggage as it evokes images of people who do not think for themselves and just do what their leader says. Followership scholar Robert E. Kelley challenges this description and notes that organizations succeed because they have engaged and skilled employees who apply critical thinking in the workplace.[17] These employees take ownership of developing themselves. They respectfully challenge organizational decisions and identify ways to improve their organization. They care about their team members and the goals of the business. Nonetheless, some in the leadership community remain conflicted on the concept of followers, especially in business organizations.[18] Regardless of what you might think about the term "follower," one thing that we can all accept is that we do not talk enough about the individuals who execute the tasks that result in organizational success.

---

[14] Barbara Kellerman, "The Future of Followership," *Strategy & Leadership* 47, no. 5 (2019): 42.

[15] Stephen C. Lundin and Lynne C. Lancaster, "Beyond Leadership….the Importance of Followership," *The Futurist* 24, no. 3 (1990): 18.

[16] Kellerman, "The Future of Followership," 42.

[17] Ibid.

[18] Jon Aarum Andersen, "On 'Followers' and the Inability to Define," *Leadership & Organization Development Journal* 40, no. 2 (2019): 274.

Effective leadership requires a competent and engaged workforce. The people you lead are a critical part of your leadership system, and you must commit to their development, as we will see in upcoming chapters. It is not enough for you to focus on your competencies and think that this will be enough for the organization. While your team members may not have the degree of power, authority, and influence you have, they still wield a certain amount of power, authority, and influence.[19] For example, software developers have the authority to commit code to a code repository while many executives do not.

There may be nothing more important than hiring individuals with the appropriate attitudes and skills into your organization. Exemplary team members exhibit good judgment, work ethic, competence, honesty, courage, discretion, loyalty, and manage their egos.[20] Your leadership system must provide an environment where team members can do their best work if the organization is to achieve its goals. It is common for many team members to believe that they have no part in the leadership system because of their role. Help followers understand that effective leadership depends on them. Their involvement is crucial. Followers are part of the leadership system and play a pivotal role in creating direction, alignment, and commitment.

The Role of Leaders

This book is for leaders, so it behooves me to pay more attention to the leader element of the leadership system. Leaders have primary responsibility for fostering conditions that lead to direction, alignment, and commitment. Leaders are accountable for organizational goals, which is probably a significant reason for focusing on people in the leader role whenever we think about leadership development. There is no question that effective leaders play an essential role in organizational success. If you do not perform certain activities and perform them well, you negatively impact team member workplace satisfaction and inhibit organizational success. People in assigned leadership roles are the primary stewards of the leadership system of any organization. They need to ensure that the leadership system is achieving the desired purpose. However, there are (at least) two types of leaders in any leadership system, emergent leaders and assigned leaders.

---

[19] Kellerman, "The Future of Followership," 42.
[20] John S. McCallum, "Followership: The Other Side of Leadership," *Ivey Business Journal (Online)*, (2013): 1–4.

Leaders—Emergent and Assigned

A few years ago, there was a morning running class that I attended at my local gym. After a while, I got to know several of the runners pretty well. We had each other's phone numbers and would text each other when one of us did not show up for class. One day I got a text from one of the ladies in the class, let us call her Camille, saying, "our instructor needs to buy herself a microphone for our class. I think it is unfair for the gym to ask her to buy herself a microphone. I would like for us to chip in and buy her a microphone she can use for class. Who's in?" Everyone who received the text responded, indicating their willingness to participate. With a single text, Camille mobilized us to raise money for our instructor's microphone.

In going along with Camille's suggestion, we allowed her to influence our actions to support a proposed goal. She emerged as our leader for a brief period. We followed Camille because we respected her and desired to help our instructor. As Northouse puts it, when people allow themselves to be influenced by an individual, regardless of that individual's title, i.e., it could be someone with less status in the organization, the individual doing the influencing is an emergent leader.[21] Every day, people emerge as leaders in their organizations because they influence those around them.

However, while leaders emerge in many group settings, organizations also assign explicit leadership responsibilities to specific individuals.[22] Examples of assigned leaders in organizations include individuals in roles with titles like "manager," "director," and "president." These leadership roles include certain forms of power and authority that those not in these roles do not have. Individuals in these roles are also the primary steward(s) of their leadership system. For example, if you are the product development team manager, you are the team's assigned leader. If you are the Chief Information Officer for a services firm, you are the assigned technology department leader. It is your responsibility to ensure leadership happens within the group(s) you lead, i.e., leaders ensure the conditions for a healthy leadership system exist. So, while being a leader does not require a formal leader title or role, specific individuals are accountable for the leadership process. But being assigned to a leadership position or role does not guarantee that (a) people will see you as their leader or that (b) you are an effective leader—the impact of your contribution to the leadership process determines that.

---

[21] Northouse, *Leadership: Theory and Practice* 7th ed, 8.
[22] Ibid.

Do We Really Need Assigned Leaders?

People often ask me questions about the assigned leader role. Questions like "why do organizations need assigned leaders in the first place" and "what prevents organizations from organizing like ants?" The largest colony of ants uses algorithmic patterns to maintain its organizational structure despite covering 3700 miles.[23] Why will this not work for human organizations? Why do we need individuals with the assigned responsibility of ensuring direction, alignment, and commitment exist in the organization? My answer? Because it is hard to find many examples of successful businesses that do not have any assigned leaders responsible for maintaining the businesses' long-term viability.

D. Scott Rue proposes that we drop the static label of leader altogether.[24] The rationale for doing so is that leading is not reserved solely for those with formal leader titles. I am sympathetic to this viewpoint, yet I believe it ignores the reality that many social groups have an individual (or individuals) with the explicit responsibility for ensuring the group continues to advance forward. A firm's CEO is ultimately accountable for the organization's advancement. While there is some truth to the notion that everyone is a leader, I do not find the observation beneficial in practice. It is like saying everyone is human. Or everyone is a cook.[25] As long as individuals are specifically assigned to lead, we need to focus on how they can become better at what the organization has asked them to do. Peter Drucker noted that "Only three things happen naturally in organizations: friction, confusion, underperformance. Everything else requires leadership."[26] Some individuals need to facilitate the leadership process. If you are an assigned leader, that is you!

The need for leaders in organizations is the basis of the Law of Organizational Entropy.[27] The Law of Organizational Entropy suggests that when no one has the specific responsibility of making sure direction, alignment, and commitment exist within a group, the group descends into disorder and fails to deliver the results for which the group exists in the first place. Think about some of the groups you have been a part of where no one wanted to take on a leader assignment or the people who took it on were not competent. How well did the group function? Were they able to achieve their shared goals? In all walks of life, we observe that groups struggle to fulfill their purpose without effective

---

[23] "Largest Colony of Ants," https://www.guinnessworldrecords.com/world-records/largest-colony-of-ants/, (last accessed July 19, 2020).

[24] D. Scott DeRue, "Adaptive Leadership Theory," 131–140.

[25] Ok, I know some people who cannot cook!

[26] "Peter Drucker on Leadership," https://journal.accj.or.jp/peter-drucker-on-leadership/, (last accessed July 19, 2020).

[27] "The Law of Organizational Entropy and Faculty Innovators," https://newforums.com/law-organizational-entropy-faculty-innovators/, (last accessed July 19, 2020).

leaders. While having leaders does not guarantee success, rarely do groups demonstrate sustained excellence without assigned leaders—the leader role matters. Your effectiveness as an assigned leader depends on the quality of your contributions towards helping your organization achieve its goals.

Destructive Leadership and Management

Many popular discussions on leadership explicitly suggest that leaders are inherently better than managers. Abraham Zalenick's famous article on the difference between managers and leaders describes managers, for example, as lacking passion towards goals, whereas leaders champion organizational goals.[28] Distinctions like the one Zalenick makes between leaders and managers have resulted (possibly unintentionally) in the popular organizational perspective where individuals in assigned leadership roles are considered managers or leaders. The implication is that an individual cannot be a leader and a manager simultaneously. Unfortunately, this simplistic frame is more hurtful than helpful for (at least) two primary reasons. First, it obscures that leadership is not inherently good or bad; second, it casts management as a second-class process and characterizes management activities as work for people who are not leaders. A proper understanding of organizational leadership requires that you understand that leadership can also be destructive, i.e., leadership and leaders are not inherently good. We also need to appreciate the importance of management to the organization. Finally, an individual can be both a manager and a leader at the same time. We will first explore the concept of destructive leadership and then discuss the importance of management.

Destructive Leadership

Leadership, in and of itself, is value-neutral. Leadership is not good by default, as some would have us believe. Just because a leadership system produces the desired results, let us say, from a financial perspective, does not mean good leadership occurred. Good leadership delivers results and delivers results ethically.[29] A leadership system with bad leaders, bad influence tactics such as coercion, bad followers, or a bad goal is not a good leadership system; it is a destructive leadership system. We do not have to look far to see destructive leadership around us. A recent example is that Boeing's stock grew from $135 to $423 between January 2015 and March 2019, even though (behind the scenes) we now know of Boeing's lax approach to 737-Max safety.[30] While

---

[28] Abraham Zalenick, "Managers and Leaders: Are They Different?" *Harvard Business Review* 82, no. 1 (2004): 74–81.

[29] Kellerman, Professionalizing Leadership, 136.

[30] "Internal Boeing documents Show Cavalier Attitude to Safety," https://www.wsj.com/articles/internal-boeing-documents-show-cavalier-attitude-to-safety-11578627206, (last accessed July 19, 2020).

Boeing is an easy target because the company is public, the sad reality is that we can look within our organizations and see destructive leadership all around us. Destructive leadership is one of the reasons why so many people are dissatisfied with the work experience. These leadership systems have leaders who (knowingly and unknowingly) make work difficult for their team members. They rely on coercive tactics and hoard power. They have little to no interest in the well-being of the followers that make up the leadership systems, except when they know a lack of attention will negatively impact their image. These leaders are only concerned about their personal interests.

And yet, while it is convenient to put destructive leadership solely on leaders' shoulders, destructive leadership rarely begins and ends with those at the proverbial top, i.e., those in assigned leadership roles high up in the organization. Instead, destructive leadership results from ineffective leaders, susceptible followers, and contexts that create a safe place for destructive leadership to occur over time.[31] John Solas puts it this way, "Although the buck stops with those at the top, corporate malevolence and malfeasance are not the sole preserves of bad bosses. Those who follow them cannot evade their share of responsibility."[32] Systemic destructive leadership involves many bad actors, and those who keep quiet, look the other way, or claim that they are following instructions are complicit. While the concept of leadership might be value-neutral, in leadership—in practice, leadership in practice is not value-free. Leaders (and followers) put their core values on display as they lead within the organization—a leader who is ineffective, unethical, or immoral contributes to destructive leadership. However, a bad leader does not a good manager make.

Management

It is simple. Anyone who performs management activities is, in a sense, a manager. So, what is management? How does management differ from leadership, and what are management activities? Many scholars have attempted to distinguish management from leadership. For example, Russell Ackoff suggests that unlike leadership, where followers participate in determining goals and how to achieve those goals, management focuses on directing others on how to do what the manager wants.[33] Ackoff's definition (possibly not intentionally) leaves one feeling that management is about soullessly giving

---

[31] Christian N. Thoroughgood, Katina B. Sawyer, Art Padilla, and Laura Lunsford, "Destructive Leadership: A Critique of Leader-Centric Perspectives and Toward a More Holistic Definition," *Journal of Business Ethics*, no. 151 (2018): 628.

[32] John Solas, "The Banality of Bad Leadership and Followership," *Society and Business Review* 11, no. 1 (2016): 15.

[33] Russell Ackoff, "A Systemic View of Transformational Leadership," *Systemic Practice and Action Research* 11, no. 1 (1998): 23.

orders to employees—a commonly put forth view in much of the popular literature. However, James Krantz and Thomas Gilmore described management as focusing on the day-to-day activities required to ensure the organization functions properly and achieves its goals.[34] Management ensures operations run smoothly, and there is a degree of order and control in organizational function. Every individual in an assigned leader role, while facilitating the leadership process as the organization moves into the future, must also ensure the organization continues to achieve its operational goals—they have management responsibilities.[35]

If you have fiscal responsibility for a department, then part of the job function is to ensure that your department does not go over budget during the fiscal year. It is your responsibility to ensure your organizational structure supports organizational goals. Developing plans and prioritizing the activities of a group are management activities that leaders must perform.[36] Monitoring your team's progress towards its goals and intervening when the team is straying from the plan is also part of your responsibility. An organization will not survive long if it does not manage the systems and resources (not people) required to support the business—management is an essential business function.[37] Assigned leaders have the dual responsibility of leading people and managing the work and work environment. Valuing one set of activities in favor of the other does not benefit an organization. Instead, both sets of activities need nurturing and development. Most of the assigned leaders I have observed paid significantly more attention to managing than they did to leading. Whether you are a supervisor or a C-level executive, you must contribute to making leadership happen. The lack of effective leaders has sullied management's reputation.

A leader's style influences how they conduct managerial activities.[38] Leaders who share their power will make sure their teams are fully involved in management activities like tactical planning exercises. Conduct management activities gracefully, even when using formal authority. Ignoring managerial duties places organizational outcomes (and your job) in jeopardy. Do not lose sight of the importance of management because it is a crucial aspect of

---

[34] James Krantz and Thomas N. Gilmore, "The Splitting of Leadership and Management as a Social Defense," *Human Relations* 43, no. 2 (1990): 188.

[35] I like the term "managerial leader."

[36] Mike Young and Victor Dulewicz, "Similarities and Differences Between Leadership and Management: High-Performance Competencies in the British Royal Navy," *British Journal of Management* 19, no. 1 (2008): 18.

[37] Michael Maccoby, "Understanding the Difference Between Management and Leadership," *Research Technology Management* 43, no. 1 (2000): 57–59.

[38] Sean T. Hannah, John T. Sumanth, Paul Lester, and Fabrice Cavarretta, "Debunking the False Dichotomy of Leadership Idealism and Pragmatism," *Journal of Organizational Behavior*, no. 35 (2014): 602–603.

organizational success. But do not become so focused on management that you forget your leadership system responsibilities.

This section would not be complete without mentioning the ever-increasing "no manager" movement promoted by management scholars such as Gary Hamel.[39] People supporting this movement tend to present it as more effective for the 21st century and morally superior. However, as I mentioned earlier, I believe that anyone engaged in management activities mentioned above is a manager regardless of whether their title has a manager in it or not. Hence, I would suggest that getting rid of managers is genuinely getting rid of almost everyone in the organization!

I think it is fair to assume that the people behind the "no manager" movement are not saying that organizations need to fire everyone. If this is not the case, what could they be saying? Michael Lee and Amy Edmondson describe the "no manager" perspective as an approach with the radical decentralization of authority throughout the organization, and nothing supersedes individual authority.[40] I describe this as organizations where middle management is mainly non-existent. I do not doubt that this approach works for certain companies in varying degrees. However, all that glitters is not gold. There is no shortage of stories of how success in these manager-less firms still depends on power and navigating the informal hierarchy.[41] In other cases, firms like Google brought back managers after getting rid of them because the organization faced performance challenges without managers.[42] Having fewer managers may seem to decentralize authority, but it does not prevent power, influence, and authority issues. You need to face these issues head-on and make sure that you and the people you lead use power and authority to support employee well-being. Let us now look at authority, power, and influence.

The Authority, Power, and Influence Cocktail

Being an assigned leader brings with it numerous challenges—it is not for the faint of heart. One of the challenges leaders need to deal with is operating within their organization's hierarchical structure. As much as there has been a recent push for flatter organizations and less hierarchy in organizations, it

---

[39] Gary Hamel, "First, Let's Fire All the Managers," *Harvard Business Review* 89, no. 12 (2011).

[40] Michael Y. Lee and Amy C. Edmondson, "Self-Managing Organizations: Exploring the Limits of Less-Hierarchical Organizing," *Research in Organizational Behavior* 37, (2017): 35–58.

[41] Perform a Google search on Valve and "no managers" for more information.

[42] David Van Rooy, "Lessons From Googles' Failed Quest to Run a Business Without Managers," https://www.inc.com/david-van-rooy/take-a-sneak-peak-inside-google-and-its-world-without-managers.html, (last accessed July 19, 2020).

remains true that hierarchy still yields the best organizational results in many situations.[43] Hierarchy exists to ensure the proper functioning of the organization. While it might be easy to imagine an organization with no hierarchy, I am yet to find an actual organization with an equal distribution of power, authority, influence, and resources among team members—hierarchies are always present. Organizational scholars observe that organizations prefer hierarchy to maintain stability and control.[44] Even in startups that I have worked in, specific team members had more authority than others on the team, i.e., a hierarchy of authority. There are highly publicized organizations, such as W. L. Gore and The Morning Star Company with a reputation for being egalitarian workplaces. However, these firms still have individuals at the top who decide the egalitarian structure. Even if these organizations truly have no hierarchy, they are "exceptions that prove the rule" that most organizations prefer hierarchy. Hierarchy requires that leaders manage the trio of power, authority (formal and informal), and influence as they interact with followers. Many leaders struggle with using this trio in a healthy way, so they deserve some attention. Let us look at them.

Power

Power does not have a stellar reputation because many assigned leaders use their power as a weapon of force, i.e., harmful and oppressive behavior. However, power, in itself, is neither good nor bad. In the social sciences, power refers to the potential to get people to change their minds, attitudes, or beliefs.[45] Put another way, power is the capacity of getting people to do what they had no intention or desire to do before. Thus, how leaders use their power determines whether its usage is good or bad. Social psychologists John R. P. French and Bertram Raven initially identified six core bases of power: coercion, reward, legitimacy, expert, reference, and information that individuals have in social groups.[46] The literature on these bases of power is quite extensive. However, because you must appreciate the various forms of power you could have in your organization, I will provide a brief overview of the different bases of power.

Coercive, reward, and legitimate power are formal powers because they come from one's assigned position in their organization. You exercise coercive

---

[43] Frieda Klotz, "Why Teams Still Need Leaders," *MIT Sloan Management Review* 60, no. 4 (2019): 1–4.

[44] Deborah H. Gruenfeld and Larissa Z. Tiedens, "Organizational Preferences and their Consequences," in *Handbook of Social Psychology*, 5th ed., ed. Susan T. Fiske, Daniel T Gilbert, and Gardner Lindzey (USA: John Wiley & Sons Inc.), 1262–1267.

[45] Jeni Mcray, *Leadership Glossary: Essential Terms for the 21st Century*, (Santa Barbara, CA: Mission Bell Media, 2015), "French and Raven's bases of power."

[46] Bertram H. Raven, "The Bases of Power and the Power/Interaction Model of Personal Influence," *Analyses of Social Issues and Public Policy* 8, no. 1 (2008): 1–22.

power when you use fear and threats to get people to follow your instructions. Threatening to terminate a team member's employment if they do not complete a project is an example of coercive power at work. On the other hand, promising a team member a spot bonus for working on a project over the weekend is an example of reward power because you used your ability to reward the team member as the means of getting them to work the weekend. Legitimate power is the power that comes from the office you hold. An example of this is that the VP of a Product Development organization has the legitimate power to call a meeting with her entire organization. In contrast, a first-level manager would not have the same legitimate power. When you are no longer in that organizational position, you lose the legitimate power you once had. Whether you like it or not, your position grants you formal power, and your team members know this. Be careful with how you use your formal power.

How people see you also gives you power—personal power. Referent power is a personal power that results in team members doing what you ask because they like, respect, and admire you. If you have ever had a team member say, "I am only doing this because of how highly I think of you," then you know what it is to have referent power. Leaders with referent power have excellent interpersonal skills and healthy relationships with others. Such leaders are role models, and team members might aspire to lead like them someday in the future. Possessing an in-depth knowledge of a specific topic or subject area can also be a source of power if others consider you an expert. If your team considers you the "change expert," "Salesforce expert," or the "conflict resolution expert," and follows the guidance you provide in these areas, then you have expert power. The last personal power is information power, and this is power based on having information others might need to accomplish their goals. For example, if you know whom to call to order supplies but others on your team do not, you have information power. Based on my experience, personal power is more impactful than formal power because personal power remains with you even when you change positions or leave an organization.

Assigned leaders have power, and so you cannot avoid using power as you lead others—it comes with your leader position. The questions are "what powers do you rely on?" and "how do you use those powers?" Many leaders rely solely on their formal power. If you have ever worked for a leader who said that you should do something "because they said so or there would be consequences," then you experienced a form of coercive, reward, or legitimate power. These leaders give lip service to dialogue and expect people to go along with what they say without asking any questions. I am not suggesting that formal power is off-limits for assigned leaders—formal power is required to maintain a certain amount of order. However, formal power will only go so far for you as a leader. To effectively lead and have people enjoy the workplace, personal power is critical. You want people in the organization to follow your lead because they respect you and know that you care for them. You will use your power(s) as you facilitate the leadership process. The power(s) you choose to use and how you use them go a long way to determine what type of leader you are.

Power-Over Versus Power-With

Power is unevenly distributed in organizations; hence, another way to conceptualize power is through the lens of how those with more power share power with those who have less power. Mary Parker Follett developed the terms "Power Over" and "Power With" to describe how leaders share power in their organizations.[47] Leaders who adopt a power-over approach hoard their power. They use their power to coerce individuals to perform activities the individuals do not want to do. Examples of power-over are when the Director of Software Engineering dictates what techniques Software Engineering Managers will use during the discovery process without consulting with any of their managers or when a Software Engineering Manager imposes a particular Agile process on their team. In these cases, the team members have no option but to comply with the orders of their leaders. Many individuals desire assigned leader positions because they want to have power over others. People who desire to have power-over other individuals spend much accumulating power as well. They are power-seeking.

Leaders who use a power-with approach seek to share their power. These leaders work to keep the distribution of power in the organization in a healthy balance. The goal of sharing power is so that everyone can maximize their contributions to organizational progress. Power-with encourages employee participation in making decision-making that impacts the employee and the organization. An example of the power-with approach would be a manager who works with their team members to identify the most appropriate product development discovery process. Or a director facilitating team members as they make technology choices for a new product line. Instead of hoarding power, the leader shares their power with others and at the same time encourages everyone to use the power they have. They routinely use their power to enable others in the organization. Leaders who adopt a power-with approach are power-giving.

Let me repeat. If you are a leader, you have power. At a minimum, you have power stemming from your position in the organization. Some of your power might also come from your expertise in a particular subject area. Information you have that others do not have also gives you power. Pay close attention to

---

[47] Pauline Graham, *Mary Parker Follett—Prophet of Management: A celebration of writings from the 1920s*, (Boston, MA: Harvard Business Press, 1995): 23–24.

the source(s) of your power and how you use your power within the leadership system. If you default to coercive or reward power, understand that you will only see desired behaviors for a short period because power based on coercion or rewards requires continual oversight. On the other hand, when you share your power—such as involving others in decision-making—you foster commitment and dedication, leading to overall job satisfaction for everyone and better organizational results.[48] As you share power with people in your organization, they will come to respect you, and from that, you increase your personal power. Having power is not the problem. How you choose to exercise your power is what truly matters.

Formal Authority

As previously mentioned, authority is often a source of power. Ronald Heifetz argues that "social living depends on authority."[49] Formal authority refers to the right an individual has to act in the organization. The amount of authority an individual has is often directly correlated to their position in the organization, i.e., the higher up in the organization an individual is, the more authority they often have. A middle manager might have the authority to purchase software up to an expense of $20,000. In contrast, the organization might give a director more purchasing authority with the right to spend up to $250,000 on software.

Unfortunately, authority is often seen (just like power) as a negative when it comes to leadership. Formal authority complicates leadership because self-aware leaders (and followers) wonder whether followers respond to their requests solely due to the formal authority the leader has. Several people have even suggested that good leadership does not involve authority.[50] These observations advise leaders against using their formal authority while leading others. But is this sound advice? Can effective leadership occur without any authority?

In their reflection on authority, Boas Shamir and Galit Eliam-Shamir posit that formal authority can both amplify and dampen leadership.[51] When leaders do not exercise their formal authority to address wrongdoing, the individuals in their charge question the leader's ability to lead. In addition, team members are left to wonder if the leader is paying attention to what is happening around

---

[48] Olivier Doucet, Marie-Eve Lapalme, Gilles Simard, and Michel Tremblay, "High involvement management practices as leadership enhancers," *International Journal of Manpower* 36, no. 9 (2015): 1058–1071.

[49] Ronald Hefeitz, *Leadership Without Easy Answers*, (Boston, MA: Harvard University Press, 1998), 49.

[50] Boas Shamir and Galit Eliam-Shamir, "Reflections on leadership, authority, and lessons learned," *The Leadership Quarterly* 28, no. 4 (2017): 578–583.

[51] Ibid.

them. Zachary Green and René Molenkamp note that authority must be (a) clearly defined, (b) taken up accordingly, and (c) accompanied by the tools to exercise it.[52] How you use your formal authority is of the utmost importance. Use your formal authority to establish and maintain organizational rules. Formal authority also helps you transmit cultural norms in the organization. Calling a meeting to appreciate and recognize teams would be an example of how you could let the rest of the department know that appreciation matters to you. Ensure that formal authority is situated—with the people and context—where it best serves the organization. Thus, formal authority, when used correctly, serves to benefit the organization. However, formal authority is not enough to lead organizations. Effective leaders must have informal authority as well.

Informal Authority

No discussion on leadership and authority is complete without a discussion on informal authority. Unfortunately, many conversations on authority focus on formal authority and ignore informal authority altogether. By default, authority in the workplace comes from an individual's position in the organization. However, unlike formal authority based on your office, informal authority comes from the trust and respect that followers give you.[53] As previously discussed, formal authority provides you with certain rights because of the office you occupy. Informal authority has nothing to do with your office; instead, informal authority is the authority others choose to give you because they trust you, respect you, believe in you, and want to follow you. Followers decide whether they will grant their leaders informal authority.[54] You cannot demand or force informal authority; you can only behave in ways that might lead people to grant you informal authority. You can tell you have informal authority when people willingly support objectives even when they disagree with them. Factors that enhance your informal authority include developing good relationships with team members and exhibiting behaviors that people in the organization appreciate. Without informal authority, you will face significant challenges because formal authority only goes so far. People will comply due to your organizational position, and compliance is rarely good enough. Therefore, work on increasing your informal authority. Remember, formal authority comes from your position, whereas informal authority comes from the people.

---

[52] Zachary Gabriel Green and René J. Molenkamp, "The BART system of group and organizational analysis: Boundary, authority, role and task," (2005). https://baddfa7d-5c43-4bec-b3f5-eefad7099302.filesusr.com/ugd/a50107_ebe83be1ff374b40 8cd39ef407fab110.pdf.

[53] Ronald Hefeitz, *Leadership Without Easy Answers*, 101.

[54] Hefeitz, *Leadership Without Easy Answers*, 101–102.

Influence

Effective leadership requires that leaders know how to influence others in the leadership system. CCL identified influence as one of the four core leadership skills required by those intending to lead others.[55] Those with excellent influencing skills persuade and convince others on what actions to take. These individuals leverage their personal power and informal authority as part of influencing others. We all have experience working with people adept at getting others to change their minds without resorting to force or coercion. Collaboration with superiors and peers is not an option in organizational life. You cannot rely on formal power or formal authority when working with these individuals; instead, you must be able to influence them. Imagine a software development manager who believes there is a better way to perform some process in the organization, but changing that activity requires tradeoffs and approval from their manager. Getting the process changed will require that the manager find a way to influence their manager. If you do not develop your influencing skills, you will ultimately resort to coercive methods. Having the ability to influence others is critical for effective leadership process facilitation. Influencing others relies on being able to communicate your desires effectively. Develop your communication skills. Unclear messages inhibit your ability to influence others.

If you want to establish direction, maintain alignment, and foster commitment within your organization while minimizing resistance, adopt influencing tactics that produce the best outcomes. Gary Yukl, Charles F. Seifert, and Carolyn Chavez recommended that leaders use rational persuasion, consultation, inspirational appeals, and collaboration as the primary influence tactics because they yield the best results.[56] Rational persuasion involves using logic and facts to explain why individuals need to participate in attaining the goals. Influencing through rational persuasion requires time commitment and patience because you need to explain to people why you want to go down a particular path.

Another way of influencing is through consultation. Consultation engages team members in an activity that requires their support. Unfortunately, I have witnessed many leaders develop fully baked plans and expect their teams to execute the plan without asking any questions. These leaders are surprised when their team members are resistant to the plan. You can reduce resistance by involving people in creating the plan. For example, let us say you believe that your team needs to modify their software development approach to

---

[55] "The Core Leadership Skills You Need in Every Role," https://www.ccl.org/articles/leading-effectively-articles/fundamental-4-core-leadership-skills-for-every-career-stage/. (last accessed July 19, 2020).

[56] Gary Yukl, Charles F. Seifert, and Carolyn Chavez, "Validation of the extended Influence Behavior Questionnaire," *The Leadership Quarterly* 19, no. 5 (2008): 614.

match client expectations. Instead of developing a new approach on your own, consult with your team. Explain the current challenges to them and ask them to identify new ways of working that will benefit the client. By consulting the team, you provide them an opportunity to participate in designing their future.

In some situations, you can influence others by inspiring them. An inspirational appeal means that you address the people's core values, principles, and ideals. If rational persuasion is speaking to the head, then an inspirational appeal is speaking to the heart. It is arousing the emotions of people, so they commit to group objectives. Speaking to your team members' hearts necessitates that you understand their values, principles, and ideals. You need to know what matters most to the individuals you lead, and you need to help them see how their aspirations come to life through the activities you are asking them to support. An inspirational appeal can be helpful during transformative change.

Last, when you make it clear to team members that you will support them as they take on an initiative, you use collaboration as an influence tactic. People take comfort in knowing that their leader will be right in there in the trenches with them. Knowing they have your support is critical when team members must take on a difficult challenge, which they may not feel fully qualified to take on. Providing team members with the assurance that you will provide all the resources they need to succeed at the task removes their fear of failure and encourage them to take on the challenge. I had firsthand experience with influence through collaboration when I had to take on new leadership responsibilities in a different group. I was concerned with the request because of the stories I had heard about how difficult it was to work in that group. However, my manager committed to working with me in the new role and providing me the support I would need to succeed at the job. Because of this leader's support, I decided to take the role.

The four influence tactics are not mutually exclusive. You may have to use all of them in a single scenario where you need to present facts, consult, inspire, and collaborate as part of how you influence team members, peers, and superiors. In one leadership situation, the context was that a department had a reputation for being a place where people did not want to work. The department needed to change. I first appealed to the departmental leaders' values and reminded them that I knew that each one of them wanted to belong to a workplace where people could do their best work. Next, I presented them with facts in the form of survey results that showed the department's poor reputation. After appealing to their hearts and heads, I asked for their help in developing actions to improve the workplace. Finally, I committed to them that I would provide the support to enact what we decided.

It is essential to recognize that these influence tactics require a significant amount of effort, time, and patience. Impatient leaders will find influencing others through these tactics hard. I have met many leaders who believe that it is a waste of their time to use these influence tactics, so they resort to coercive and brute force methods. Instead of relying on coercion, exercise patience. If you want team members to commit to a particular activity, take the time to provide them with information that helps them understand why the activity is worthy of their commitment.

Power, Authority, and Influence—The Interplay

Individuals in assigned leader positions must lead followers while negotiating the realities of power, authority, and influence as they work towards achieving organizational goals. Mishandling any of these factors can harm leader effectiveness and undermine the ability to achieve desired goals. As a result, leaders always need to assess how they use power, authority, and influence as part of their leadership approach. A short story might help illustrate this point.

A few years ago, an individual I know (let us call him Okeke) joined an organization in an executive position. Okeke's position in the organization afforded him significant formal power and formal authority. He had responsibility for setting the direction of his department, and what he said became the law of the land. At the onset, there were no problems in Okeke's department. Team members followed Okeke's instructions and directives. Okeke used his formal power and formal authority to establish how he wanted the department to function. However, Okeke rarely consulted with team members in the department and made most decisions by himself. For a while, everything went fine.

However, after a few months, Okeke began to experience resistance from team members. They ignored his directives and openly opposed him during team meetings. It was not long before team members complained about Okeke to other senior leaders in the organization. Before he knew it, Okeke had a revolt on his hands—no one wanted to work with him anymore. The situation went from bad to worse, and Okeke quickly became powerless. His authority no longer mattered. It was not long after this that Okeke was fired and found himself looking for another job. What had gone wrong? While many factors possibly contributed to Okeke's termination, one major contributing factor was that Okeke had failed to grow his informal authority and personal power with his team. People initially followed him because of his organizational position. But this only lasted for a while. Eventually, people wanted to follow him for other reasons than the office he occupied. They wanted to accept his influence for reasons beyond Okeke's organizational position. Okeke failed to realize this, thinking he could control his team using his formal power and formal authority. Unfortunately for him, he was wrong, and it cost him dearly. Informal authority and personal power are becoming increasingly critical for leaders to have. Avoid making the same mistakes Okeke made by growing your personal power and informal authority while using highly effective influence tactics.

Leaders Make a Difference

You need to use your authority, power, and influence as part of making leadership happen. When leadership happens, groups achieve shared goals. Formal power and authority are needed to put organizational structures in place—even self-managing organizations have a CEO who determined that the organization would be self-managing. So formal power and authority have their place. However, dependence on formal authority and power for goal attainment only generates compliance; it does not generate a long-lasting commitment to organizational goals. Unfortunately, many leaders use surveillance-based methods in the leadership process. Surveillance requires keeping a watchful eye on followers' behavior to ensure followers' performance aligns with desired organizational goals.[57] This approach leads to disengaged and demotivated team members.

You want engaged team members. You want team members to see how their contribution makes them part of a mission more significant than themselves. Be intentional about how you use your power, authority, and influence. Subsequent chapters will show you how you can use them to nurture an organization where team members thrive while working. As a result, you can make a meaningful difference in the workplace.

Takeaways

- Organizations need leadership. Leadership is more than skills, traits, or a single individual. It is the process of maintaining direction, alignment, and commitment in a group to pursue a shared goal. The leadership system consists of context, followers, and leaders.

- As an assigned leader, you are primarily responsible for ensuring direction, alignment, and commitment in your group.

- You have formal power and formal authority based on your leader role. However, formal authority and formal power are limited tools of leadership.

---

[57] Raven, "The Bases of Power," 2.

- Increase your personal power and informal authority. Share your power with others and use highly effective influence methods like rational persuasion, consultation, inspirational appeal, and collaboration.

- Leadership is value-neutral, and yet, the result of the leadership process is not value-free. Leadership can be bad or good. Good leadership is both effective and ethical.

- Balance the demands of leading the organization while ensuring the organization functions properly daily. Failure to pay attention to both leadership and management activities negatively impacts your organization.

- Use your power, authority, and influence to foster an environment where people thrive while working together to achieve organizational goals.

The Agile Game

We are uncovering better ways of developing software by doing it and helping others do it.

—The Manifesto for Agile Software Development[1]

It would be inappropriate to write a book about leading product development teams without saying something about the process of software development. Some individuals go as far as to suggest that software is eating the world.[2] Software continues to play an increasingly vital role in business success in almost every sector imaginable. Many product and service companies rely on software solutions as part of their business strategy. Many businesses have undergone (or are undergoing) a "digital transformation," which means they are automating many of their processes using software. Web pages, desktop applications, and mobile apps have replaced activities performed with pen and paper. An audit recovery company with 40 people who manually review hundreds of receipts in the hopes of identifying rebates their clients did not take advantage of decided to develop an automated software-based process that scanned the receipts and used algorithms to identify missed rebates. Suddenly, a process that took weeks now took minutes. Walk into a restaurant, bank, or school, and you will observe software playing an integral part in how

---

[1] https://agilemanifesto.org/.
[2] Marc Andreessen, "Why Software Is Eating the World," https://a16z.com/2011/08/20/why-software-is-eating-the-world/ (last accessed July 19, 2020).

© Ebenezer C. Ikonne 2021
E. C. Ikonne, *Becoming a Leader in Product Development*,
https://doi.org/10.1007/978-1-4842-7298-5_2

employees do their jobs. Everywhere we look, software is part (or even at the heart) of business operations.

The software situation is made more complex because organizations often need to modify their existing software (or create new software) in response to changes around them. The competitive landscape for many businesses is dynamic and ever-changing. What is hot today is replaced by a new hot idea tomorrow. Consumers and clients need new capabilities, and businesses need to provide these capabilities and provide them quickly if the business wants to remain viable. The competition is not standing still. They also make changes to provide their customer base with improved service. Ergo, the ability to develop software (and develop it well) has become a core competency that many businesses need.

Many organizations claim to practice Agile Software Development (Agile) as a response to business demands. Others say they practice it because it would be unpopular not to do so. I would not be surprised if you lead within an organization that has chosen Agile for one reason or the other. Understanding Agile is essential for leaders who want their teams to adopt it. So, before digging into how to lead product development organizations, I will share what Agile means to me. It is also crucial that you understand that Agile is not a panacea, so I share some of the limitations, criticisms, and challenges Agile faces in organizations.

What Is Agile?

Agile has become the approach most software development organizations claim is the backbone of their product development approach.[3] A search on the Internet for Agile and Agile-related roles yields thousands of results.[4] The Scrum Master role—a role in Scrum, an Agile process framework—has been described as one of the fastest-growing technology roles.[5] Agile has become a booming industry with various certifications focused on managing the software development process, increasing technical skills, and even recently, developing leadership capabilities. People refer to Agile leadership, Agile organizations, Agile-this, and Agile-that. You would not be wrong to think that there is a standard definition of Agile. You would be wrong because one does not exist.

---

[3] It is hard to find a software development organization that does not claim that it is "Agile."

[4] A search near Atlanta, Georgia returned over 2004 Agile-related jobs.

[5] Joe McKendrick, "Why the Hottest Technology Job This Year May Be the Scrum Master," https://www.zdnet.com/article/hottest-tech-job-this-year-may-be-scrum-master/ (last accessed July 19, 2020).

Agreeing on a single and shared definition of Agile seemingly presents a significant problem. Ask 10 people "what is Agile," and you will get 30 different responses. I have lost track of the number of debates on social media where a group of people tried (and failed) to reach a consensus on a standard definition of Agile. For some people, Agile is a software development approach. Others define Agile as an approach to adapting to changes in the business landscape. Some definitions of Agile attempt to have it represent every good leadership and management idea known to humanity. If a practice is beneficial, it automatically is a part of Agile. For other individuals, Agile, like quality, does not have a definition. You know Agile when you are practicing it.

What started as a description of a software development approach has crossed the chasm and has become part of the mainstream lexicon and now means different things.[6] As Agile has become popular, it has suffered the fate of Jerry Weinberg's Law of Raspberry Jam.[7] Agile has come to mean whatever anyone wants it to mean, and hence a shared definition accepted by everyone does not (and probably will not) exist. However, I will offer my definition of Agile after providing a brief review of Agile's history.

Brief Review of the History of Agile

For decades, product development teams faced (and continue to face) the challenge of developing software that met the needs of stakeholders. Not only did product development teams have to meet an initial set of identified needs, but the teams also had to change the software as needs evolved with business changes. As a result, an organization's software systems changed over time. Many organizations had a software development approach that was highly sequential and deferred any form of meaningful feedback until the end of (or late in) the software development process illustrated by Figure 2-1. The sequential, waterfall-like, little to no feedback, large-batch software development approach can be found in a software development paper written by Winston Royce where Royce advised against a sequential approach, because it delayed feedback till late in the software development process.[8] Unsurprisingly, this approach does not work well for developing business applications because by the time the software was available for use, it no longer met business needs—business needs had changed during the software development process.

---

[6] For more on crossing the chasm, please refer to Geoffrey Moore's book Crossing the Chasm: Marketing and Selling High-Tech Products to Mainstream Customers.

[7] Jerry Weinberg's Law of Raspberry Jam: The more you spread it, the thinner it gets.

[8] Winston W. Royce, "Managing the Development of Large Software Systems," http://www-scf.usc.edu/~csci201/lectures/Lecture11/royce1970.pdf (last accessed July 19, 2020).

System Requirements → Software Requirements → Analysis → Program Design → Coding → Testing → Operations

Figure 2-1. Sequential Software Development

The frustration of providing software that did not meet stakeholders' needs led software developers in the United States and Europe to devise different approaches to improve software development outcomes. These approaches assumed that, in many cases, it is impractical to understand stakeholder needs upfront fully; instead, understanding grows throughout the product development process. The approaches also recognized how important it was to receive feedback throughout the development process. In 2001, 17 software development practitioners discussed the different software development approaches that each practitioner had experienced success with. Their discussions considered the different practices and techniques each of the attendees used as part of software development. Such practices and methods included Adaptive Software Development, Scrum, Extreme Programming, Test Driven Development, and Modeling languages.[9] The result of their dialogue was a set of values and principles they felt represented a better way to meet needs through software development. They memorialized these values and principles in a document referred to as the Manifesto for Agile Software Development.[10] The four values are

- Individuals and Interactions Over Processes and Tools

- Working Software Over Comprehensive Documentation

- Customer Collaboration Over Contract Negotiation

- Responding to Change Over Following a Plan[11]

The manifesto also outlines 12 principles, which are

- Our highest priority is to satisfy the customer through early and continuous delivery of valuable software.

- Welcome changing requirements, even late in development. Agile processes harness change for the customers' competitive advantage.

---

[9] Philipp Hohl et al., "Back to the Future: Origins and Directions of the "Agile Manifesto" – Views of the Originators," *Journal of Software Engineering and Research* 6, no. 15 (2018): 11–15.

[10] Caroline Mimbs Nyce, "The Winter Getaway That Turned the Software World Upside Down: How a Group of Programming Rebels Started a Global Movement," https://www.theatlantic.com/technology/archive/2017/12/agile-manifesto-a-history/547715/ (last accessed July 19, 2020).

[11] "Manifesto for Agile Software Development," https://agilemanifesto.org/ (last accessed July 19, 2020).

- Deliver working software frequently, from a couple of weeks to a couple of months, with a preference to a shorter timescale.

- Business people and developers must work together daily throughout the project.

- Build projects around motivated individuals. Give them the environment and support they need, and trust them to get the job done.

- The most efficient and effective method of conveying information to and within a development team is face-to-face conversation.

- Working software is the primary measure of progress.

- Agile processes promote sustainable development. The sponsors, developers, and users should be able to maintain a constant pace indefinitely.

- Continuous attention to technical excellence and good design enhances agility.

- The best architectures, requirements, and designs emerge from self-organizing teams.

- At regular intervals, the team reflects on how to become more effective, then tunes and adjusts its behavior accordingly.[12]

It is important to note that the manifesto recognizes the importance of the values on the right side; however, it says that the left side's values are more valuable. Improving personal work experience was a significant motivation for several of the Agile manifesto contributors.[13] I like to think that they wanted software developers to experience "joy at work."

The Agile approach was for people who wanted to work in a highly collaborative workplace with a high level of transparency. It was also highly dependent on motivated people with a continuous improvement mindset, i.e., people with a passion for identifying better ways of developing software. To succeed with Agile meant having the willingness to adopt technical practices like pair-programming, user stories, and test-driven development. Teams who adopted Agile also wanted to work directly with their stakeholders. The Agile approach also made it clear that uncertainty was a friend and not a foe. Unlike traditional

---

[12] Ibid.
[13] Hohl et al., "Back to the Future," 2.

approaches that focus on achieving high certainty levels (especially at the beginning of the product development process), Agile embraces uncertainty.[14] Also, the Agile approach had implicit expectations of the kind of people that would thrive with the approach.

A review of Agile values and principles shows that the original contributors to the manifesto believed in the importance of communication, motivated individuals, and customer satisfaction in the software development process. Several software development methods and frameworks that influenced Agile (and those that came after) incorporate practices that attempt to demonstrate the 4 values and 12 principles of Agile in action. Examples of such methods and frameworks include Scrum, Extreme Programming (XP), Crystal, and Disciplined Agile Delivery (DAD). Arun Kamepally and Tejaswini Nalamothu, in their review of Agile methods, suggested the themes of Agile include "focus on delivering small, quick iterations of software, and focus on pleasing the customer or client."[15] Product development organizations that adopted Agile did so because they wanted to respond to business needs quickly.

Agile as a Software Development Culture

Agile is more than just a set of values, principles, and practices. Because Agile has the constituent elements of culture, I consider it a software development culture. Ed Schein states that culture has three levels—tacit assumptions, espoused values, and artifacts.[16] An in-depth look at the Agile manifesto, frameworks, and methods reveals the presence of tacit assumptions, espoused values, and artifacts (practices). A tacit assumption is an unspoken belief accepted as true. People take tacit assumptions for granted and rarely speak about them, so they exist unconsciously. The need for people to collaborate is an example of an Agile tacit assumption, and this tacit assumption is at the heart of principles four, five, and six in the manifesto. Other examples of tacit assumptions include "the inevitability of change" and "self-organization produces positive results."[17] Table 2-1 lists the common assumptions behind the Agile values and principles. These assumptions are neither right nor wrong; however, they influence how Agile practitioners approach software development.

---

[14] Subhas Misra, "Agile Software Development Practices: Evolution, Principles, and Criticisms," *International Journal of Quality and Reliability Management* 29, no. 9 (2012): 976.

[15] Arun Kumar Kamepally and Tejaswini Nalamothu, "Agile Methodologies in Software Engineering and Web Engineering," *International Journal of Education and Management Engineering* 6, no. 5 (2016): 6.

[16] Edgar Schein, *Organizational Culture and Leadership*, (San Francisco, CA: Jossey-Bass, 2010), 17–30.

[17] Daniel Turk, Robert France, and Bernhard Rumpe, "Assumptions Underlying Agile Software-Development," *Journal of Database Management* 16, no. 4 (2005): 66–76.

Table 2-1. Assumptions Behind Agile Software Development Principles and Values. Source: Daniel Turk, Robert France, and Bernhard Rumpe, "Assumptions Underlying Agile Software-Development," 76–82

Assumptions	Description
The Visibility Assumption	Project visibility can be achieved solely through the delivery of working code.
The Iteration Assumption	A project can always be structured into short fixed-time iterations.
The Business People Interaction Assumption	Business people teams are available for frequent interaction when needed by developers.
The Team-Communication Assumption	Developers are located in a time and place such that they are able to have frequent, intensive communication with each other.
The Face-to-Face Assumption	Face-to-face interaction is the most productive method of communicating with customers and among developers.
The Documentation Assumption	Developing extensive (relatively complete) and consistent documentation and software models is counterproductive.
The Changing-Requirements Assumption	Requirements always evolve because of changes in technology, customer needs, and business domains, or even because of the acquisition of new customers.
The Cost-of-Change Assumption	The cost of change does not dramatically increase over time.
The Team-Experience Assumption	Developers have the experience needed to define and adapt their processes appropriately.
The Self-Evaluation Assumption	Teams are willing and able to evaluate themselves.
The Quality-Assurance Assumption	The evaluation of software artifacts (products and processes) can be restricted to frequent informal reviews, reviews, and code testing.
The Application-Specific-Development Assumption	Reusability and generality should not be the goals of application-specific software development.
The Continuous-Redesign Assumption	Systems can be continuously redesigned (refactored) and still maintain their structural and conceptual integrity.

Source: Daniel Turk, Robert France, and Bernhard Rumpe, "Assumptions Underlying Agile Software-Development," 76–82.

The 4 values and 12 principles represent the espoused values that guide the Agile approach. Espoused values are a culture's strategies, goals, and philosophies.[18] Many Agile frameworks also have their specific values. For example, the Scrum process framework has commitment, courage, focus, openness, and respect.[19] Commitment in Scrum means that individuals and teams will do their best to accomplish what they said they would. Scrum teams show courage by speaking up when they believe that specific actions or decisions are not in the team's or organization's best interest. Teams also show courage when the team takes risks or tries new approaches to novel challenges. Because Scrum teams value focus, they are supposed to keep their eyes on shared team goals and minimize distractions. The openness value refers to the team's willingness to change based on learning that occurs. Finally, Scrum team members treat each other and their stakeholders with respect.

Artifacts are visible aspects of a culture.[20] Many Agile frameworks could also qualify as an Agile cultural artifact. All frameworks and methods have practices and techniques that give the observer a sense that the team might have tried to adopt an Agile approach. An example of an XP artifact is pair programming. Pair programming is a technique where two people work together on the same workstation on the same task. More recently, a newer technique known as mob programming has emerged. In mob programming, the entire team uses a single workstation to work on the same task.[21] Teams that adopt XP also have a "Daily Stand Up Meeting," where team members gather to discuss challenges and make plans for the day. Other XP artifacts include user stories, unit tests, continuous integration, and acceptance tests.[22] Each practice demonstrates an XP value which in turn reflects an Agile value and principle. For example, unit tests and acceptance tests reflect the principle of "technical excellence" and make it easier for teams to modify systems and "satisfy the customer through early and continuous delivery of valuable software."

Viewing Agile through the lens of Schein's cultural levels makes it possible to see Agile as a software development culture with specific goals in mind. Furthermore, the first lines of the Agile manifesto give this view some credence as the original contributors observed that they discovered an approach to software development they found beneficial for them and their stakeholders.

---

[18] Schein, *Organizational Culture and Leadership*, 19–21.

[19] Ken Schwaber and Jeff Sutherland, "Scrum Values," https://www.scrumguides.org/scrum-guide.html#values (last accessed July 19, 2020).

[20] Schein, *Organizational Culture and Leadership*, 17–18.

[21] "Mob Programming," https://www.agilealliance.org/glossary/mob-programming (last accessed July 19, 2020).

[22] "The Rules of Extreme Programming," http://www.extremeprogramming.org/rules.html (last accessed July 19, 2020).

Based on Agile history and an organizational cultural lens, I define Agile as a software development approach focused on creating a positive working environment where teams meet stakeholder needs through regular software delivery. Stakeholders include everyone involved in the software development process.

Limitations and Challenges

Many product development organizations claim to use Agile as their primary product development approach. However, Agile success reports are primarily anecdotal. Surveys or weak case studies report how teams and organizations benefited from adopting Agile. These forms of evidence, while valid to a degree, are also often limited in applicability. The lack of evidence is a reason why several people consider Agile just another marketing ploy.[23] Yet, even without extensive empirical evidence, many practitioners promote Agile as a cure-all for all business challenges. They often present Agile as having no limitations and working well in any context. And yet, several of the original contributors to Agile caution against viewing Agile as a silver bullet.[24] In that spirit, it is important to review several limitations of Agile. Understanding these limitations will help you make better decisions as you support your product development teams.

Agile Is Not a Panacea

An excellent way to identify limitations with Agile is through the lens of the assumptions behind its principles.[25] Where these assumptions do not hold, workplaces may find it challenging to use Agile practices and techniques. Agile requires team members who have expertise with Agile practices and methods. But as Adam Solisnski and Kai Petersen note, a shortage of knowledgeable and skilled Agile practitioners (managers and team members alike) limits an organization's chances of succeeding with Agile.[26] Another assumption is that team members possess strong social skills because Agile methods are highly collaborative. And yet, not everyone is interested in collaborative methods.[27] I have consulted with many teams with team members who preferred their cowboy coder or hero developer role. I also have worked with many individuals

---

[23] Hohl et al, "Back to the Future," 2.

[24] Ibid, 23.

[25] Turk, France, and Rumpe, "Assumptions Underlying Agile Software-Development," 76–82.

[26] Adam Solinski and Kai Petersen, "Prioritizing Agile Benefits and Limitations in Relation to Practice Usage," *Software Quality Journal* 24, no. 2 (2016): 468.

[27] Kieran Conboy and Sharon Coyle, "People over Process: Key Challenges in Agile Development," *IEEE Software* 28, no. 4 (2011): 54.

who preferred working in isolation. These individuals had no interest in learning new programming techniques (especially techniques that required collaboration with peers on the team). Finally, not every developer truly buys into the Agile approach. Team members who want to show up, do their work, barely engage, and go home will probably struggle in an Agile context.

Teams also struggle with Agile when remote work challenges the assumption of face-to-face communication. Face-to-face communication makes it easier to develop social presence and build personal relationships, making it easier for team members to collaborate on complex work.[28] However, the reality of the 21st century is that more and more companies continue to invest in various forms of distributed product development for various reasons. For example, the 2019 coronavirus pandemic made distributed product development the norm in many countries. The various configurations for distributed product development are a single team with distributed team members, multiple distributed teams with collocated team members, and multiple distributed teams with distributed team members.[29] Each configuration introduces a set of challenges to Agile and makes it increasingly difficult to adhere to Agile principles and practices. For example, when working with distributed teams, it becomes vital to capture critical information in documentation because information can get lost in translation; however, this practice goes up against the value of "comprehensive documentation" and the principle of "face-to-face conversation." Also, serendipity becomes less of a factor in the workplace. Distributed product development can also impact a team member's ability to work with "business people daily" when product developers and business people are in separate geographies.

Large-scale product development endeavors also challenge many of the underlying Agile assumptions. Large-scale product development requires the coordination of many teams working together on a shared goal. The number of teams and the software's complexity makes it difficult for everyone working together to communicate face-to-face. Because of team size and the software project or product size, not every team member can work with business people daily. Comprehensive documentation becomes essential in these scenarios. I have been a part of large-scale product development efforts that required greater management control and formalized processes than smaller product development efforts. Instead of "working software" being the primary measure of progress, other forms of reporting (like status reports and Gannt charts) become the primary measure of progress. Over the last decade,

---

[28] Reza Barkhi, Ali Amiri, and Tabitha L. James, "A Study of Communication and Coordination in Collaborative Software Development," *Journal of Global Information Technology Management* 9, no. 1 (2006): 46.

[29] Imran Ghani et al, "Challenges in Distributed Agile Software Development Environment: A Systematic Literature Review," *KSII Transactions on Internet and Information Systems* 13, no. 9 (2019): 4560–4561.

approaches like the Scaled Agile Framework (SAFe)[30] and Large Scale Scrum (LeSS) have attempted to address these challenges. Currently, there is a lack of empirical studies on how well teams do with these scaled Agile approaches, and practitioners are left to rely on weak case studies and lots of anecdotes.

Leaders responsible for large-scale product development efforts will need to augment the Agile approach with other tried-and-true techniques.[31] Early in my career, I was reluctant to make these accommodations because I felt I would dilute the Agile approach's essence. Perfect Agile meant so much to me, so complementing Agile with traditional approaches was not much of an option. It took me a few failures to learn that Agile is no more than one approach to meeting business needs. It was okay to deviate from specific values and practices if the situation required it as long as I continued to foster a workplace in which people found meaning and experienced joy at work while achieving business goals.

It is crucial to remember: Agile is not the goal. Agile relies on some assumptions about your product development context, and there are times when these assumptions do not hold true. You must adopt approaches necessary for your team and organization to achieve its desired objectives. Be transparent about this process and do not claim an Agile-only approach when it is apparent that this is not the case. Ultimately, your approach must take into consideration the desired goal.

Practicing Agile? Easier Said Than Done

Agile adoption and practice poses a significant challenge for many organizations. Several practitioners have noted that we are now in the Agile Industrial Complex age (AIC).[32] The AIC is best described as the attempted widespread imposition of Agile within organizations by individuals in senior leadership positions. I say attempted because the imposition rarely succeeds anyway. Business leaders engage consulting firms to help them design an imposition strategy for their organization leading to the mass commercialization of Agile. As Martin Fowler noted in his keynote at Agile Australia in 2018, AIC has become one of the most significant challenges organizations need to address as they attempt to use Agile in how they get work done.[33] Despite executives' motivation for teams to adopt Agile, anecdotal evidence suggests that many organizations struggle to reap the proposed benefits of Agile. Instead, the

---

[30] Practitioners frequently debate whether SAFe is an Agile approach.

[31] Turk, France, and Rumpe, "Assumptions Underlying Agile Software-Development," 76–84.

[32] Daniel Mezick, "The Agile Industrial Complex," https://newtechusa.net/aic/ (last accessed July 19, 2020).

[33] Martin Fowler, "The State of Agile Software in 2018," https://martinfowler.com/articles/agile-aus-2018.html (last accessed July 19, 2020).

imposition sucks the life and joy out of team members, and teams struggle to provide products that address stakeholder needs. I have met numerous product development practitioners who have written off Agile because of how senior leaders imposed it on the rest of the organization. In some organizations, the adoption is so weak that it has led practitioners to describe the situation as "Agile in Name Only" (AINO).

AINO is characterized by teams going through the motions with certain Agile practices, while failing to reap any benefits from the practices. The long and short of it is that the teams never adopt the underlying values and change their tacit assumptions. For example, I have worked with teams in an AINO environment with a daily standup every morning from which the team learns nothing, and after the standup, team members barely collaborate. In other cases, the teams work in two-week Sprints but barely interact with the customers or clients who need the system's capabilities. In fact, in some cases, they did not even know who used the software. In one situation, an organization invested millions of dollars creating Agile team rooms with all the bells and whistles. Leaders followed the construction changes by imposing arbitrary tight deadlines that caused people to work over 60 to 70 hours every week continuously. The leaders in that organization did not trust team members to remain focused on organizational objectives without deadlines. This is no different from claiming your organization has a fun culture because you have a recreation room with ping-pong tables, but you pack team member schedules, making it impossible for them to play ping-pong during work hours. The presence of ping-pong tables does not a fun culture make.

Another challenge is that many software developers are left disillusioned and frustrated with their work experience that involves Agile because of the hyper-focus on managing product development (especially using Scrum) and little focus on good product management and software engineering practice. Agile requires technical excellence, which depends on solid product and software development techniques and practice. Unfortunately, these technical practices do not receive the same amount of attention as the process frameworks. It would not be a stretch to propose that most organizations claiming to practice Agile spend more time monitoring progress than providing their teams with the resources and support required to improve their product development competency. All of this happens in the name of Agile. Conformance to the process results in product development teams taking technical shortcuts, which prevents software change agility. Agile becomes management's surveillance mechanism.

Agile also has a reputational challenge. There is ample evidence that many organizations and teams struggle to practice Agile in their organizations for various reasons. First, teams that use Agile do not always succeed, i.e., Agile does not guarantee success. Second, costs associated with failed Agile software delivery attempts are estimated to be billions of pounds.[34] Third, some industry analysts suggest that Agile is simply another IT fad that harms (and does not help organizations).[35] On the other hand, ardent Agile practitioners believe strongly in the Agile approach and cite other reasons as the source of Agile failures.

While it is tempting to assign a single cause to Agile adoption failure, a review of Agile adoption failures shows that a lack of leader support, organizational culture mismatch, and a misunderstanding of Agile values and principles routinely contribute to Agile adoption failures.[36] Leaders impact each of these causes because they influence organizational context and culture. Ed Schein observed that leaders embed and transmit the culture they desire for their organization.[37] If the organizational culture does not foster the conditions for Agile, team members will struggle to practice Agile. Many leaders struggle to facilitate a leadership process that supports Agile because they do not want to change their leadership paradigms. Fewer leaders know how to have conversations when Agile alone may not be appropriate for the organizational challenge. The Agile industry has responded to leadership challenges by developing Agile Leadership certification programs from Scrum.org and the Scrum Alliance organization.[38] However, it is undetermined how impactful these programs are. I remain skeptical of their efficacy.

If You Choose Agile, Lead the Way

Many organizations desire to use an Agile approach (or incorporate some Agile aspects into their product development approach). Yet, many organizations struggle to do so. Leaders exist in every organization, and whether we like it or not, influence how an organization accomplishes its goals. Leader support for Agile is necessary if organizations and teams are to succeed with it. Product Development leaders have a significant role to play if they want their teams to adopt Agile techniques and practices. Your leadership approach will have to foster an environment where Agile can thrive.

---

[34] Alex Rolf, "UK Wasting €37 Billion a Year on Failed Agile IT projects," *Payments Cards & Mobile,* https://www.paymentscardsandmobile.com/failed-agile-it-projects/ (last accessed July 19, 2020).

[35] Cliff Saran, "Agile development an 'IT fad' That Risks Iterative Failure," *ComputerWeekly. com,* https://www.computerweekly.com/news/450418205/Agile-development-an-IT-fad-that-risks-iterative-failure (last accessed July 19, 2020).

[36] Mariangela Pinton and Alvair Silveria Torres Junior, "Human Aspects of Agile Transition in Traditional Organizations," *Journal of Technology Management & Innovation* 15, no. 3 (2020): 62–73.

[37] Schein, *Organizational Culture and Leadership,* 181–206.

[38] Scrum Alliance and Scrum.org have "agile" leadership certifications. More found here https://www.scrumalliance.org/get-certified/agile-leadership/cal-1 and https://www.scrum.org/professional-agile-leadership-certification.

However, it is hard to succeed if leaders actively work against (even if it is inadvertent) Agile. This occurs when leaders make decisions and take actions that make it difficult for their teams to practice Agile. But why would leaders do such a thing? Do they not agree with the values and principles outlined in the manifesto? Are they not fans of having teams that can quickly respond to change as needed? I do not think so. I believe that many leaders desire the benefits of Agile; it just so happens that they do not know which leader-behaviors support Agile. As Edward Deming famously said, "Best efforts are essential. Unfortunately, best efforts, people charging this way and that way without the guidance of principles, can do a lot of damage."[39] Without a solid understanding of how to lead teams practicing Agile, leaders get in the way of their team's success. My goal is to help you understand how you can lead in a manner that amplifies (and does not dampen) your team's ability to adopt and practice Agile.

I want to reiterate that Agile does not guarantee organizational success as much as some its most ardent proponents might suggest. Agile, with its practices, enables teams to modify software products in response to business changes when needed. And yet, Agile alone is not enough for organizations to remain viable and competitive. For the organization to thrive, all the other departments in the organization must do their jobs and do them well. Agile will not overcome poor business strategy, poor product management, poor marketing, or poor customer service. However, Agile can play an essential role in an organization that wants to adapt quickly to changing business circumstances. While Agile does not guarantee organizational adaptability, the inability to move quickly in software product development can also hinder organizational adaptation. So, firms that understand the inherent uncertainty of the future and want to make sure they are well-positioned to adapt will also want to make sure the organization has product development agility and has leaders who can effectively lead in these contexts. You need the competencies required to lead in organizations where continuous adaptation to change is a necessity.[40] Ineffective leadership approaches will hinder (and not help) your product development teams and the organization.

There is no product development process panacea. Businesses dependent on high-performing product development teams require leaders like you to foster the conditions for excellence. These teams will want to adopt a product development that incorporates Agile values and principles in many cases. While Agile exists to help organizations deliver software in response to stakeholder needs, teams can only effectively practice Agile if they have the support required. The benefits of the Agile approach will not happen in a vacuum—Agile requires effective leaders and leadership. The leader insights in

---

[39] W. Edward Deming, *Out of the Crisis*, (Cambridge, MA: MIT Press, 2000), 19.

[40] Robert J. Bloome, "Leadership, Complex Adaptive Systems, and Equivocality: The Role of Managers in Emergent Change," *Organization Management Journal* 9, no. 1 (2012): 16.

the upcoming chapters assume your teams have adopted a product development approach influenced by Agile and use examples and stories that occurred within such a context. However, the upcoming chapters also provide guidance that will benefit leaders in contexts where Agile is not the de facto approach. The recommendations apply in many creative work contexts, i.e., the recommendations work for leaders in domains outside of product development. If you desire to lead in a way that contributes to a joyful workplace and produces excellent results—even if your teams chose something besides Agile—the upcoming chapters will help you do that.

Takeaways

- Agile is a software development approach focused on meeting changing people's needs.

- Agile is not a panacea, has limitations, does not account for every aspect of product development, and may not work in every context.

- Understanding the strengths, weaknesses, and underlying assumptions of Agile is vital if you intend to adopt it as part of your product development approach.

- Focus on fostering an environment where people thrive and achieve organizational goals even if Agile is not the chosen approach.

Making Sense of Cultural Plurality

Traditions are the guideposts driven deep in our subconscious minds. The most powerful ones are those we can't even describe, aren't even aware of.

—Ellen Goodman[1]

A nation's culture resides in the hearts and in the soul of its people.

—Mahatma Gandhi[2]

It is not uncommon for leaders to assume that their leadership approach, based on their cultural values and worldview, works in different national cultures. I made this mistake in the early 2000s while establishing a software development team in Bangalore, India. I assumed that my leadership

---

[1] Ellen Goodman is an American journalist.
[2] Mahatma Gandhi was a nonviolent social protest pioneer.

© Ebenezer C. Ikonne 2021
E. C. Ikonne, *Becoming a Leader in Product Development*,
https://doi.org/10.1007/978-1-4842-7298-5_3

approach—developed in the United States—was appropriate for my new teams. Unfortunately, I did not appreciate the cultural differences between the two countries and how these differences would impact the leadership process. As a result, the leadership process had a rough start.

I learned how a simple behavior—the headshake—can impact leadership. The Indian headshake can mean different things depending on the situation.[3] I mistook team member's headshakes as disagreement when they agreed with me. In fact, team members rarely disagreed with me in public—which was another cultural difference I had to learn through this process. Another assumption I made was that team members desired a hands-off approach and that anything else would be considered micromanagement and inappropriate. I also assumed that communication would primarily be verbal. I had no appreciation for the high-context culture that I was a part of. People would not share their opinions during meetings. I would find out about dissatisfaction much later.[4] Looking back on it now, growing up in Nigeria—a country with many cultural similarities to India—enabled me to leverage familiar cultural norms and eventually connect with my team. At that point in my career, I did not know how big an impact national culture can have on the leadership process and was fortunate that I had a multicultural background.

As my experience shows, national culture influences the leadership process. Individuals interpret leader behaviors (signs and symbols) within their cultural context. Failing to understand how national culture impacts the leadership process will hinder your effectiveness as a leader. This chapter will look at why you need to understand how national culture impacts your leadership system and why you need to consider your team members' cultural backgrounds as you lead. Throughout the chapter, I will provide recommendations that will help you leverage cultural diversity on your teams.

National Culture and Its Dimensions

National culture refers to commonly held norms, customs, and behaviors of people in a sovereign nation. National culture shows up in the workplace because we bring our culture to work. As the famed Nigerian writer Chinua Achebe observed, "When a tradition gathers enough strength to go on for centuries, you don't just turn it off one day." Leaders who ignore national culture do so at their own risk. The most widely cited works on differences between national cultures come from Hofstede Insights[5] and the GLOBE

---

[3] "India Headshakes: What They Mean," https://www.youtube.com/watch?v=Uj56IPJOqWE (last accessed July 19, 2019).

[4] Neha Patel, Nataliz Vila-López, and Ines Kuster-Boluda, "Difference Between American and Indian Consumers' Visual Images," *Cross Cultural Management* 20, no. 1 (2013): 53–54.

[5] See https://www.hofstede-insights.com/ for more information on Hofstede insights. (last accessed July 19, 2020).

(Global Leadership and Organizational Behavior Effectiveness) Project.[6] From Geert Hofstede's study of employees at IBM in the 1960s, Hofstede, Gert Jan Hofstede, and Michael Minkov identified the following six dimensions of national culture: power distance, individualism, masculinity, uncertainty avoidance, long-term orientation, and indulgence described in Table 3-1.[7]

Table 3-1. Hofstede Dimensions and Descriptions. Source: Geert Hofstede, Gert Jan Hofstede, and Michael Minkov, Cultures and Organizations: Software of the Mind, 3rd ed., (New York, NY: McGraw-Hill, 2010)

Hofstede Dimension	Description
Power Distance (PD)	The extent to which the less powerful members of institutions and organizations within a country expect and accept that power is distributed unequally.
Individualism-Collectivism (IDV)	Individualism pertains to societies in which the ties between individuals are loose; everyone is expected to look after him- or herself and his or her immediate family. Collectivism pertains to societies in which people from birth onward are integrated into strong, cohesive in-groups, which throughout people's lifetime continue to protect them in exchange for unquestioning loyalty.
Masculinity-Femininity (MAS)	A society is called masculine when emotional gender roles are clearly distinct: men are supposed to be assertive, tough, and focused on material success, whereas women are supposed to be more modest, tender, and concerned with the quality of life. A society is called feminine when emotional gender roles overlap: both men and women are supposed to be modest, tender, and concerned with the quality of life.
Uncertainty Avoidance (UAI)	The extent to which the members of a culture feel threatened by ambiguous or unknown situations.
Long-Term versus Short-Term Orientation (LTO)	Long-term orientation is the fostering of virtues oriented toward future rewards—in particular, perseverance and thrift. Short-term orientation is the fostering of virtues related to the past and present—in particular, respect for tradition, preservation of "face," and fulfilling social obligations.
Indulgence versus Restraint (IDG)	Indulgence stands for a tendency to allow relatively free gratification of basic and natural human desires related to enjoying life and having fun. Restraint reflects a conviction that such gratification needs to be curbed and regulated by strict social norms.

[6] See http://www.globeproject.com/ for more information on the GLOBE Project.
[7] Geert Hofstede, Gert Jan Hofstede and Michael Minkov, *Cultures and Organizations: Software of the Mind*, 3rd ed., (New York, NY: McGraw-Hill, 2010).

Each dimension has a corresponding index that represents the dimension. The Hofstede study is not without its fair share of criticism. In his review of the use of Hofstede's cultural dimensions in accounting research, Hichem Khlif identified the following criticisms:

- Outdated data

- Assumptions of ethnic homogeneity in one country

- The close connection of cultural dimensions with socio-economic data

- The IBM data are not representative of the world

- The inapplicability of the five dimensions to all countries and cultures[8]

Despite criticisms, Hofstede's model continues to serve as a reference source for cross-cultural studies.[9] The model provides leaders with the awareness of how national culture can impact their leadership practice.[10] Cross-cultural theories continue to evolve. It is also critical to understand that Hofstede's dimensions score at the national level, so stereotyping individuals based on their cultural heritage is wrong. Instead, the dimensions provide a general frame of reference to remind you of cultural differences while you lead. Using the dimension index scores for the United States, Nigeria, India, China, and Sweden displayed in Table 3-2, I will share how you might need to adapt your leadership approach when you have team members from these different nations.

Table 3-2. Hofstede Index Scores for Several Countries

Nation	PD Index Score	IDV Index Score	MAS Index Score	UAI Index Score	LTO Index Score	IDG Index Sore
United States	40	91	62	46	26	68
Nigeria	80	30	60	55	13	84
India	77	48	56	40	51	26
China	80	20	66	30	87	24
Sweden	31	71	5	29	53	78

---

[8] Hichem Khlif, "Hofstede's Cultural Dimensions in Accounting Research: A Review," *Meditari Accountancy Research* 24, no. 4 (2016): 545–573.

[9] Sunil Venaik and Paul Brewer, "Avoiding Uncertainty in Hofstede and GLOBE," *Journal of International Business Studies* 41, no. 8 (2010): 1296.

[10] Michael Minkov and Geert Hofstede, "Is National Culture a Meaningful Concept? Cultural Values Delineate Homogenous National Clusters of In-Country Regions," *Cross-Cultural Research* 46, no. 2 (2012): 133–159.

Power Distance

Power distance refers to the degree to which members of society encourage the unequal distribution of power.[11] In nations with high power distance, people accept or tolerate the unequal distribution of power among group members. Individuals with less power defer to individuals with more power in high power distance societies. Leaders operate with more power than the rest of the group and often default to power-over approaches. For example, the expectations in the workplace could be that team members expect you to provide direction and instructions (over consulting). Individuals with a high-power distance cultural background might not appreciate a leader who does not practice a power-over approach. They might view this as an abdication of the leader role.

In nations with low power distance, individuals expect a near equal distribution of power. They desire that those with more power share their power with those who have less and do not use their power to oppress others. This expectation can also make its way into organizations with individuals desiring democratic and participative forms of working. Individuals in a low power distance society might expect unfettered access to their leaders. They may also expect leaders to accept their feedback. In societies with low power distance, team members consistently try to level the workplace's power playing field.

On the surface, power distance may not seem meaningful because we see power abuse in both low power distance and high-power distance countries. And yet, how people navigate hierarchy in an organization often reflects the power distance in their country. Let us consider how power distance could impact a team from Nigeria with a leader from the United States—two countries that I am familiar with. Nigeria has a high-power distance score of 80, while the United States has a low power distance score of 40. The low power distance score in the United States suggests that the leader will not let their organizational position deter them from working directly with their members. However, the high-power distance background for the team members from Nigeria might mean that they do not expect an accessible leader. With the Nigerian team members, power distance becomes even more significant if the leader is older than the team member. Not only does the team have to respect their leader's position in the organization, but they also must respect their age. Referring to an individual in a "higher position" by their first name is a sign of disrespect. It took months for me to refer to my professors by their first names while in graduate school. Individuals show respect for those with more power in Nigeria differently from how individuals show respect in the United States.

---

[11] Hofstede, Hofstede and Minkov, *Cultures and Organizations*, 61.

I experienced the impact of high-power distance while leading software development teams in India with a power distance score of 77. Even though I had a trusting relationship with many team members, they would often defer to me to decide what was best for the team. To them, I was their leader, and they expected me to make decisions. They consistently found it odd when I asked for their opinion on specific items or when I would want the group to arrive at a consensus before we decided what to do. We had to work together until we all became comfortable with a shared power approach. The irony of this situation is that it had taken me a few years to become comfortable with low power distance as I had grown up in a high power distance society. When your power orientation does not match your team's power orientation, there can be conflict and tension.

The conflict is more significant if you attempt to practice Agile in a high-power distance setting because Agile presumes low power distance. Agile promotes consensus-based decision-making using the information produced from working software. Team members—across the business—are expected to work together to solve problems regardless of title or status with leaders using their power to foster an environment where team members can do their best work. Leaders are not supposed to use their power to primarily control or command their teams; instead, power is for support. If you want to practice Agile in a country with high power distance, you will need to determine how to adapt the Agile approach to fit that context. For example, an Indian organization modified its authority structures and provided team members with leadership roles while maintaining the organizational structure.[12] Pay attention to power distance. It impacts what people expect from you and how people work together.

Individualism

The individualism dimension refers to how much interdependence people encourage in their society.[13] Do people focus on themselves and their immediate family, or do they focus on their broader community? It is the difference between an "I" focus and a "We" focus. The GLOBE project further analyzes how these dimensions function at both the organizational and societal levels.[14] How people view themselves relative to their social groups is often a reflection of their national culture.

---

[12] Balasubramaniam Ramesh et al., "Conflicts and Complements Between Eastern Cultures and Agile methods: An Empirical Investigation," *European Journal of Information Systems* 26, no. 2 (2017): 228.

[13] Hofstede, Hofstede and Minkov, *Cultures and Organizations,* 92.

[14] Michele J. Gelfand, Dharm P. S. Bhawuk, Lisa Hisae Nishi, and Daniel J. Bechtold, "Individualism and Collectivism," in *Culture, Leadership, and Organizations: The GLOBE Study of 62 Societies*, ed. Robert J. House et al., (Thousand Oaks, CA: Sage Publications, 2004), 437–513.

The individualism dimension determines whether people prefer to work alone and for themselves or value working in groups and accomplishing goals with other people. The part of the African proverb, "If you want to go fast, go alone. If you want to go far, go together," that resonates within a group reflects their preference. Certain national cultures promote individualism more than others. Leaders may face an uphill battle with constructs that promote collectivism—such as teamwork—when leading teams (or individuals) with an individualistic orientation.

The United States is an example of a country that scores high on individualism with 91. The implication is that individuals focus on their personal goals ahead of any group goals. Some researchers have suggested that individualism is a primary reason why 2020 COVID19 stay-at-home orders faced significant resistance in the United States.[15] People were more interested in their rights. But we do not have to look at the COVD19 behaviors for evidence of individualism in the United States. All we need to do is look at the reward systems we see in organizations. Even though many organizations strongly suggest that teamwork is essential, individual rewards and incentives such as Salesperson of the Year are more common than team awards. It seems that many leaders do not recognize the mixed messages that a reward system focused on individuals sends after a corporate speech on the merits of teamwork.

Nigeria is an example of a collectivistic society with an individualism score of 30. Community well-being is essential. It is expected that individuals take care of the people in their community. For example, when a family member is well-positioned in a firm, it is expected that they actively work to bring members of their social group (family members, close friends, etc.) into the firm as well. Loyalty to the social group is critical in collectivist societies, and people in collectivistic societies prefer that the group they also belong to receive rewards and recognition. In collectivistic cultures, everyone who is part of the group shares the group's success and failure. An individual's success is determined by how well their community does. Success in collectivistic societies is often measured by how many people a successful person helped.

Please pay attention to the individualism-collectivism dimension and how it impacts you and your team. High-performing teams require that individuals look beyond themselves and focus on the greater good for the team.[16] People from national cultures high on collectivism may have an easier time working on teams than people with a high individualism orientation. If you are a leader with an individualistic orientation, you might experience dissonance when

---

[15] Bo Bian, Jingjing Li, Ting Xu, and Natasha Z. Foutz, "Individualism During Crises," https://papers.ssrn.com/sol3/papers.cfm?abstract_id=3626841 (last accessed July 29, 2020).

[16] J. Richard Hackman, *Leading Teams: Setting the Stage for Great Performances*, (Boston, Mass: Harvard Business School Press, 2002).

trying to get people to work together for the greater good. In fact, I will go as far as to suggest that leaders need to have a collectivistic orientation to lead teams effectively.

Excellent leadership happens when team members work together for the greater good of the team and the broader organization. However, in high individualism cultures, recognition and appreciation (e.g., promotions and bonuses) focused on the individual challenge teamwork—an Agile tacit assumption. A leadership process that engages everyone will require that the group manage the individualism-collectivism tension that exists. Introduce practices that encourage collectivism on your teams in high individualistic contexts. For example, modify your recognition programs so that team achievements become a prominent symbol in the organization.

Masculinity-Femininity

Another national cultural dimension is the degree to which members of society compete against each other and pursue success. Hofstede et al. called this dimension masculinity.[17] Individuals in masculine societies focus on winning, finishing first, and demonstrating their ability to get things done. Coincidentally, both Nigeria and the United States are examples of more masculine countries. Nigeria has a masculinity score of 60, while the United States has a masculinity score of 62. You might see the masculine dimension appear as individuals, teams, and departments compete for ideas, promotions, and recognition. People feel the need to prove they are right during conversations. Not having answers to questions is often seen as incompetence or lack of knowledge, and saving face is commonly practiced.

On the other hand, Sweden is considered an example of what would be considered a feminine society with a masculinity score of 5. Feminine societies concern themselves with others' well-being. They tend to promote fairness, justice, and equality more than their masculine counterparts. People value highly participative and consensus-based approaches to work in these societies. Organizations in feminine countries may lean toward an egalitarian style of leadership and management. Leaders engage their teams in organizational decision-making. People integrate work into their holistic lifestyle.

Like the individualism dimension, the masculinity dimension impacts how people work together in an organization. Our definition of leadership stresses the importance of team member participation in determining how to achieve team goals and desires that everyone has their voice heard. This is especially crucial for software product development teams that adopt an Agile approach. Competition between team members and teams is discouraged; instead, cooperation, coordination, and collaboration are encouraged. Agile

---

[17] Hofstede, Hofstede, and Minkov, *Cultures and Organizations,* 140.

frameworks and methods require a working style where team members support and look out for each other's best interests as they work together. Agile values conflict with the values promoted in highly masculine societies. So, if you are leading a product development team in a masculine society—like in the United States—encourage collaboration within and between teams. Continuously focus the team on its shared goals. Make it safe for everyone to respectfully express their thoughts on even the most difficult of topics. You must pay attention to team member well-being, especially in masculine societies where a "results at any cost" work ethic might be prevalent.

Uncertainty Avoidance

Societies handle uncertainty stemming from not knowing the future differently. Some communities embrace change and try to make the best of the fact that many aspects of the future are unknowable. Other cultures work hard to protect themselves from the surprises that the future will bring. These societies do not appreciate ambiguity. GLOBE defines uncertainty avoidance as "the extent to which members of collectives seek orderliness, consistency, structure, formalized procedures, and laws to cover situations in their daily lives."[18] Cultures high in uncertainty avoidance have lots of rules to protect them from the unknown. Societies low in uncertainty avoidance go with the flow and are less anxious.

The United States has a lower uncertainty score of 46, suggesting that society is moderately open to trying new ideas and experimenting with new problem-solving approaches. People might not go out of their way to prevent uncertainty; instead, they embrace it. Such societies do not have too many rules to protect themselves from the future. Managers in organizations in the United States show lower uncertainty avoidance by being comfortable with a degree of ambiguity and not expecting every bit of detail clarified for them.[19] Managers have some freedom to improve work methods without requiring approval in every situation. While people in the organization pay attention to rules, what matters more is doing the right thing, even if it means breaking the rules on occasion.

High uncertainty avoidance countries put controls in place to reduce uncertainty and minimize ambiguity. Do not be surprised that individuals from these societies do not appreciate big surprises. They value stability and order and hence try to achieve clarity of what the future might bring. Germany is an example of a country with a higher uncertainty avoidance score of 65. A study

---

[18] Mary Sully de Luque and Mansour Javidan, "Uncertainty Avoidance," in *Culture, Leadership, and Organizations: The GLOBE Study of 62 Societies,* ed. Robert J. House et al., (Thousand Oaks, CA: Sage Publications, 2004), 603.
[19] Kris Portz and John C. Lere, "Cost Center Practices in Germany and the United States: Impact of Country Differences on Managerial Practices," *American Journal of Business* 25, no. 1 (2010): 45–51.

of managers in Germany showed that their jobs and responsibilities are clearly defined, so they do not have to deal with ambiguity around how they successfully perform their job.[20] These managers can become highly competent at their job because they have a clear set of expectations that do not change without notice. High uncertainty avoidance discourages people from stepping out of their comfort zone and taking risks like changing employers or trying new roles in their organization.

Uncertainty avoidance can either amplify or dampen your teams' willingness to try new methods of working. Agile methods encourage experimentation and embrace uncertainty as part of the product development process. Individuals and teams are encouraged to learn through testing new ideas. You need to demonstrate your willingness to take risks and embrace uncertainty. If you or your team members are not comfortable with uncertainty, adapting to change may prove challenging. Patience is vital in these situations as team members in high uncertainty avoidance cultures may desire clearly defined roles and responsibilities. A lack of clarity leads to ambiguity, which ultimately results in discomfort. Consider the use of boundary, authority, resources, and task (BART) to reduce ambiguity in the right places.[21] Reduce uncertainty about tasks by being specific about task completion requirements. Make it clear who has the authority to make certain decisions to reduce ambiguity around authority.

Long-Term Versus Short-Term Orientation

Hofstede et al. describe long-term orientation as the fostering of the virtues of perseverance and thrift.[22] These virtues have a focus on future rewards. Societies can also have a short-term orientation with an orientation that fosters the virtues of respect for tradition, saving face, and fulfilling social obligations.[23] Societies with a short-term orientation focus on the past and what is happening in the present. Short-term orientation communities optimize for immediate feedback, while long-term orientation communities optimize for delayed feedback. China ranks number one in long-term orientation with a score of 87. Social interactions in China happen within the context of the long-term.[24] People spend meaningful time thinking about how

---

[20] Ibid.

[21] Zachary Gabriel Green and René J. Molenkamp, "The BART System of Group and Organizational Analysis: Boundary, Authority, Role and Task," (2005). https://badd-fa7d-5c43-4bec-b3f5-eefad7099302.filesusr.com/ugd/a50107_ebe-83be1ff374b408cd39ef407fab110.pdf. (last accessed July 19, 2020).

[22] Hofstede, Hofstede, and Minkov, *Cultures and Organizations*, 239.

[23] Ibid.

[24] Sungmin Ryu and Chul Moon Woo, "Long-Term Orientation as a Determinant of Relationship Quality Between Channel Members," *The International Economics & Economics Research Journal* 8, no. 11 (2009): 1–9.

their actions might impact their future. Because they have a long-term outlook, people in societies with a long-term orientation are also more prone to adapt to changing circumstances.

Long-term orientation also impacts organizational life. Leaders with a long-term orientation focus on future results (and not just immediate results). Decisions that yield long-term results occur in favor of decisions that only impact the short-term. Specific values, such as learning and self-discipline, are also more prevalent in organizations where leaders have a long-term orientation.[25] Organizations invest in developing their team members because they expect team members will remain with the organization for a long time. Leaders believe their organization is running a marathon (and not a sprint). So, questions such as "if we treat an individual team member this way today, will we be able to treat other team members similarly in the future?" are of the utmost importance because leaders in these contexts value consistency over time.

The United States is an example of a society with a short-term orientation score of 26. People are generally more concerned with what they can accomplish in the present and want to make sure their rights and freedom are honored.[26] Tradition matters a great deal in societies with a short-term orientation. People remain loyal to past events, even if the events cannot help them succeed in their current situation. The "microwave mentality," i.e., we need results now, is prevalent in short-term orientation nations. In the workplace, leaders focus on short-term outcomes. Because the goals are short-term, leaders often find themselves having a view of the organization that differs from those in other roles. For example, a software development manager's concern might be how a product can be released in the shortest time possible while team members worry about the product's technical viability post-release.

Product development organizations need a balance of short-term and long-term orientation. The goal is to deliver value (most often via software) regularly and frequently from a short-term perspective. Agile planning practices focus more on the short-term horizon. The short-term horizon aligns with embracing uncertainty and focusing on what is in view. Simultaneously, Agile practices such as test-driven development, test automation, and continuous integration exist to make it easier for teams to modify their software over the long-term.

Your challenge is to help your organization have the right balance of long-term or short-term orientation by helping teams see when short-term orientation is more appropriate and when long-term orientation is more appropriate. My experience leading teams in cultures with short-term orientation is that long-

---

[25] Hofstede, Hofstede, and Minkov, *Cultures and Organizations*, 235–276.
[26] Ibid.

term practices face significant resistance because they do not provide immediate benefit. Teams with a primary disposition towards the short-term do not want to learn and practice software development techniques like pair-programming because the benefits of the practice exist in the future. It can be challenging to invest in the long-term when the average tenure for leaders (especially senior leaders) in any position is three to five years. You might not be in your current position when the impact of the long-term decisions you made occurs. There is a lot of pressure to focus solely on immediate results. However, if you want to impact people's lives, you must consider leaving a long-term, lasting impact.

Teams with a long-term orientation might struggle with focusing on short-term goals. In many cases, teams in these environments enjoy long-term planning and can struggle to adopt the iterative nature of Agile, with plans changing every couple of weeks. Spend time helping these teams connect the dots between short-term goals to support long-term goals. Helping teams appreciate making quick decisions that will benefit them in the future is a critical task for you in this setting. Because teams have their eyes set on a long-term future prize, they may be reluctant to engage in any leisure time as they will feel that leisure will get in the way of accomplishing future objectives. Encourage these teams to take breaks and to have fun. As the saying goes, "All work and no play makes Jack a dull boy."

Indulgence Versus Restraint

The last Hofstede dimension is indulgence. The indulgence dimension measures the degree to which members of society control their desires and impulses.[27] Do people in society delay gratification, or do they need to get what they want immediately? Societies high in restraint are described as restrained societies, while societies that are not highly restrained are considered indulgent societies. Nigeria is an example of a nation with a high indulgence with a score of 84. Nigerians love to celebrate, enjoy themselves, and have fun. Nigerians spend millions (USD) on elaborate funerals, weddings, and birthday parties.[28] People in indulgent cultures tend to describe themselves as happy, and Nigeria was once considered the happiest nation on earth despite its economic challenges.[29] The United States also scores relatively high on the indulgence scale, and it is not uncommon for people to overspend to acquire the items they desire. They also may not follow specific rules if those rules will prevent them from meeting their desires. While work is

---

[27] Ibid.

[28] Temi O Wright, "The Local Context for Organizing," *The Journal of Business Diversity* 19, no. 2 (2019): 148.

[29] "Nigeria: The happiest place on earth," https://www.theguardian.com/global/2011/jan/04/nigerians-top-optimism-poll (last access July 19 2020).

essential in indulgent cultures, play is also crucial. If the workplace does not make room for play, employees in indulgent countries may become unhappy.[30]

China is a low indulgence nation with a score of 24; hence it is considered a more restrained culture. Society focuses primarily on the needs required for survival and control over satisfying their desires. Society places limits on how much enjoyment is acceptable. In low indulgence cultures, the emphasis is on work, and leisure time is not as emphasized in work settings, i.e., activities that encourage socializing or play may not be highly encouraged. Work ethic receives more praise in low indulgent cultures than it does in high indulgent cultures.[31] Because work ethic receives so much praise, people in low indulgent cultures risk overworking themselves. People in low indulgent cultures are less likely to try new ideas that challenge the current way of thinking or working, and so introducing new methods for getting work done may face some resistance.

Highly indulgent cultures are more compatible with Agile. Even though cross-functional teams address challenges, we cannot forget that individuals make up the team. Agile values and principles demand that leaders foster a workplace where team members can maintain a healthy balance between work and play. A high indulgence culture is more likely to encourage events where team members can socialize and get to know each other. Harnessing the culture to promote these Agile values is your responsibility. Providing opportunities for leisure will also help individuals remain motivated in the organization. It is easy to lose sight of making sure individuals and teams can work at a sustainable pace. The results are disengaged team members and poor performance. In one organization, we established a social committee that made sure we had fun events scheduled during the year. Encourage your teams to make sure they spend time together celebrating their achievements. Departmental outings and birthday celebrations, while seemingly small, make a big difference.

If you are leading product development teams in a low indulgence orientation context, you have a different challenge on your hands. Teams in low indulgence (high restrained) societies may find team building activities and games as learning instruments during work time a distraction because play during work is not encouraged. Pay attention to how teams respond to games at work because play and work are separate activities. It is common for business to come before pleasure. People may also not want to talk about their family or social life at work—that is a private matter that is not appropriate for work. Find other culturally acceptable and appropriate ways to increase play and relaxation on the team.

---

[30] I once received feedback that an organization was no longer fun because the leaders did not bring in cake to celebrate birthdays.

[31] Zongyun Zhou, Xiao-ling Jing, Yulin Fang, and Doug Vogel, "Toward a Theory of Perceived Benefits, Affective Commitment, and Continuance Intention in Social Virtue Worlds: Cultural Values (Indulgence and Individualism Matter)," *European Journal of Information Systems* 24, no. 3 (2015): 250.

Are Cultural Dimensions Useful?

There is no denying that scholars continue to debate the usefulness of the Hofstede model (and national culture models more broadly). However, there are two reasons why I believe the model is useful. First, Ramya Vankateswaran and Abhoy Ojha argue that many criticisms incorrectly assume that Hofstede intended for the model to represent reality perfectly when that is not the case.[32] The Hofstede model provides subjective and pragmatic insight into the general collective behaviors of people in different nations and societies.[33] It helps us understand (even if imperfectly) cultural differences that may exist. Second, based on my experience living and working in multiple cultures, I am convinced that different national cultures impact the leadership process in unique ways. Hence, the model can provide value to leaders because becoming an effective leader requires that you understand that people often bring some core values and norms into the workplace. As a reminder, not everyone will conform to the generally observed cultural values and norms.[34]

So, it is wrong to stereotype people from a given country based on their score for each Hofstede dimension. For example, not every Nigerian is indulgent, and not every American (or American organization) has a short-term orientation. I imagine that as you read this section, some of your preferences differed from your country's preference. You (like me) may also adjust your behaviors based on where you find yourself. For example, power distance does not matter as much when I am with fellow Americans; however, power distance becomes more critical when I am in the company of Nigerians. Hofstede's dimensions provide insight into the potential cultural norms and values that influence how groups of people might respond to workplace challenges. The model can help leaders make sense of their leadership system.[35] Having the ability to anticipate and recognize these responses ahead of time is to your advantage. Understanding the impact of national culture on how you and your teams operate is valuable knowledge for a leader.

It is easy to become enamored with a single dimension and overlook the others. I made this mistake with my first team in India. My relentless focus on lowering power distance meant that I missed the opportunity to use other cultural dimensions to benefit our product development approach. For example, in the first few years working with the teams, I missed the opportunity to encourage and reward teamwork through the collectivist cultural value. Lower uncertainty avoidance also meant that team members were more

---

[32] Ramya T. Venkateswaran and Abhoy K. Ojha, "Abandon Hofstede-based Research? Not Yet! A Perspective from the Philosophy of Social Sciences," *Asia Pacific Business Review* 25, no. 3 (2019): 425.

[33] Michael Minkov and Geert Hofstede, "The Evolution of Hofstede's Doctrine," *Cross Cultural Management: An International Journal* 18, no. 1 (2011): 10–20.

[34] Hofstede, Hofstede, and Minkov, *Cultures and Organizations*, 40.

[35] Venkateswaran and Ojha, "Abandon Hofstede-based Research?," 418.

willing to try new practices and working arrangements.[36] And while high power distance often comes across as a negative, the teams were not resistant when I provided them with directives. Over time, I discovered how these cultural values help me become a better leader for my teams.

You need to pay attention to the tension between your product development approach and the national cultures in the leadership system. Most Agile methods encourage a egalitarian approach to work. Team members are encouraged to express their opinions and provide feedback to one another, but not all cultures encourage this degree of openness between individuals. Agile methods also attempt to balance short-term and long-term needs, and individuals from certain cultures may be uncomfortable with either the long-term or short-term orientation. Agile face resistances in practically every society due to value conflicts. In some cultures, power distance is high, with distinct power differences between a manager and the individuals they support. Your goal is to find ways to use power distance to amplify your Agile approach in these cultures. The interactions on teams in these cultures may look vastly different from teams' interactions in a culture where power distance is low. Each cultural dimension either makes it easier or harder to lead product development teams. It is your responsibility to identify the cultural conflicts that will get in the way of effective leadership. Once you identify these conflicts, determine what changes you can make to your leadership approach, your product development method, or both to harness the power of the cultures represented in your organization.

What Makes an Outstanding Leader?

It is prudent to consider Hofstede's cultural dimensions while leading product development teams, but you will also benefit from considering the leader expectations of the people based on their cultural heritage. One of the many assumptions in Western leadership literature is that all societies have the same expectations of their leaders. Unfortunately, the Western perspective has become the de facto perspective on leadership, ignoring the fact that "what effective leadership and leader looks like" differs in various societies. To understand who people in different countries consider effective leaders, we turn to the GLOBE Project. The result—the statistical analysis of survey data from a questionnaire with 112 leader attributes and behaviors—is six global leader dimensions.[37] Each global dimension consists of more specific

---

[36] Hajer Ayed, Benoît Vanderose, and Naji Habra. 2017. Agile Cultural Challenges in Europe and Asia: Insights from Practitioners. In Proceedings of the 39th International Conference on Software Engineering: Software Engineering in Practice Track (ICSE-SEIP '17). IEEE Press, 153–162.

[37] Peter W. Dorfman, Paul J. Hanges, and Felix C. Brodbeck, "Leadership and Cultural Variation," in *Culture, Leadership, and Organizations: The GLOBE Study of 62 Societies*, ed. Robert J. House et al., (Thousand Oaks, CA: Sage Publications, 2004), 669–713.

dimensions. The six global leader dimensions with their specific supporting dimensions are

- Charismatic: Leaders inspire and expect high performance from the people they lead. The source of their inspiration comes from firmly held values and beliefs.
  - Supporting dimensions: Visionary, inspirational, self-sacrifice, integrity, decisive, and performance-oriented.
- Team Oriented: Leaders focus on developing and sustaining teams within their social groups. They achieve this by providing the group with a common goal or purpose.
  - Supporting dimensions: collaborative team orientation, team integrator, diplomatic, malevolent, administratively competent.
- Participative: Leaders involve others in making and executing decisions.
  - Supporting dimensions: Non-participative and autocratic.
- Humane Oriented: Leaders support those they lead. They do so with compassion and generosity.
  - Supporting dimensions: Modesty and humane orientation
- Autonomous: Leaders do not involve others and are highly independent.
- Self-Protective: Leaders engage in practices that shield the group from criticism and ensure they can save face.
  - Supporting dimensions: Self-centered, status-conscious, conflict inducer, face-saver, and procedural.

People in different countries rated the leadership dimensions based on the following scale:

- 1 = greatly inhibits a person from being an outstanding leader.
- 2 = somewhat inhibits a person from being an outstanding leader.
- 3 = slightly inhibits a person from being an outstanding leader.
- 4 = has no impact on whether a person is an outstanding leader.

- 5 = contributes slightly to a person being an outstanding leader.

- 6 = contributes somewhat to a person being an outstanding leader.

- 7 = and contributes greatly to a person being an outstanding leader.

The GLOBE Project conducted its study on leadership and national culture across ten culture groups or clusters. The clusters are Eastern Europe, Latin America, Latin Europe, Confucian Asia, Nordic Europe, Anglo, Sub-Saharan Africa, Southern Asia, Germanic Europe, and the Middle East. Each cluster contains culturally similar countries. Table 3-3 summarizes the leadership scores for perceived outstanding leadership based on the GLOBE leadership dimensions for the United States, Nigeria, India, and France.

Table 3-3. GLOBE Leadership Dimensions for Several Countries

Nation	Charismatic	Team Oriented	Participative	Humane Oriented	Autonomous	Self-Protective
USA	6.12	5.8	5.93	5.21	3.75	3.15
Nigeria	5.76	5.65	5.18	5.49	3.62	3.89
India	5.85	5.72	4.99	5.26	3.85	3.77
France	4.93	5.11	5.9	3.82	3.32	2.81
China	5.56	5.57	5.04	5.19	4.07	3.8
Sweden	5.84	5.75	5.54	4.73	3.97	2.81
GLOBE Average	5.83	5.76	5.33	4.89	3.85	3.47

People in the United States describe outstanding leaders as charismatic, team-oriented, and participative. Team members expect leaders to inspire them with a compelling vision, provide them with a goal or purpose, and then include them in making and implementing decisions. While a leader may achieve organizational results without these behaviors, it is unlikely people will consider them outstanding. In addition, there is less of an expectation for leaders to treat those they lead with compassion and care. This is not to suggest that team members do not want leaders to care about them; instead, this dimension does not contribute heavily to determining whether the leader is outstanding (or not). The GLOBE results suggest that an autonomous leadership style has little to no impact on effective leadership in the United States. In contrast, if leaders try to save face or create conflict, they may slightly inhibit the perception of being an outstanding leader.

The GLOBE studies show that Nigerian society has a slightly different view on which dimensions constitute outstanding leader behaviors. While charismatic, team-oriented, and participative leader behaviors matter, humane-oriented behaviors matter more in Nigerian society than in the United States. In fact, Nigeria scores below the GLOBE average for all behaviors except humane-oriented behavior. Autonomous leader behaviors slightly inhibit leadership, while a self-protective leader style has little impact on the perception of leader performance. It is not uncommon for Nigerians to spend a few minutes inquiring about family members before discussing work-related items. Team members expect leaders to show they care about their needs and support them. Also, protecting the group from shame is critical.

The GLOBE scores for France tell a different story. The participative dimension of leadership has the most impact on society's perception of effective leaders. People expect leaders to foster an environment where they can freely express their opinions on achieving team goals. They want leaders to give them a seat at the table and expect to make and implement decisions. Being involved is more important to team members in France than experiencing charismatic and team-oriented leader behaviors. The results also suggest that humane-oriented leadership might get in the way of being perceived as an outstanding leader. So, team members would not expect leaders to go out of their way to exhibit compassion and support. Autonomous and self-protective leadership negatively impacts an individual's perception of leaders. People do not appreciate leaders who constantly try to save face.

Our last example will come from the region the GLOBE Project refers to as Southern Asia and will focus on India. India's effective leadership profile is different from the United States, Nigeria, and France's profiles. The GLOBE Project suggests that people in India view charismatic and team-oriented leaders as outstanding. People expect leaders to inspire them and provide them with clear goals and objectives while at the same time supporting them as they tackle their objectives. Conversely, involving people in decision-making is not seen as a vital leader behavior in India as it is in France and the United States. People also consider a display of compassion and concern for their well-being a behavior of outstanding leaders. Unlike France, the absence of autonomous and self-protective leader behaviors does not significantly impact people's perception of an effective leader in India.

The results of the GLOBE Project study show that different societies value different leader behaviors. Some societies value charismatic leaders. They expect their leaders to paint a compelling vision that inspires them to reach for the stars. They want their leaders to act with integrity and to lead sacrificially. Acting decisively and achieving results are valued leader attributes because people desire strong and assertive leaders. In other cases, people want leaders to involve them in decision-making, and autocratic leader behaviors are not appreciated. People also want to participate in the activities that result from their decisions. In some societies, face-saving happens frequently, and the leader is required to do all they can do to avoid having their group experience shame and embarrassment. Leaving team members out to dry is not acceptable.

Then again, in some groups, people frown when their leaders exhibit self-protective behaviors. They want to face the consequences of their actions. They also want their leaders to step up and be accountable. Other groups expect that their leader spends time helping the team develop its competencies, i.e., they want hands-on and heavily engaged leaders who know what they are working on and the struggles they face. Disengaged leaders that lead from afar or do not involve others are not highly valued or respected in these settings. Whether a leader is outstanding, in some societies, depends on how much care and compassion they provide members of their society. How much help the leader is willing to offer in support of an individual's need goes a long way to determine whether society views a leader as outstanding or not.

Make time to understand the leader expectations of the people you lead. Their societal heritage will influence their expectations. Adapt your behaviors when and where appropriate. This is not a recommendation to forgo your core values and principles. Neither is it a suggestion to lose your identity through compromise. Instead, it is a challenge for you to adapt your approach to fit the leadership context. Chapter 7 will take a deeper look at tools to help you adapt to your environment, but for now, note that adapting how you support the people you lead is vital for effective leadership. Do not assume that what worked for you in one culture or with one individual will work for you in another culture or another individual. As we will see in the next section, due to globalization, leaders now have no choice but to adapt.

Becoming a Multicultural Leader

Both the Hofstede Insights and GLOBE Project suggest different national cultural values that leaders must work within. When Hofstede conducted his original studies between 1967 and 1973, it was highly probable that nearly all of a firm's employees came from the country of their employment; this is no longer the case. Globalization—organizations operating on an international scale with employees from different countries—has changed many organizations' makeup. Businesses now comprise people from different parts of the world—each bringing their unique cultural background to the organization. For example, a product development department can easily have people from the United States, India, China, Mexico, Nigeria, Australia, and many other countries. Many American-founded firms are now multinationals with CEOs that hail from other countries. For example, Microsoft's CEO Satya Nadella, credited for Microsoft's turnaround, grew up in India. It would not be far-fetched to suggest that his collectivist cultural heritage influenced his approach to leading Microsoft's cultural change. Your cultural heritage will impact how you facilitate the leadership process.

Cultural values also impact how employees interact with you as they participate in the leadership process. We have learned that it is naive to assume that because all your team members live and work in the United States, they share the same values and have the exact leader expectations as you. The 21st-century product development leader is most likely going to lead people of different nationalities in their organization. For example, you may have a team member from Nigeria who agrees with you in public—even though they disagree with you—because they default to high power distance. The values they hold dear discourage them from disagreeing with you, their leader, in public. Cultural values affect how people expect you to interact with them. Effective leadership requires that you intentionally consider cultural diversity while leading multicultural groups.

Developing your cultural intelligence and awareness will help you become a more effective leader. My time in India made me a more empathetic leader. It also helped me become more open to different ideas. So, how can you develop your cultural intelligence? Cultural agility expert Paula Caligiuri recommends individuals establish peer-level interactions with people from different cultures to develop cultural agility.[38] These interactions will help you learn about other cultures and, at the same time, provide you a safe environment in which you can practice new skills they have learned. These peer-level interactions are most beneficial when all the peers are developing their cultural intelligence together. Reciprocal mentoring ensures that both individuals help each other improve their cultural intelligence and, at the same time, build trust with each other.[39] It is tempting to think that developing cultural intelligence only matters when people come from different countries. However, it is also a fact that people from the same country can come from different cultural backgrounds. You are better off not making assumptions about your team members' cultural heritage; instead, exhibit curiosity and develop your cultural intelligence.

What happens if you cannot travel to foreign countries or cannot find a peer in your organization with a different cultural background? How can you develop your cultural awareness and intelligence? I think the answer is relatively straightforward. Spend time learning about each team member's cultural values directly from them. Make it safe for people to share their background information, beliefs, and values in one-on-one and group sessions.

---

[38] Paula Caligiuri, *Cultural Agility: Building a Pipeline of Successful Global Professionals*, (San Francisco: CA, Jossey-Bass, 2012), 145–146.

[39] Desai Sheetal, Srinivasa Rao, and Jabeen Shazi Shah, "Developing Cultural Intelligence: Learning Together with Reciprocal Mentoring," *Human Resource Management International Digest* 26, no. 3 (2018): 38–40.

Organize activities like potlucks and ask everyone to bring a dish from their country that they enjoy. Explore information from Hofstede's Insights and the GLOBE Project with your team members. Ask them to describe what behaviors would make you an outstanding leader. The more time you spend learning about your team member's cultural heritage, the more you develop your cultural awareness, and the more effective a leader you will become.

Takeaways

- Culture is more than the way a group of people behaves. Culture also includes what a group of people believe and what they value. National culture affects leaders and the leadership process.

- Globalization has resulted in multicultural product development organizations.

- Hofstede's dimensions of power distance, individualism-collectivism, masculinity-femininity, uncertainty avoidance, long-term and short-term orientation, and indulgence-restraint provide a lens on cultural differences at the national level.

- The GLOBE Project identifies that people from different nations have different expectations of their leaders across the dimensions of charismatic, team-oriented, participative, humane-oriented, autonomous, and self-protective.

- You need to increase your cultural intelligence and awareness to lead within multicultural organizations effectively.

- Develop your cultural awareness and cultural intelligence by spending time with team members from cultures different from yours.

- Harness cultural diversity for product development excellence.

Organizational Culture: Friend or Foe?

You only begin to understand culture when you try to change it.

—Ed Schein

Culture eats strategy for breakfast.

—Unknown[1]

"Our culture is terrible!" said the team members speaking to me. I had recently been hired to lead a software engineering team at a small company and was meeting with team members to learn more about them and the organization. I asked them to share what they thought about the software development organization—its strengths and weaknesses. Unfortunately, all I

---

[1] "Culture eats strategy for breakfast," https://quoteinvestigator.com/2017/05/23/culture-eats/ (last accessed July 19, 2020).

© Ebenezer C. Ikonne 2021
E. C. Ikonne, *Becoming a Leader in Product Development,*
https://doi.org/10.1007/978-1-4842-7298-5_4

heard were complaints. This was not the first (and I doubt it will be the last) time in my career that people would complain about the culture of their team, department, or even company.

We are in love with the concept of organizational culture. Our fascination with organizational culture may explain why the word "culture" is used so much in business.[2] A Google search on "why is organizational culture important" returns around 177 million results. Organizational magicians sell organizational culture as the magic elixir that determines business success. Many leadership books stress the importance for leaders to "build" or "create" an organizational culture that will lead to business success. There is no shortage of stories on how organizational culture change leads to business transformation, such as W. Warner Burke's detailed account of the critical role organizational culture played in British Airways' (BA) transformation. Burke implies that its transformation would not have succeeded without a corresponding change in the BA organizational culture.[3] Stories like that of the British Airways transformation reinforce the notion that organizational culture plays a critical role in any firm's success.

What is organizational culture, and what does organizational culture have to do with leadership in product development organizations? How does organizational culture impact employee well-being? Which organizational culture(s) espouses that a people-focus is critical for goal achievement. What responsibilities do you have when it comes to your organization's culture? These are the questions this chapter aims to answer. As we explore leadership and organizational culture, I will provide you with organizational culture diagnostic instruments in addition to recommendations for leading product development teams in different organizational cultures. We will also discuss the concept of organizational climate and its relationship to organizational culture. But before we look at organizational culture, we must first understand the concept of organization.

The Organization—What Is It?

In general terms, an organization is a group of people working together towards a shared purpose. When viewed through a rational frame, an organization is a vehicle through which people achieve all sorts of goals.[4] Most of us belong to one or more different organizations in our professional and

---

[2] "Why Is Organizational Culture Important," https://www.google.com/search?q=why+is+organizational+culture+important (last accessed July 28, 2020).

[3] W. Warner Burke, *Organizational Change: Theory and Practice*, (Thousand Oaks, CA: SAGE, 2018), 250–259.

[4] Gareth Morgan, *Images of Organization*, (Thousand Oaks, CA: Sage Publications, Inc., 2006), 15.

personal life. For example, if you work for a company, then you belong to an organization. Maybe you belong to a faith group, ethnic association, or sports club—these are also organizations, albeit different kinds. Jon Aarum Andersen suggests that business organizations (corporations) exist to achieve their owners' goals, i.e., your firm is not a democracy. Employees in firms work together to achieve the goals of the firm's principals. Sometimes these principals are also employees, like in the case of a startup, and in other cases, the principals hand over the keys of their business to others to take care of for them. For other types of organizations (e.g., political and religious), the aim is to achieve the leader's goals or common goals.[5] Anyone hired into an leader position in a firm—starting with the CEO—is a steward of the organization. These individuals need to ensure the firm attains its goals.

At face value, the perspective that you (and other leaders) are stewards (and not owners) might be difficult to accept because it may not align with your daily experience. All communication surrounding goals and plans comes from leaders. Employees do not see (or may not even know) the owners of the firm. The CEO is the face of the firm, and so it makes sense to believe the CEO is the ultimate decision-maker. However, the CEO is most likely accountable to a Board of Directors (or something similar). The Board of Directors is then accountable to a set of principal owners. The Board and the owners must approve any plans the firm's CEO develops. Ultimately, the owners (principals) chart the business course. Even though the principals may be mostly hands-off, they must still approve the firm's executive leadership plans.

It is easy to conclude that the company we work for—the signer of our paycheck—is the only unit of analysis when discussing organizational culture. However, if we consider an organization as "a consciously coordinated social entity, with a relatively identifiable boundary, which functions on a relatively continuous basis to achieve a common goal or a set of goals,"[6] we discover other organizations within the large organization. To illustrate this point further, consider Kelechi, a product development manager who works for corporation XYZ. First, Kelechi belongs to the XYZ organization. Second, she belongs to the product development department. Finally, but equally as important, Kelechi leads Team ABC. The organizations Kelechi belongs to are shown in Figure 4-1. Her employment in XYZ company makes Kelechi part of (at least) three organizations. Her team's goals must support all the other organizational goals, or else she runs the risk of being in misalignment with her other organizations. The consequences of misalignment are often dire and can lead to the termination of her employment.

---

[5] Jon Aarum Andersen, "On 'followers' and the Inability to Define," *Leadership & Organization Development Journal* 40, no. 2 (2019): 275–276.

[6] Stephen Robbins, *Organizational Theory: Structure, Design and Applications*, (Englewood Cliffs, NJ: Prentice Hall, 1990), 4.

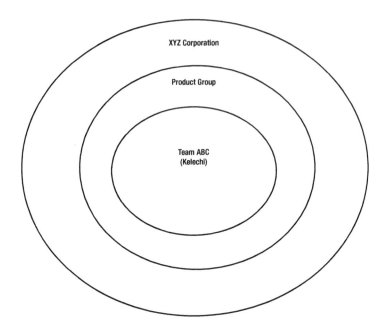

Figure 4-1. Kelechi belongs to multiple organizations

It then means that when we talk about an organization and its culture, we must be specific about the organization under observation. Is it a discrete team within the organization, a department such as the product development department Kelechi belongs to, or the firm as a whole? In many cases, when people refer to organizational culture, they have the department or business they belong to in mind. And yet, discrete teams are also organizations and hence have an organizational culture. When you think about organizational culture, start at your assigned organizational unit. For example, a manager, director, and vice president have different organizational boundaries because their leadership scope is different. The manager is responsible for the teams they lead. A director may be responsible for multiple managers and multiple teams. A vice president could have responsibility for the entire department. Your business organization is also part of a larger environment. In addition to national culture, other factors such as the business environment, geopolitical affairs, economy, and societal shifts are part of the environment that organizations operate within. We saw several businesses increase their commitment to inclusion and diversity after the social justice protests in the summer of 2020. Thus, an organization's culture is not immune to outside influences.

Each leader's first concern is the culture(s) of their assigned organization. I am not suggesting that a product development team manager should not care about their department's culture(s). On the contrary, they need to because their department's culture impacts their team's culture. However, I have observed that many managers are so focused on their department's organizational culture that they ignore the culture they influence daily—their teams' culture—and miss opportunities to improve it.

While a rational description of "organization" might be a collection of people who belong to a shared structure working together to achieve some larger aim, we also have mental image(s) of the organization we belong to. These images influence our behavior. Gareth Morgan proposes the following images of organization:

- Machine

- Organism

- Brain

- Culture

- Political System

- Psychic Prison

- Flux and Transformation

- Instruments of Domination[7]

Each metaphor provides a different perspective on how you might think about an organization. Most people hold predominant views of what an organization is to them. Whenever I ask people to rank these metaphors based on their organizational experiences, I get all kinds of results. When you rank these metaphors, what comes first, second, and third? Why? How does your primary view of organizations influence how you do your job? Having the ability to see organizations through various lenses equips leaders with information to contribute to the leadership process. Throughout the remainder of this book, we will refer to these images where appropriate. Let us briefly review organizational climate before looking at organizational culture.

Organizational Climate

People often use organizational culture and organizational climate interchangeably, but they are not the same.[8] Organizational climate refers to how individuals feel about their work environment at any given time.[9] Team

---

[7] Gareth Morgan, *Images of Organization*, (Thousand Oaks, CA: Sage Publications, Inc., 2006).

[8] Ogbonna and Harris, "Organizational Culture," 36.

[9] Aysen Berberoglu, "Impact of Organizational Climate on Organizational Commitment and Perceived Organizational Performance: Empirical Evidence from Public Hospitals," *BMC Health Services Research* 18, no. 399 (2018): 2–3.

members' immediate perception of the organization is the organizational climate. It is not uncommon for corporations to conduct a quarterly organizational survey that provides information on how employees feel about the organization. This information exposes the current organizational climate (and not necessarily the organizational culture). When people ask during job interviews, "what is the culture here?" they are really asking (in many cases) "what is the current climate here?" While they might be interested in the organization's deeply held beliefs and values, they are most likely more interested in learning what it is like to work in the organization then and there. While organizational culture does influence organizational climate, you must understand the difference between the two. The way you lead day in and day out plays a crucial role in determining your organization's climate, and over time, these behaviors shape organizational culture. Now, it is time to unpack organizational culture.

What Is Organizational Culture?

A single definition of organizational culture that organizational theorists agree with does not exist. Ed Schein defines culture as "the accumulated shared learning of that group as it solves its problems of external adaptation and internal integration; which has worked well enough to be considered valid and, therefore, to be taught to new members as the correct way to perceive, think, feel, and behave in relation to those problems."[10] That is a mouthful. Simplifying a bit, we could say that culture reflects how a social group responds to environmental demands based on their previous experiences. Schein (and other organizational culture theorists) offers a rational definition of organizational culture. Other definitions of organizational culture adopt more of a subjective-interpretive frame with less focus on rationality. Lee Bolman and Terence Deal suggest that an organization's culture becomes visible through the symbols (myths, sagas, rituals, heroes and heroines, etc.) that it has.[11] Organizational culture results from employee responses to the symbols—these responses are not always predictable and can be full of surprises. We can also understand the importance of culture from how people respond when outsiders or newcomers challenge well-established symbols and rituals such as the end-of-year company party. Many aspects of culture become deeply ingrained and relatively stable over time.

---

[10] Schein, *Organizational Culture and Leadership*, 6.
[11] Lee G. Bolman and Terrence E. Deal, *Reframing Organizations*, (Hoboken, NJ: Josey Bass, 2017), 242–257.

Significant debate exists over whether culture is a property of an organization that leaders can manipulate or whether an organization is a culture. Over the years, my perspective on this topic has shifted. I started with the perspective that culture is an organizational variable that leaders need to control and direct for optimal results. Most business books promote this viewpoint. However, after further research and reflecting on my leadership experiences, it is evident that an organization IS a culture. Organizational culture is not a standalone property that leaders create and then manipulate; instead, organizational culture emerges from social interactions within the organization.[12] That is, how people interact with each other while pursuing organizational objectives leads to organizational culture. Leaders embed and transmit organizational cultural values through actions that serve as symbols to their organization.[13] You must understand how to interpret and make sense of organizational culture to influence it. If you primarily view culture as something an organization HAS, then I hope you come to see culture as something that an organization IS by the end of the chapter. The IS perspective undergirds the remainder of this chapter.

Many definitions of organizational culture agree that organizational culture consists of people's values, beliefs, and tacit assumptions. Some of these values may appear in employee handbooks, such as "treat everyone with respect," or "we value open, honest, and direct communication." However, each organization also has assumptions that are tacit and unspoken. An example of a tacit assumption might be, "do not say anything that may hurt people's feelings" or "relationships matter more than experience." These definitions suggest that organizational culture is unitary, i.e., the organization has a culture that most people agree with and uphold. While this might be the popular perspective of organizational culture in leadership literature, it is not the only perspective. While studying a firm, Joanne Martin observed that employees had different perspectives on their firm's culture. She categorized these perspectives as the integration, differentiation, and fragmentation perspectives.[14] Each perspective provides a unique approach for making sense of an organization's culture. The approaches are outlined in Table 4-1.

[12] V. Lynn Meek, "Organizational Culture: Origins and Weaknesses," *Organization Studies* 39, no. 4 (1988): 463.

[13] Abinash Panda and Rajen Gupta. Understanding Organizational Culture: A Perspective on Roles for Leaders. *Vikalpa*. no. 26. (2001): 3–19.

[14] Joanne Martin, *Cultures in Organizations: Three Perspectives*, (New York, NY: Oxford University Press, 1992).

Table 4-1. Organizational Culture Perspectives

Perspective	Integration	Differentiation	Fragmentation
Orientation to consensus	Organization-wide consensus	Subcultural consensus	Multiplicity of views (no consensus)
Relation among manifestations	Consistency	Inconsistency	Complexity (not clearly consistent or inconsistent)
Orientation to ambiguity	Exclude it	Channel it outside subcultures	Focus on it
Metaphors	Clearing in jungle, monolith, hologram	Islands of clarity in a sea of ambiguity	Web, jungle

Integration View—A Single Organizational Culture

If you have ever sat in a meeting where you are working on defining the culture for a team, department, or firm, you know the integration view. The integration view is the most popular perspective on organizational culture. Whenever people make general statements about their organization's culture like "leaders care for their people" or "we value diverse opinions," that is the integration view. The integration view promotes organization-wide consensus, consistency, and clarity with the exclusion of ambiguity within the entire organization.[15] The default unit of analysis for the integration view is generally at the level of a business unit (or a group with a Profit & Loss statement); however, the integration view also applies when there is more than one organizational unit under consideration. Organization-wide consensus means that different groups within the organization agree on certain core beliefs. For example, individuals may agree that everyone on the product development team has an equal voice. The integration view assumes consistency in how values, e.g., "open, honest, and direct," are understood and practiced. This shared understanding of values ensures employees know what matters most, especially when making tough decisions. An illustration of a shared global value could be how the organization handles when a team member loses a loved one, e.g., sending flowers. If people receive the same layoff treatment regardless of which department they belong to, this represents an integrated culture. The integration view of organizational culture does not tolerate those with divergent opinions. New hires need to be a cultural fit, and cultural misfits eventually find themselves looking for new jobs.

A predominant characteristic of the integration view is that organizational culture is considered a critical determinant of organizational effectiveness.[16] This view is more in line with the "culture is a property" take on organizational

---

[15] Ibid, 46–52.
[16] Ibid, 59–61.

culture. Many leaders focus on changing organizational culture with the hopes that these changes improve organizational effectiveness. Ironically, empirical evidence that validates the link between organizational culture and organizational effectiveness is mixed.[17] Nonetheless, some evidence may suggest that organizational culture is associated with organizational performance.[18] As we know, not all that matters can be measured (at least not easily). The integration view also presents the leader as the organizational cultural change champion. The leader becomes the hero who is supposed to establish an organizational culture that leads to organizational excellence. This view is consistent with the image of the organization as a machine.[19] Organizational culture becomes the fuel that ensures the organization—the machine—runs smoothly. It is the leader's responsibility to shape organizational culture. Leadership literature—academic and popular—contains many stories of how leaders supposedly single-handedly transformed their organization's culture all by themselves. The leader is at the center of the organizational culture change in the integration view. Unfortunately, such organizations are in danger of succumbing to the leader attribution error.[20] The leader attribution error places the success and failure of an organization solely on its leader(s).

And yet, the integration view can benefit your leadership practice. There will be people in the organization who appreciate a degree of consensus, consistency, and clarity. Consensus, consistency, and clarity provide the comfort required for people to do their job and do their job well. They know what to expect from you and the organization at large. Ensuring that team members know desired values and behaviors is your responsibility as their leader. Making sure people understand values and behaviors goes beyond having everyone reading the employee manual—it will not capture many of the tacit assumptions required for team effectiveness. If your team needs to make some cultural changes, they will look to you to lead and support these changes. Schein extensively details how leaders embed and transmit cultural norms and values through signs and symbols.[21] People take their cultural cues from the behaviors you model in the organization.

---

[17] Boon-Seng Tan, "In Search of the Link Between Organizational Culture and Performance: A Review From the Conclusion Validity Perspective," *Leadership & Organization Development Journal* 40, no. 3 (2019): 356–368.

[18] I Charles A. O'Reilly III, David F. Caldwell, Jennifer A. Chatman, and Bernadette Doerr, "The Promise and Problems of Organizational Culture: CEO Personality, Culture, and Firm Performance," *Group & Organization Management* 39, no. 6 (2014): 595–625.

[19] Morgan, *Images of Organization*.

[20] J. Richard Hackman, *Leading Teams: Setting the Stage for Great Performances*, (Boston, MA: Harvard Business School Press., 2002)

[21] Edgar Schein, *Organizational Culture and Leadership*, 181–206.

In my experience, developing a shared set of core values and then engaging in dialogue on behaviors that reflect these values is crucial and is work that you need to make sure happens. Culture work is never complete. It requires passion, commitment, intentionality, and focus. I learned this while leading the team with the organizational culture complaints mentioned at the beginning of this chapter. That first meeting with the team left me wondering if I had just made the biggest mistake of my career. Even though many years have passed since that meeting, I still remember how depressed and miserable everyone sounded. Their comments made it evident that no one was happy working at the company. Unknown to me, almost everyone on the team was looking for a new job. I had a team that was ready to head out the door! I even considered asking the CIO for another opportunity within the company. Fortunately, I did not.

I needed something to bring the team together before we spoke about goals, roadmaps, or other software development activities. So, I decided to conduct an activity and ask the team members to write down what they thought our shared values could be. We wrote down value statements in the form of "We value…" Examples of value statement that team members wrote down included the following:

- We value treating each other with respect.
- We value asking for help when we face a problem we cannot solve.
- We value working together as a single team.
- We value improving our software development process.
- We value doing what we say we will do.

We then identified behaviors that would demonstrate each shared value and committed to those behaviors. Then we identified behaviors that did not reflect our shared values and committed to minimizing those behaviors. For example, the team agreed that if someone were stuck on a problem for longer than 20 minutes, they would ask someone else on the team for help. Working with the team to co-create team values helped develop a team (organizational) culture that provided a sense of consistency for everyone.

Differentiation View—Multiple Subcultures

And yet, not everyone supports espoused organizational values. For example, several individuals on my product team disagreed with the value statements we developed and decided to leave the team (and the organization). This area of difference is the focus of the differentiation perspective. Differences are due to the presence of subcultures that differ from the proposed unitary culture.[22] The differentiation view acknowledges the various subcultures within an organization and studies how these subcultures interact. For example, the product development department and the operations department often represent two subcultures. Taking it a step further, the product and engineering department could also have multiple subcultures within their department. Anytime people point out material differences between groups, they are most likely pointing out a different subculture. Leaders who only have an integration perspective find multiple subcultures frustrating because their focus is on creating a single culture. Trying to create a single culture is futile. An observation such as "I do not want to work in that group because I do not like X, Y, or Z" often indicates cultural differences. However, you must avoid the temptation to try and fix a culture just because it is different.

The differentiation perspective provides insight that is invaluable to you. To take a differentiation view means that you look for inconsistencies and subcultural consensus.[23] Inconsistencies show up when groups do not see people treated the same way or do not share the same experiences across the organization. I recall a situation where several departments in an organization were upset that another department could leave work in the middle of the day for social activities while other departments could not leave till after 4 p.m. It did not matter that each department had different work demands—this department had a different set of social activity norms. It was a cultural inconsistency—and not a good one. As mentioned previously, it is essential to recognize that multiple subcultures can exist within the same group, e.g., two software development teams in the same department can have cultural differences. Software developers form a subculture based on their skills (and often consider culture superior to other cultures) within a larger product development department. In the same token, product management managers belong to the manager subculture.

The differentiation view shows that there is little agreement on what organizational culture elements lead to organizational effectiveness.[24] Unlike the integration view, which posits that a single organizational culture enhances

---

[22] Martin, *Cultures in Organizations: Three Perspectives*. 83.

[23] Ibid, 85–94.

[24] Jossy Matthew, "Organisational Culture and Effectiveness: A Multi-Perspective Evaluation of an Indian Knowledge-Intensive Firm," *Employee Relations: The International Journal* 41, no. 3 (2019): 543–545.

organizational effectiveness, the differentiation view posits that a single organizational culture results from one group dominating other groups.[25] For example, the department which had social activities in the middle of the day eventually had to get back on the "corporate plan" and only leave for social activities after 4 p.m. Many team members were displeased with the decision. In their minds, it was just another example of the "other culture" dominating their department. In addition, different subcultures have different definitions of organizational effectiveness, so it can be challenging to reach a consensus on defining organizational effectiveness. For example, software developers may think organizational effectiveness is high software quality. In contrast, product managers may think organizational effectiveness is getting product features to market as quickly as possible. These culture clashes hinder organizational effectiveness.

Unlike the integration view that places the locus of organizational change with the leader, the differentiation perspective views organizational culture change through how a subculture changes in response to environmental stimuli. Thus, the differentiation view seeks to answer questions such as: how did the department adapt when asked to change their social activity hours or how did various groups in the business change in response to the coronavirus pandemic and company work-from-home requirements?

The differentiation perspective is beneficial because it enables you to acknowledge multiple subcultures within a single organization. It would be naïve for you to think that everyone experiences the espoused values of the organization similarly. It is hard to achieve this level of consistency in a group that consists of more than a handful of people. Recognizing that the organization's subcultures will have different shared beliefs is crucial, especially when the different subcultures have shared tasks. Events, signs, or rituals that you may consider trivial might be significant to another subculture, as the story about outings during business hours illustrated. As a leader, taking the time to appreciate the values that matter to the subcultures you work with is critical, especially if you want to influence across organizational boundaries. Once you know what matters to other groups, you can adopt an approach that considers their values.

It is also vital to detect inconsistencies in an organization's culture that might hamper organizational effectiveness. While it is true that we always have subcultures, some champions of the differentiation perspective do acknowledge that there are values that can benefit the entire organization—even though the adoption of these values may override the preferred values of other groups.[26] For example, if your organization espouses treating people with respect and fairness, it is your job to make sure you address any inconsistencies

---

[25] Ibid, 101–104.
[26] Martin, *Cultures in Organizations: Three Perspectives.*

immediately. Sometimes subcultures create rules to protect individuals who do not live up to broader organizational values and norms. I have worked in several organizations where leaders went against company values by protecting brilliant jerks who made life miserable for other people because these jerks were subject matter experts and would be difficult to replace. Do not be this type of leader. Appreciate the beauty of the subcultures in your organization while upholding values that transcend any subculture.

Fragmentation View—Conflict and Confusion

In many cases, it is hard to find consensus on shared beliefs, and instead, people are confused (in different ways) about their organization's culture—even within a discrete team. The fragmentation perspective on culture focuses on the ambiguity, complexity of relationships between the various cultural expressions in the organization, and the diverse interpretations of culture that prevent consensus.[27] Fragmentation is evident when people provide varied and contradictory responses to questions about cultural norms or values. For example, I remember being part of a leadership team that attempted to change an existing organizational norm. Despite our best attempts to clearly state the new norm, managers presented the new norm to their teams differently. This caused team members to have various interpretations of what the norm entailed. Many of these interpretations were utterly wrong. It was unclear what was acceptable and what was not. Some individuals believed the norm did not apply in certain situations, and they could do whatever they desired. The fragmentation perspective focuses on cultural ambiguity and clarifies that even subcultures experience ambiguity around cultural norms and values. For example, many software development organizations struggle with a shared understanding of how to make technology choices.

While there is no doubt that ambiguity is ever-present, the jury is still out on whether ambiguity benefits organizational effectiveness. One study observed that an organization's cultural ambiguity hurt organizational effectiveness because of confusion on the behaviors consistent with espoused values.[28] The new norm that my leadership team attempted to introduce created noise that took focus away from matters of more importance in the organization and had us spending hours addressing the new norm. However, other studies suggest that ambiguity can help with adaptability and creativity in the organization.[29] The absence of defined rules for every situation can provide people with the freedom and flexibility needed to try new ideas. For example, the confusion surrounding how new technology is selected allows a software

---

[27] Ibid, 130.
[28] Matthew, "Organisational Culture and Effectiveness," 545–546.
[29] Martin, *Cultures in Organizations: Three Perspectives*, 158.

developer to test a JavaScript framework without getting approval from anyone in the organization. If the JavaScript framework works well, that developer becomes a hero or heroine.

The fragmentation perspective challenges the idea of ordered organizational change offered by the integration (leader-led) and differentiation (subculture-led) perspectives. The fragmentation perspective supports the image that the organization is an instrument of domination.[30] The ambiguity and uncertainty highlight the perspective that the organizational norms benefit a select few—the organizational elite. However, the perspective does not provide much guidance on how to change an existing organizational culture.[31] Because ambiguity and inconsistency will always exist in an organization, understanding how to facilitate change with this reality is essential. The lack of extensive literature on leading within a fragmentation perspective is unfortunate because leaders need to know how to deal with multiple cultural interpretations without becoming frustrated or discouraged. Frustrated leaders resort to coercive and punitive measures when encountering multiple cultural interpretations in the organization that they do not know how to handle.

Many leaders view fragmentation as an indication that something is wrong with their organization that they need to fix. But the fragmentation perspective is helpful because it forces us to acknowledge the ambiguity and the lack of clarity throughout our organization. It is improbable that everyone in the organization has the same view on espoused values. People have different experiences, which leads to different interpretations. Use the results of employee surveys to look for sources of ambiguity that significantly dampen organizational effectiveness. Sometimes these ambiguities are improper or unethical, and you should address them as quickly as you can. An example of ambiguity in product development organizations is the promotion criteria. All too often, team members have different interpretations of what is required to get to the next level in the organization. You need to address ambiguities like this to the best of your ability.

It is easy to assume or even desire that everyone (even within the same department) shares the same underlying cultural assumptions. Such thinking ignores the fact that people are different and have different worldviews, as discussed in Chapter 3. Trying to eliminate all forms of inconsistency and ambiguity in the organization is a waste of time. Instead, consider embracing the tension caused by multiple views on the organization's culture. Harness the tension to learn more about how people view the organization. Not all divergent viewpoints are harmful. In fact, diversity in thought and action can benefit the organization if leveraged appropriately. I recall a manager who challenged his company's espoused values of empowerment because he could

---

[30] Morgan, *Images of Organization*.
[31] Ibid, 159–162.

not share company talking points directly with his team. In his mind, being an "empowered leader" included regularly providing his team with updates about the firm. His feedback led to the firm providing talking points to managers. The fragmentation view looks for ways to take advantage of identified inconsistencies within the culture.

Uncovering Hidden Perspectives

So why should you care about multiple perspectives of organizational culture? And how will these perspectives help you become a more impactful leader? You need to care about these perspectives because they provide you with a holistic understanding of your organization's culture. Each perspective provides insightful nuggets on your organization's culture that the other perspectives do not provide. Many leaders are only familiar with the integration perspective because it is the perspective that receives the most attention. And yet, ignoring the differentiation and fragmentation perspectives prevents you from obtaining insights only available through those perspectives. Martin refers to insights that are not available through our default view as "hidden perspectives."[32] Within these hidden perspectives often lies cultural realities that amplify or dampen organizational effectiveness. As a leader, you want to make sure your organization's cultures support organizational goals.

The integration perspective is popular because some evidence does suggest that having a set of shared assumptions and values benefits organizations.[33] However, do not fall for the myth that leaders build or create cultures. Remember, leaders influence organizational culture through their symbolic actions. Pay attention to the differences between subcultures in the organization—especially subcultures that need to collaborate. Team members will have unique perspectives on the organization's culture.[34] Look for indicators that show a lack of consensus and the presence of ambiguity in how people make sense of cultural norms so that you can explore the ambiguity. Continually assess your organizational culture through the cultural lens of integration, differentiation, and fragmentation so that you influence culture in the appropriate places. Also, invest time learning about other groups' subcultures because doing so will help you understand their shared assumptions and values. The knowledge you gain leads to wisdom making you more effective. It will help you relate to the other group both positively and productively. It is not that different from learning a new language in a foreign country. Speaking the new language breaks down

---

[32] Ibid, 175–176.
[33] O'Reilly III, Caldwell, Chatman, and Doerr, "Promise and Problems of Organizational Culture," 595–597.
[34] Emmanuel Ogbonna and Lloyd C. Harris, "Organizational Culture: It's Not What You Think…," *Journal of General Management* 23, no. 3 (1998): 35–47.

communication barriers that exist and makes you an honorary member of the other group's subculture. Pay attention to the various cultures and subcultures you influence.

Organizational Culture Typologies

We have already established that organizations are multiple cultures. It should then come as no surprise that no two organizational cultures are the same—even for successful companies in the same industry like Delta Air Lines and Southwest Airlines. To help leaders make sense of organizational cultures, researchers have developed different organizational culture typologies. Organizational typologies describe cultures based on specific dimensions, such as their leadership and management approach. Some typologies consider the customer's role in the organization, while other typologies consider employee interaction models. Diagnostic models such as the Westrum typology consider how an organization processes information to determine whether the organization is pathological (power-oriented), bureaucratic (rule-oriented), or generative (performance-oriented).[35] And then again, how organizations execute their strategy is another dimension found in certain organizational culture typologies. There is an abundance of cultural typologies that leaders can use to diagnose their organization's culture. Some typologies reflect an integration perspective, while others allow for differentiation. If you use a typology that has an integration perspective, do not forget its inherent limitations. At best, the typology reflects a dominant perspective within the organization. It does not, however, reflect the entire perspective. I am not aware of organizational culture typology that accounts for fragmentation.

We will explore two of the more popular organizational culture typologies, the Schneider Model and the Competitive Values Framework (CVF). These instruments help you diagnose your organization's culture so that you can determine the best way to influence the culture in a different direction (if necessary). However, as previously mentioned, do not lose sight of the differentiation and fragmentation views in the organization while using these typologies.

[35] Ron Westrum, "A typology of organizational cultures, "*Quality and Safety in Health Care* 13 no. Suppl 2, (2004): ii22–ii27.

The Schneider Model

William Schneider identified four core organizational culture types—control, collaboration, competence, and cultivation—of successful organizations.[36] Each culture reflects whether the organization focuses on actuality or possibility (content) and whether the organization has a personal or impersonal approach to decision-making and judgments (process).[37] Thus, while an organization will display aspects of the different organizational culture types, a look under the covers shows that many organizations have a core organizational culture type. They are either primarily control, collaboration, competence, or cultivation. In addition, leaders' predominant or default behavior(s)—every leader has a combination of behaviors—plays a significant role in fostering and reinforcing their organization's core culture, as we will see in the following sections. As you review Schneider's culture types and the leader behaviors, ask yourself the following questions:

- Which leader archetype(s)—commander, coach, visionary, or steward—do I think best describes me?

- Which leader archetype(s)—commander, coach, visionary, or steward—would the people I lead say best describes me?

Figure 4-2 shows the mapping between the four cultures and the personal-impersonal and actuality-possibility axes.

---

[36] William E. Schneider, "Why Good Management Ideas Fail: The Neglected Power of Organizational Culture," *Strategy & Leadership* 28, no. 1 (2000): 26–27.

[37] William E. Schneider, *The Reengineering Alternative: A Plan for Making Your Current Culture Work* (Burr Ridge, Illinois: Irwin Professional Publishing, 1994), 105.

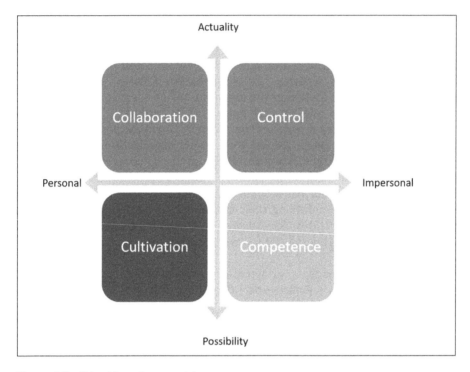

Figure 4-2. Schneider culture model

Each culture has an associated archetype shown in Table 4-2.

Table 4-2. Schneider's Organizational Culture Types. William E. Schneider, The Reengineering Alternative: A Plan for Making Your Current Culture Work (Burr Ridge, Illinois: Irwin Professional Publishing, 1994), 105

Culture type	Organization archetype	Leader archetype
Control	Military	Commander
Collaboration	Family or Sports Team	Coach
Competence	University	Visionary
Cultivation	Religious institution	Steward

Control Culture—Leader as Commander

The control culture archetype is the military. It focuses on ensuring certainty in all aspects of organizational life. What matters most is that the organization achieves its goals, i.e., getting stuff done. In organizational units with a core culture of control, leaders institute processes and practices to ensure that everything runs like a machine. These organizations will have procedures for all operational functions. Leaders in these organizations traditionally adopt a "command-and-control" leadership style characterized by directives and commands. In many cases, team members assume that the manager knows best and can address all system issues. Risk-taking is discouraged, and a business-as-usual process is encouraged. Organizations with a control culture are obsessed with maintaining their market dominance and ensuring the organization's survival. Many of the organizations I have worked in display the control culture. And many (if not most) leaders default to commander behaviors and practices.

The control culture is all about certainty, and yet product development is full of uncertainty. As such, if you find yourself leading product development teams in an organization with a control culture or even working with a department with a control culture, you may experience some hardship. These other departments will expect precision and accuracy unavailable in product development. The best approach I have found for succeeding in these environments is to release impactful software frequently. Frequently releasing software was the approach I adopted when I took on the director role for a product development department team in a control culture organization. The team previously spent months working on features before the features made it into production. Hence, the operations team wanted precise estimates from our teams before we started working on new product features. We responded by releasing small software increments that helped the operations team. We created a release pipeline with automated tests, which gave us the comfort needed to release often. Once we had our release infrastructure in place, we began to release software frequently, and it was not long before the desire for precise estimates became infrequent.

Collaboration Culture—Leader as Coach

Some organizational cultures focus more on affiliation and belonging. Schneider called cultures with these core attributes the collaboration culture because they operate like a family or athletic team.[38] Organizations showing a collaboration culture are concerned with what their customers think of them. They place much effort into creating synergies inside and outside the organization.[39] Relationships are the lifeblood of collaboration cultures. Leaders focus on coaching in these organizations and creating an exceptional experience for everyone involved with the organization. Also, psychological safety is a crucial concern in these organizations. Psychological safety is a

---

[38] William E. Schneider, "Why Good Management Ideas Fail, 27.
[39] Ibid

shared belief that taking interpersonal risks on the team will not have negative repercussions.[40] An example of an interpersonal risk could be sharing bad news or having a dissenting opinion. The family-like atmosphere provides a safe environment for learning. Leaders encourage egalitarianism and participative decision-making. Software startups often reflect a collaboration culture.

The collaboration culture is a good match for Agile methods because Agile promotes collaboration and addressing customer needs which this culture supports. An Agile principle encourages the daily interaction between everyone involved in the product development process.[41] It is vital to foster this culture's tacit assumptions and values in your organization as a product development leader. Encourage collaboration throughout the organization by example. Make it easy for individuals and teams to work together. Provide them with opportunities to develop their teamwork skills. Foster a workplace where everyone can meaningfully participate in the product development process.

Competence Culture—Leader as Visionary

Organizations with a competence core culture focus on setting themselves apart from others in their industry—they focus on what might be possible. Achieving what other firms have not achieved is the primary driver of this culture. As Schneider puts it, these organizations bring to market products and services that meet people's needs in extraordinary ways—they look entirely different from anything else on the market.[42] Apple is an example of an organization that demonstrated a competence culture focused on distinguishing its products from other firms' products. Products such as the iPod and iPhone set Apple apart from other players in its space. Leaders in organizations with a core culture of competence demand excellence from their workforce, focus on output, and expect a lot of work to get done. They are pacesetters.[43] There is little patience for individuals who need developmental help, and these organizations focus on hiring the proverbial "A-player" to remain competitive.

How does the Agile approach fit into this culture? If you are a leader in an organization with a competence core culture, then the regular delivery of high-quality software-based solutions that Agile encourages is essential. High-quality product delivery requires that teams have a mastery of product

---

[40] Amy C. Edmondson, "Psychological Safety and Learning Behavior in Work Teams," *Administrative Science Quarterly* 44, no. 2 (1999): 350–383.

[41] The Agile principle states that "Business people and developers must work together daily throughout the project."

[42] Schneider, "Why Good Management Ideas Fail," 27.

[43] William E. Schneider, *The Reengineering Alternative*, 7.

development technical practices (for example, product discovery and software development design principles). The competence culture produces top-notch solutions. However, the impersonal and competitive approach encouraged by competence cultures runs counter to some of the tacit assumptions of Agile. For example, many studies show that technical competence is not the sole predictor of team success. Team members' ability to work together goes a long way to determine how much success a team will achieve. Organizations with a competence culture may rely on specific individuals' brilliance (at the expense of team performance). In addition, the competence culture may lead to unsustainable and unhealthy work habits. If you do not manage this, team members may engage in unhealthy competition, hurting team outcomes. Therefore, healthy integration of work and other aspects of life is essential in the competence culture.

Cultivation Culture—Leader as Steward

Some organizational cultures have a core focus on people development. These organizations strive to provide an environment where the pursuit of noble goals and ideals transcending the organization is the primary objective—a cultivation culture. Cultivation culture's archetype is religious systems.[44] Organizations with a cultivation core culture measure themselves by looking at the difference they make in society, not just by what their profit-and-loss statements say. They also pay attention to whether employees are achieving their dreams and desires. Examples of cultivation culture organizations would be organizations that, before corporate social responsibility became popular in the 21st century, championed corporate social responsibility. Leaders in such organizations challenge their workforce to strive for ideals more significant than themselves and provide team members opportunities to give back to society through volunteering and other community service programs. These organizations also focus on helping their customers achieve their goals. W.L. Gore is an example of a cultivation culture organization.[45]

If you are leading teams in an organization with the cultivation culture as its core culture, focus on establishing congruence between product development values, principles, and organizational values. Continuous improvement is part of the Agile approach and meshes with the cultivation culture's focus on team member development. Autonomy and employee commitment are crucial in cultivation cultures.[46] Form teams with motivated and trustworthy individuals and then challenge them by presenting them with goals that inspire. In the cultivation culture, it is all about significance through difference-making.

---

[44] Ibid
[45] Ibid.
[46] Ibid

The Competing Values Framework

Robert Quinn and Kim Cameron developed the Competing Values Framework (CVF). The CVF attempts to categorize organizational culture based on how organizations use an internal focus-external focus and stability-flexibility approach to achieve organizational effectiveness.[47] The internal-external dimension indicates where the organization focuses, i.e., does the organization focus on its inner workings, or does the organization focus on its customer interactions? The stability-flexibility dimension represents whether an organization takes steps to foster stability and increased certainty versus flexibility and uncertainty. CVF produces four organizational culture types: clan, adhocracy, hierarchy, and market with their distinct characteristics.[48] Table 4-3 shows the four cultures and their dimensions. Even though most organizations have aspects of all four cultures, like Schneider's model, CVF posits that an organization will have a dominant culture at any given time.

The clan culture reflects a family-like structure with a focus on collaboration. Attention to creativity, experimentation, and entrepreneurship characterize the adhocracy culture. When leaders emphasize meeting financial goals and dominating the marketplace, they reinforce the market culture. Finally, the hierarchy culture focuses on control through defined internal structures, directives, and policies to ensure the organization runs smoothly. Quinn and Cameron note that the clan and market cultures oppose each other while the hierarchy and adhocracy oppose each other and compete.[49] Thus, there is tension between various cultural types. Figure 4-3 shows the culture types of the Competing Values Framework.

---

[47] Kim S. Cameron and Robert E. Quinn, *Diagnosing and Changing Organizational Culture*, (San Francisco, CA: Jossey-Bass, 2011), 38–41
[48] Ibid.
[49] Ibid.

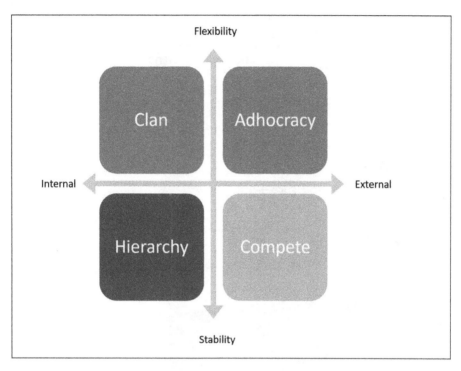

Figure 4-3. Competing Values Framework

The Organizational Culture Assessment Instrument (OCAI)[50] is an instrument that enables you to assess the present and preferred organizational cultures perceived by individuals in your organization. You can use the results from the assessment to develop organizational culture action plans. The results will also help to highlight the integration, differentiation, and fragmentation perspectives within your organization. To illustrate how you can use the OCAI assessment, I have provided OCAI assessment results for four software engineering teams. The results show how team members felt about their organization's culture and the cultural changes they desired.

The OCAI results are in Table 4-3.

---

[50] "OCAI One: Discover Your Culture in 15 minutes," https://www.ocai-online.com/ products/ocai-one (last accessed July 19, 2020).

Table 4-3. OCAI Results from Four Software Engineering Teams

	Now	Preferred
Clan	32.19	36.13
Adhocracy	20.36	25.61
Market	25.19	18.04
Hierarchy	22.25	20.22

The results are shown in Figure 4-4.

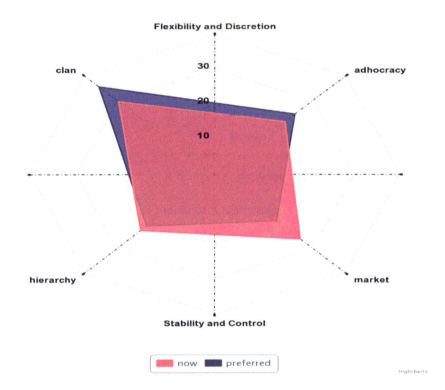

Figure 4-4. OCAI results visualized

Clan Score—We Function Like a Family

The clan culture type received the highest score in the assessment, reflecting that team members felt they belonged to a culture focused on collaboration and team building. Team members expressed high levels of trust in each other. Many of them felt psychological safety was high on their team. They also appreciated their managers' leadership and management style and described their managers as friends, mentors, and coaches because managers did not micromanage. Managers supported team members and nurtured a workplace where team members could do their best work. Managers also took the teams out to lunch and coordinated special team events where everyone got to interact with each other. Team members described their teams as largely self-managed cross-functional teams with significant autonomy.

While the results presented the clan culture as the predominant culture type, the preferred results show that team members still desired more of the clan culture experience. They desired increased internal support and flexibility. Teams viewed enterprise mandates as restricting their autonomy. Team members also wanted leaders to provide more development opportunities.

Adhocracy Score—We Do Not Innovate Enough

The adhocracy culture type received the lowest "now" score. Team members did not consider their work highly innovative, creative, or necessarily exciting because they mostly enhanced existing products with small features. Team members also provided feedback that they did not consider the broader organization particularly innovative. Even though the organization conducted "innovation days," team members noted that their innovations, when they had the opportunity to do them, rarely made it past the innovation exercise. It was "innovation theater." Some team members also expressed displeasure with the organization's decision to outsource new work because they wanted to do the work themselves.

The difference between the "now" and "preferred" scores is over 5 points which is significant. The "preferred" score indicated that team members would like to see more focus on product innovation with their participation in discovering new ideas and products instead of taking feature requests like orders. While most team members did not believe that the organization needed to become a "research and development" organization, they wanted the space to try new ideas and take risks when developing new solutions. Teams wanted the opportunity to experiment and to try new ideas.

Market Score—We Have to Hit Our Numbers

After the clan culture, most team members considered the values of market culture most dominant. A constant focus on the financials at town halls and other team meetings reinforced the perspective that achieving business financial outcomes and defeating the competition was essential to business leaders. Team members felt that stretch goals and arbitrary deadlines existed just to make sure the teams worked hard. Team members did not consider their immediate leaders hard-driving or pushy; however, they viewed senior leaders in the organization as hard-driving. The teams consistently referred to two large initiatives with unreasonable timelines. Unreasonable timelines are a common observation in market culture organizations. They believed that the organization committed to unattainable goals to attract customers and sold solutions that did not yet exist to avoid losing market share. The commitments led to the teams working under significant stress and pressure to create products sold before they existed.

The difference between the "now" and "preferred" numbers represented the largest delta in either direction (increase or decrease) for all culture types. Team members preferred that the market culture become the least dominant organizational culture in the organization. Understandably, this culture type is the least desirable as it is in opposition to and competes with the clan culture (which received the highest score). So, there will always be tension between these two culture types.

Hierarchy Score—It Does Not Feel Like a Hierarchy

The teams expressed a low perception of the hierarchy culture. While a hierarchy existed in the organization (team members report to a manager who reports to a manager), team members did not consider the organization highly formal or bureaucratic. However, several team members felt like the rollout of the enterprise processes, e.g., mandating synchronized work cadences and a single way of structuring work, had made their work difficult. They also considered the formal enterprise processes that existed for acquiring equipment or software unnecessary protocol and burdensome. Like the market culture, team members desired a slight decrease in hierarchy culture behaviors; however, it is safe to say that the team members did not perceive the hierarchy culture negatively.

Why Does Organizational Culture Matter?

Organizational culture is how an organization goes about doing its business. Doing its business includes how it achieves its goals and desires. It also includes how the organization treats people and how people feel about the organization. It reflects what matters to the people with the most power and authority in the organization i.e., the norms, values, and behaviors these individuals care about and want others to model and encourage. Organizational culture is essential, and yet it is messy and difficult to influence. It is your responsibility to determine what organizational culture you want to support your organizational goals. A look around the business landscape reveals successful companies in the same industry, all with different organizational cultures. In other words, there are successful companies with control or market core culture. Other successful companies have a cultivation or clan culture. There is not one organizational culture that is a panacea. Your organizational culture choice needs to reflect the core principles and values you want guiding your organization. Your organization's culture must not prevent organizational excellence and business success.

The organizational culture models we have looked at provide a set of tools you can use to make some sense of your organization's culture. These tools allow you to get a broad sense of what has led to the group's success or what might be contributing to its current struggles. Every organization demonstrates attributes of all of Schneider's and CVF's organizational types. However, organizations tend to have a cultural preference or a default cultural stance. Often leaders show up to a new role and do not pause to understand the firm's culture—both the implicit and explicit elements. As a result, they fail to recognize the leader behaviors (signs and symbols) people expect and ignore existing cultural norms. If the leader cannot make the necessary adjustments, they may find themselves outside looking in or working with disengaged and demotivated individuals and teams. And yet, I must remind you, these tools are not exhaustive and should only be used to lead you down a path of inquiry. The map is not the territory.

Understanding organizational culture is critical from an adaptation perspective, as we will see later. Meaningful organizational change often requires a shift in core values and attitudes. These cultural values have been central to organizational success, leading people to hold on tightly to them. Correctly identifying core cultures provides insight into how elements of the organization like control, leadership, finances, relationships, and even decision-making work. Also, remember that there will be other organizational cultures your teams interact with that have conflicting values. In situations like this, become an ambassador for your team and find ways to work between cultures.

Organizational culture types (like the clan and the cultivation culture) show that firms can have a people-focus and still achieve audacious goals. Promote an organizational culture that focuses on fostering a workplace experience where people thrive. Any organizational culture type (collaboration, cultivation, clan, adhocracy, or some combination) that attends to the needs of employees is worth nurturing. Achieving business goals and attending to the needs of employees do not have to be at odds with each other, as some might suggest. Striking a healthy balance is what you must do.

Organizational culture is always present, but not every organizational culture exhibits deep concern and care for employee well-being. Based on my research and experience, this inattention to employee well-being is a primary reason many employees are dissatisfied with their workplace experience. So, the question you need to answer is: what kind of culture do I want my organization to have, and what will I do to foster it? Whether you like it or not, people look to you to determine what is acceptable (or not) in the organization. You influence organizational culture through your actions and interactions. Nurture an organizational culture that focuses on team member well-being and organizational excellence.

While leaders, at all levels, influence organizational culture, it is critical that if you are an executive, you recognize the outsized influence you have on your organization's culture. Your words and actions send powerful signals throughout the organization. You significantly impact how people experience your organization by what gets your attention and what you ignore. Your leadership approach sets the tone for how others lead within the organization. So, if you want an organization where people thrive, you need to commit to fostering such an organization, and it behooves you to co-create great experiences with the people you are assigned to lead. Chapters 5 through 8 will cover my preferred approaches for doing this. At the heart of my approaches is a commitment to an organizational culture where people experience joy at work. However, I must let you know that these approaches are not always popular because they challenge the control, stability, and impersonal attitudes prevalent in many organizations. And yet, even though you may face challenges, I remain convinced that adopting these approaches is well worth it.

Takeaways

- Effectively leading requires understanding the role organizational culture plays as part of the leadership context.

- While organizational culture explains why organizations act in specific ways, organizational climate expresses how people feel about the organization. Many organizational culture elements are enduring, while organizational climate is more temporal.

- A unitary view of culture limits your ability to affect change. Applying an integration, differentiation, and fragmentation perspective will help you identify common cultural themes, cultural islands, and organizational ambiguities.

- Every organization has multiple competing cultures. Cultural typologies such as the Schneider model and Competing Values Framework (CVF) can help you understand your organization's dominant culture(s).

- Do not use organizational (or corporate) culture as an unactionable abstraction. Address specific elements of the culture.

- How you show up as a leader influences organizational culture.

- Foster an organizational culture where people can thrive while they work. Employee well-being and organizational excellence are not mutually exclusive.

Leading with a Heart of Service

The First Responsibility of a Leader is to Define Reality. The last is to say Thank You. In between, the leader is a Servant.

—Max De Pree[1]

Service is the rent each of us pays for living. It is the very purpose of life, and not something you do in your spare time.

—Marian Wright Edelman[2]

In the previous chapter, we explored the complex phenomenon that is organizational culture. Organizational culture is a product of everything that happens in your firm—including how you develop products. Effective leaders provide their teams with the support needed to achieve organizational goals. An Agile principle is to "Build projects around motivated individuals. Give them the environment and support they need, and trust them to get the job done."[3] Adhering to this principle means fostering a culture focused on attending to

---

[1] Max De Pree, *Leadership Is An Art*, (New York, NY: Currency, 2004), 11.
[2] Marian Wright Edelman is an American children's rights activist.
[3] "Manifesto for Agile Software Development," http://agilemanifesto.org/ (last accessed July 19, 2020).

© Ebenezer C. Ikonne 2021
E. C. Ikonne, *Becoming a Leader in Product Development*,
https://doi.org/10.1007/978-1-4842-7298-5_5

peoples' needs within the organization. As a result of the desire to meet peoples' needs, service becomes of the utmost importance to leaders.

Many leaders assert that people are the most crucial part of the organization. Sadly, their actions often indicate otherwise. People, and the relationships between people, are the most critical part of any organization. Any leader who understands this will be genuinely interested in serving the people assigned to them and meeting their needs. A service-oriented leadership approach is necessary for this. Servant leadership is a leadership theory and practice with attending to people's needs as its core focus. In fact, servant leadership is so people-centered some descriptions of it consider attending to followers' needs, the most critical focus area for leaders.[4]

Servant leadership is not a new leadership approach, but it has become trendy in leadership publications since the 2000s.[5] Leadership researchers attribute the success of Starbucks and Southwest Airlines, for example, to the servant-leadership approach of these organization's executives.[6] Cheryl Bachelder (former CEO of Popeyes Louisiana Kitchen) credits servant leadership for Popeye's growth in restaurant sales, profits, and unit growth rates.[7] There is also empirical evidence that supports the effectiveness of servant leadership. For example, researchers found that servant leadership led to improved organizational performance because the leadership style encouraged organizational learning.[8] Other researchers discovered that servant leadership leads to increased trust between leaders and followers in the organization.[9] Servant leadership seems to make a difference.

Servant leadership generates a positive experience for employees and potentially benefits an organization's bottom line. So why do we not see more leaders adopting behaviors that focus on the needs of the people they lead? How come many employees have such a bad experience with their leaders?

---

[4] A. Gregory Stone, Robert F. Russell, and Kathleen Patterson, "Transformational Versus Servant Leadership: A Difference in Leader Focus," *Leadership & Organization Development Journal* 25, no. 4 (2004): 354–355.

[5] Mark T. Green, Richard A. Rodriguez, Carol A. Wheeler, and Barbara Baggerly-Hinojosa, "Servant Leadership: A Quantitative Review of Instruments and Related Findings," *Servant Leadership: Theory and Practice* 2, no. 2 (2015): 77.

[6] Peter Ortiz, "Servant-Leadership—Bring Your Employees to the Table," *The International Journey of Servant-Leadership* 2, no. 1 (2006): 483–488.

[7] Carol Bachelder, "Serve the People," in *Servant Leadership in Action: How Can You Achieve Great Relationships and Results*, eds. Ken Blanchard and Renee Broadwell (Oakland, CA: Polvera Publishing, 2018): 385.

[8] Ali Iftikhar, Syed Azeem Ahktar, and Arshad Zaheer, "Impact of Transformational and Servant leadership on Organizational Performance: A Comparative Analysis," *Journal of Business Ethics* 116, no. 2 (2013): 433–440.

[9] Sen Sanjaya and Andre Perketi, "Servant Leadership as an Antecedent of Trust in Organizations," *Leadership & Organization Development Journal* 31, no. 7 (2010): 643–663.

My research has uncovered three main reasons. First, many leaders find the "servant" in servant leadership unattractive. Second, leaders who claim that they are servant leaders do not adequately understand servant leadership. Third, servant leadership is not pervasive in practice is because it requires a significant paradigm shift, a shift many leaders are not ready to make.

In this chapter, I explain servant leadership and how adopting its philosophy will help you become a more impactful leader. No leadership theory is without challenges, so I also share the limitations and criticisms of servant leadership. In the next chapter, I will share some real-life examples of servant leaders in the workplace. But first, we start with understanding servant leadership.

What Is Servant Leadership?

As a formal leadership theory, servant leadership began in a 1970 essay written by Robert K. Greenleaf. In the essay titled "The Servant as Leader," Greenleaf described a type of leader and leadership philosophy that differed from the prevailing self-centered, authoritative, and controlling forms of leadership of his time (which continue to dominate the business landscape even in the 21st century). The approach was countercultural when Greenleaf wrote the essay, and it is still countercultural to this day. As Greenleaf presented it, servant leadership was an approach to leadership that resulted from a deep desire to serve others.[10] Greenleaf said the following about servant leadership in the essay:

> "The servant-leader is servant first... It begins with the natural feeling that one wants to serve, to serve first. Then conscious choice brings one to aspire to lead. That person is sharply different from one who is leader first, perhaps because of the need to assuage an unusual power drive or to acquire material possessions... The leader-first and the servant-first are two extreme types. Between them there are shadings and blends that are part of the infinite variety of human nature."

> "The difference manifests itself in the care taken by the servant-first to make sure that other people's highest priority needs are being served. The best test, and difficult to administer, is: Do those served grow as persons? Do they, while being served, become healthier, wiser, freer, more autonomous, more likely themselves to become servants? And what is the effect on the least privileged in society? Will they benefit or at least not be further deprived?"[11]

---

[10] Robert K. Greenleaf, *The Servant as Leader*, (Indianapolis: Robert K. Greenleaf Center, 1991).
[11] Ibid, 6.

Servant leadership has a distinct moral focus. According to Greenleaf, servant leaders lead out of their desire to see those they lead develop, become more independent, and eventually serve others. Since Greenleaf's essay, many researchers have further developed and refined the servant leadership theory. Julie Irving and Julie Berndt describe servant leadership as a follower-considerate approach to leadership in which addressing the needs of followers are the highest priority for the leader.[12] Peter Ortiz observes that "Servant-leadership requires the company leadership to place the employees' needs above its own. It is a leadership style in which employees have a stake in the company's well-being and in which their voices and actions on strategic decisions are sought out and valued."[13] Gregory Stone, Robert Russell, and Kathleen Patterson note that servant leaders provide their followers with significant latitude to do their jobs because they trust their followers.[14] Attending to employees' needs is the number one concern of servant leadership, and servant leaders focus on providing those in their care with the resources they need to excel at their jobs. These leaders make sure that employees have a voice and that they listen and respond to employee voices.

Servant leadership upends the traditional approach to leadership and creates a paradox because of the combination of leader and servant in servant leadership.[15] Much of traditional leadership practice ignore or downplay the needs of team members. On the other hand, servant leadership places employees' needs alongside organizational needs. Servant leadership asserts that meeting employee needs goes beyond achieving organization goals (which many organizations find a way to do anyhow); servant leadership leads to an engaged and dedicated workforce—something missing from many organizations today. Leaders validate their interest in serving their followers when they ask, "will this action or decision provide the opportunity for the people in my care to have a meaningful and joyful experience in this organization?"

These definitions of servant leadership could leave you with the notion that servant leadership is a leadership approach where you do whatever team members desire, i.e., you are at their beck and call. For example, if the software developers believe the organization needs to change its cloud provider vendor, e.g., move from AWS to Azure, then, as a servant leader, you need to do as they say. Such conclusions miss the essence of servant leadership.

---

[12] Justin A. Irving and Julie Berndt, "Leader Purposefulness Within Servant Leadership: Examining the Effect of Servant Leadership, Leader Follower-Focus, Leader Goal Orientation, and Leaders Purposefulness in Large U.S. Healthcare Organization," *Administrative Sciences* 7, no. 10 (2017): 1–20.

[13] Ortiz, "Servant-Leadership—Bring Your Employees to the Table," 484.

[14] Stone, Russell, and Patterson, "Transformational versus Servant leadership," 354.

[15] Enoch Wong "Not Just Simply Looking Forward: An Exploration of Greenleaf's Servant-Leadership Characteristic of Foresight," *The International Journal of Servant-Leadership* 10, no. 1 (2014): 90.

Servant leadership means that you support team members by helping them perform their jobs to the best of their abilities. You do this in support of your firm's goals. Unlike other leadership approaches that encourage you to lead by coercion, servant leadership challenges you to lead your organization by providing service to those you lead. Your power, authority, and influence enable you to serve others.

Strategic Servant Leadership

Servant leadership consists of two parts—a strategic part and an operational part.[16] The strategic aspect of servant leadership is future-focused and concerns itself with ensuring the organization continues to move in its desired direction. The operational aspect of servant leadership focuses on supporting team members and employees and ensuring that team members have what they need to excel at their tasks. Both parts require your attention, and so in the next section, we will take a deeper look at these parts.

Establishing a Direction

Michael Coetzer, Mark Bussin, and Madelyn Geldenhuys describe the functions of strategic servant leadership as (1) to set, translate, and execute a higher purpose vision and (2) to become a role model and ambassador.[17] While Coetzer et al. chose "vision" as the symbol that you need to establish, I suggest that what matters is that you ensure a shared direction exists for your group. You can articulate direction through a vision, mission, purpose, objective, priorities, or a goal depending on the situation. Regardless of how you decide to establish direction, consistently involve your team in the process. Remember that leadership only succeeds when the group moves towards the desired direction. The shared objective will require the group's collaborative effort to achieve.

It is not enough, however, for a shared direction to exist. Team members must also understand where they are going. They need to know why the direction matters to them, their organization, and (in some cases) society. Everyone should understand how their role contributes to moving the organization in its desired direction. It is your responsibility to help your teams understand the desired direction. It is not uncommon that individuals in assigned leadership positions lack clarity on organizational direction. Start with yourself and make sure the organization's direction is clear to you.

---

[16] Ken Blanchard, "What Is Servant Leadership," in *Servant Leadership in Action: How Can You Achieve Great Relationships and Results*, eds. Ken Blanchard and Renee Broadwell (Oakland, CA: Polvera Publishing, 2018), 3–14.

[17] Michiel Frederick Coetzer, Mark Bussin, and Madelyn Geldenhuys, "The Functions of a Servant Leader," *Administrative Sciences* 7, no. 5 (2017): 12–15.

Clear communication is critical to make this happen. Continually develop your communication skills to make sure you can communicate with clarity within your organization. Effective leaders often use stories to stress the importance of the organization's goal and to inspire team members.

It is essential to remember that understanding does not mean agreement. People may disagree with the direction, but they need to understand it. Work with your teams to translate organizational objectives into action items that they can contribute to. I have used various symbolic tokens such as vision statements, purpose statements, and organizational priorities to convey our desired direction to team members. Whatever tactic you might use, ensure that it has the outcome of making the shared direction come alive for people through their work as much as is possible. Once the team has goals, objectives, or priorities, you can work with the team to develop plans for achieving them.[18]

Even though it is your responsibility to provide those you lead with what they need to achieve organizational goals, I do not advise that you determine what is needed by yourself. I learned that determining the method for achieving goals while not involving teams leads to resistance and poor results. Instead, involve the teams in identifying how the team will achieve its goals. Liberating Structures provides a collection of techniques to unleash creativity with your groups.[19] Involving the team upfront differs from the standard practices of many leaders. Traditionally, many organizations rely heavily on scientific management philosophy, which proposes that the leader knows best and can design the optimum method for achieving team goals by themselves. These approaches assume the leader is the expert, which is not the case in creative work contexts. Instead of developing strategy and tactics on your own, taking a service approach causes you to ask teams and team members, "what do you need from me to achieve our shared goal?" They need to know that you will provide them with the support they need. Team members also need to see your support through your commitment to team goals. If team members sense that your commitment is wavering or you do not intend to support them fully, they may also lose interest in the goal.

Setting an Example

The second aspect of strategic servant leadership is modeling the behaviors you want to see from those you serve. Servant leaders "model the way."[20] For example, if you want team members to treat each other with respect,

[18] Ken Blanchard, "What Is Servant Leadership," 8–9.

[19] Liberating Structures Menu, "https://www.liberatingstructures.com/ls-menu/."

[20] James M. Kouzes and Barry Z. Posner, *The Leadership Challenge: How to Make Extraordinary Things Happen in Organizations* 6th ed., (Hoboken, NJ: Jossey-Bass, 2017), 45–92.

you must lead by example and treat everyone with respect. If you want team members to include diverse opinions, include diverse opinions in your meetings. Consistently do what you expect others to do. People need to be able to learn how to lead through service by watching how you lead. Your actions should promote servant leadership, and you need to champion attending to others' needs whenever the opportunity presents itself. People need to see that attending to needs is a concern of the highest order for you. Do not claim to be a servant leader and then act counter to what you claim. Leading through service results in the development of other-centered leaders.

Strategic servant leadership also requires a commitment to personal development. A motive for developing your leadership capabilities is so you can improve how you serve those you lead. Leaders with a heart of service ask themselves the question, "what do I need to improve about myself so I can more effectively serve the people in my care?" Ask the individuals you lead this question and decide the best way to modify your behaviors based on the answers you receive. For example, imagine you receive feedback that you need to listen more and talk less during team meetings. Then commit to becoming a better listener. I once had my direct supports ask that I stop sending late night or early morning emails because those emails placed additional stress on them (even though I told them they did not have to respond to those emails). To serve them more effectively, I stopped sending emails at those times and have tried hard not to do that ever since—even though I still slip up occasionally. Leading through service requires a commitment to personal evolution. If you do not provide a safe space for your team to provide you with feedback, you are genuinely not committed to becoming a more effective leader.

Operational Servant Leadership

Servant leadership also has an operational aspect to it. After all, the organization needs to accomplish its goals if it is to remain viable. Thus, while the strategic dimension requires that you put conditions in place for long-term success by providing direction and setting an example, the operational dimension requires that you provide team members with the support they need to achieve goals. Servant leaders do this by (a) aligning, caring, growing talent, and (b) continuously monitoring work progress and improving how teams perform their work.[21]

---

[21] Coetzer, Bussin, and Geldenhuys, "The Functions of a Servant Leader," 15–17.

Caring for Team Members

It is challenging to serve your team members if you do not care for them. I would go as far as to suggest that if you cannot find it in your heart to care for someone you directly support, you or that individual needs to change groups. Servant leadership research posits that altruistic love undergirds the leader's desire to serve others.[22] It is taboo to speak about love in many workplaces; however, I agree that love is at the heart of servant leadership. How can you serve others if you are genuinely not concerned with their well-being? Checking in on people to see how they are doing outside of the workplace is an example of what caring leaders do. Such behaviors come from recognizing that the relationship between you and the people you lead transcends just getting the work done. It is more than a transactional relationship. Many leaders misuse their one-on-ones with team members by using them solely for status updates. In doing so, these leaders miss an opportunity to understand how they can help team members achieve their career aspirations and goals. However, not everyone responds favorably to this level of care and concern. Some people find it odd or uncomfortable because they may have never had a leader who took a holistic interest in their life except something in their life interfered with achieving organizational goals. That is okay. Allow relationships to develop at their own pace. Ensure healthy working conditions for team members and proactively prevent conditions that induce stress or burnout. Caring for your team members means that you do not take their health and welfare for granted. Institute practices that support working at a sustainable pace. You also make sure that no one in the organization is taking advantage of others. Do not turn a blind eye to bullying or intimidation that often occurs in the workplace, regardless of how talented the bullies might be.

Serving your team members means offering them positions where they are most likely to succeed. Equip teams so that they have what they need to accomplish their goals. Ensure people have the authority, resources, information, and accountability required by the task.[23] Understanding each team member's strengths avoids creating a situation where a team member has a task beyond their competency level. For example, a software development manager serving their software development team would make sure an entry-level developer does not end up with a task that requires significant experience because that would not set up the developer for success. Similarly, promoting a team member into a managerial leadership position because they have excellent technical skills but lack the social skills required for the managerial

---

[22] Peter Mulinge, "Altruism and Altruistic Love: Intrinsic Motivation for Servant Leadership," *The International Journal of Servant Leadership* 12, no. 1 (2018): 337–370.

[23] Kimball Fisher, *Leading Self-Directed Work Teams: A Guide to Developing New Team Leadership Skills*, 2nd ed. (New York, NY: McGraw-Hill Education, 1999).

position would not be in the team member's and organization's best interest. Asking an individual or team to accomplish a task they have no means of achieving is cruel.

Provide Teams with Development Opportunities

A vital aspect of operational servant leadership is the development of those you lead. Servant leadership posits that the best way to achieve organizational objectives is to ensure that people in the workplace experience growth, development, and general well-being.[24] However, just like you cannot force a flower to grow, you cannot force a team member to develop. Personal development is ultimately the responsibility of the team member. Provide team members with opportunities that allow them to maximize their potential and perform their jobs at the highest level possible. Support team members when they take on stretch opportunities. Research shows that when leaders foster conditions that allow employees to perform their roles well, employees experience intrinsic and extrinsic job satisfaction.[25] Satisfied team members are also more likely to commit themselves to organizational objectives. Also, ensure the team has development opportunities. Teams need to learn how to work better together. Provide consistent and constructive feedback and feedforward to your teams. A leader with a heart of service keeps their eyes open for development opportunities that may benefit the people they lead.

Let us look at a quick example of supporting a product development team member. Capturing user stories is a common Agile practice. Imagine you have a team member who participates in capturing user stories. Unfortunately, this individual does not do this activity well, thus impacting the software development process. How could you respond from a place of care and service? First, you could support the team member by providing them with the training they need. Second, you could pair the team member with someone who can support them while they learn. How about a senior team member whose role requires speaking in front of large crowds but they have a fear of public speaking? You could serve the team member by helping them find public speaking classes and providing them with speaking opportunities to practice their public speaking skills. These are simply suggestions of what a servant leader might do. The more significant point is that a leader who cares will look for ways to help their team members both as individuals and in groups.

---

[24] Stone, Russell, and Patterson, "Transformational versus Servant leadership," 355.

[25] Rami Al-Asadi, Shahnawaz Muhammed, Oulaid Abidi, and Vladimir Dzenopoljac, "Impact of Servant Leadership on Intrinsic and Extrinsic Job Satisfaction," *Leadership & Organization Development Journal* 40, no. 4 (2019): 472–484.

A Commitment to Continuous Improvement

As mentioned earlier, servant leadership is follower-centric and focuses on employee needs as the primary focus area for achieving organizational objectives. This prioritization reversal can make it seem that organizational objectives are not essential, but this is not the case. Organizational objectives matter a great deal. In his review of Greenleaf's thoughts on servant leadership, Jeffrey McClellan points out that Greenleaf recognized how important it is that organizations excel.[26] Organizations exist to accomplish some identified purpose. Any organization that fails to achieve its goals will not be around for long, and team members— that the leader cares for—will no longer have jobs. Servant leadership cannot be the reason why you take your eyes off organizational objectives and goal achievement. In fact, it would demonstrate a complete misunderstanding of servant leadership to say that all that matters as a leader is attending to people's needs. However, leaders, who function from a place of service, influence organizational objectives using tactics that differ from the more common approaches where the "bottom line" is all that matters. Operational servant leadership requires that leaders continuously monitor progress towards organizational objectives and foster a continuous improvement culture.[27] Results matter to servant leaders.

You must define the measures of success and review the measures consistently. The following dimensions of performance are an example of what a manager could use with their team:[28]

- Do the right stuff.
- Do it predictably.
- Do it right.
- Do lots.
- Keep doing it.
- Do it fast.

Pay attention to feedback loops in your processes. A balancing feedback loop encourages a team to do less of what it is currently doing, and reinforcing feedback loop encourages a team to do more of what it is currently doing. The Scrum process framework (as an example) has the Sprint Review, where the team demonstrates progress towards its goal. Scrum also has the Sprint Retrospective, where teams review their process for achieving their

---

[26] Jeffrey L. McClellan, "Servant-Leadership and Organizational Outcomes," *The International Journal of Servant-Leadership* 6, no. 1 (2010): 103–122.

[27] Coetzer, Bussin, and Geldenhuys, "The Functions of a Servant Leader," 17.

[28] "Six Dimensions of Team Performance," https://mailchi.mp/79a876c00880/six-dimensions-of-team-performance-forecasting-and-metrics-with-troy-magennis#Article (last accessed July 19, 2020).

goals. Use debriefs to review progress towards organizational objectives. Consider preferring an "eyes-on, hands-off" style for how you lead your teams.[29] Have the right monitors to know how teams are progressing but leave the work to the teams. Achieving organizational goals is critical; however, you want achievement to occur because team members are committed to the organization and do their best work. Use your authority, power, and influence to influence the environment to allow individuals and teams to excel.

Leading from a place of service means fostering a continuous improvement attitude within the organization by routinely reviewing systems, policies, processes, products, and services for improvement opportunities.[30] For example, you might choose to use a method such as the Deming Cycle (Plan-Do-Check-Act)[31] as part of your team's improvement approach. Or you might prefer the Improvement Kata[32] with its four steps of

1. Get the Direction or Challenge

2. Grasp the Current Condition

3. Establish your Next Target Condition

4. Conduct Experiments to get there

Regardless of the continuous improvement technique you choose, remain committed to challenging your teams to improve how they perform their work. You need to champion new ways of working and provide any support needed to make changes. Do not allow you and your team to become comfortable with the status quo, especially when you have experienced sustained periods of success.

Servant Leadership Summary

Servant leadership involves both strategic and operational aspects. The strategic aspect requires that you facilitate setting the direction for you and your team. Find an approach for setting the direction that works for the group and bring as much clarity as possible on what the group is trying to achieve. Make sure your message is coherent and that you communicate it effectively. If you are a product development manager with a team or two, consider working with your teams to craft team goals. If you are a leader of a larger

---

[29] "Retired Gen. Stanley McChrystal's Advice to Leaders: Be More Humble," https://www. cnbc.com/2018/10/30/retired-gen-stanley-mcchrystals-advice-to-leaders-be-more-humble.html (last accessed July 19, 2020).

[30] Coetzer, Bussin, and Geldenhuys, "The Functions of a Servant Leader," 17

[31] "PDCA," https://en.wikipedia.org/wiki/PDCA (last accessed July 19, 2020).

[32] "The Improvement Kata, "http://www-personal.umich.edu/~mrother/The_Improvement_ Kata.html" (last accessed July 19, 2020).

organizational unit with other leaders, developing a set of priorities can help the other leaders understand what they need to focus on. Setting direction, however, is not a "one-and-done" deal. Like you would listen to your GPS to make sure you are heading in the right direction, you will need to regularly revisit direction with your teams to ensure that everyone still understands the direction because it will change. The hallmark of servant leadership is producing other leaders who serve those around them.

Serving others requires altruism. Operational servant leadership acknowledges that success depends on committed and equipped team members. Every interaction with team members provides you a chance to impact them positively. Give your team members the resources they need to excel at their jobs. Provide them with stretch opportunities that aid in their development. The follower focus of servant leadership is no excuse for not achieving organizational goals. Instead, collaborate with the team, monitor goal achievement progress, and take corrective actions when needed. Achieving desired business outcomes depend on effective processes, so keep improving your processes.

Characteristics of Leaders Who Serve

Leaders who attend to the needs of those they lead possess specific characteristics that enable them to do so effectively. There are various descriptions of servant leader characteristics. Larry Spears identifies ten characteristics of servant leaders based on Robert Greenleaf's work—listening, empathy, healing, awareness, persuasion, conceptualization, foresight, stewardship, commitment to the growth of people, and building community.[33] None of these individual characteristics are individually unique to servant leadership, but the combination is as each of these aspects reinforces each other. As I provide an overview of each characteristic, reflect on how much you possess the characteristic and identify improvements you need to make as you strive to become a more effective leader.

Listening

To serve others, you must be ready to listen to what they have to say. Unfortunately, many leaders struggle with listening and prefer to do all the talking. Many leaders are not even aware of how much talking they do. As the saying goes, we have two ears and one mouth for a reason. Listen before you talk. Active listening is essential to servant leadership.[34] Pay attention to team

---

[33] Larry C. Spears, "Character and Servant Leadership: Ten Characteristics of Effective, Caring Leaders," *The Journal of Virtues and Leadership* 1, no. 1 (2010): 25–30.
[34] Greenleaf, *The Servant as Leader*, 8.

members' body language and words. To show that you are listening, you may want to consider repeating what you hear people say to you. Ask questions to clarify what you think you heard. Listening does not mean that you do not talk during the conversation; instead, pick the appropriate time to speak. When you do speak, do not dominate the conversation. Genuine listening requires that you be open to having the follower influence you.[35] Listening for listening's sake does not cut it. And yet, listening does not mean that you do whatever a team member desires; instead, you first listen to the concern, after which you provide a genuine response.

Effective leaders pick up on "what is not said" because they listen carefully.[36] Reflect on how well you listen to your team members. How often do they thank you for listening to them when they speak with you? It is easy to miss vital messages from team members (especially when leading a large organization) because of distractions and other organizational pressures. Hence, it is essential to pay attention when people are speaking to you. In the virtual workplace, distractions abound because of the physical separation that exists. You will need to put more effort into making sure that you give people your full attention when they are speaking to you. Turn over your phone and put it on vibrate. Leverage the "do not disturb" feature of the messaging application you use. Ask the individual how well you listened. Use the feedback you receive to improve your listening skills. Listening helps develop trust with your team members and boosts their self-esteem.[37] If actively listening to a team member during a meeting is difficult because you are distracted, reschedule the meeting to a more convenient time. Make sure you can give people your undivided attention.

Empathy

Having empathy for team members is a crucial characteristic of leaders who care for others. Empathy is a multi-dimensional concept with affective, cognitive, and behavioral dimensions.[38] Robert Hicks defines empathy as "focus on the other person, see things from their perspective, understand the person's feelings and then communicate that understanding so that the helping relationship is strengthened."[39] Empathy is neither sympathy nor pity. Empathy does not require that you have gone through the same experience as the

---

[35] Larry C. Spears, "A Journey in Servant-Leadership," *The International Journal of Servant-Leadership* 11, no. 1 (2017): 4.

[36] Colin Coulson-Thomas, "Listening Leadership," *Effective Executive* XVII, no. 3 (2014): 11.

[37] Larry W. Boone and Sanya Makhani, "Five Necessary Attitudes of a Servant Leader," *Review of Business* 33, no. 1 (2012): 90.

[38] Malissa A. Clark, Melissa M. Robertson, and Stephen Young, "'I Feel Your Pain: A Critical Review of Organizational Research on Empathy'," *Journal of Organizational Behavior* 40, no. 2 (2019): 171.

[39] Robert Hicks, "Are You Empathetic," *Physician Leadership Journal* 3, no. 1 (2016): 52.

team member. Having empathy means you are willing to explore what your team members might be feeling—cognitive empathy—and possibly feel what they are feeling—affective empathy. It shows that you are willing to take the time to understand where they are coming from, even if you disagree with their conclusions. Empathy and disagreement are not mutually exclusive.

Research indicates that showing empathy towards team members causes them to feel unique and valued.[40] Unfortunately, however, not everyone is naturally empathetic. Many leaders have climbed up the corporate ranks without demonstrating an ounce of empathy on the way up. How they treat people is overlooked because they meet organizational objectives. Fortunately, even if you are not naturally empathetic, empathy is a skill you can develop with practice and focus.[41] How can you show empathy in the workplace? Imagine that you have a frustrated team member struggling to learn a new programming language needed for their role. Being empathetic means that you can understand why the team member feels the way they do, possibly share in their sadness, while maintaining how important it is to learn the new programming language to succeed in their role. Empathy leads to compassion and support.

Healing

Healing is a unique characteristic of servant leadership not found in many other leadership theories. Leaders serve their organizations when they work to restore relationships within their organizations. Addressing broken relationships and fostering harmony where you lead is part of how you serve others. Spears notes that leaders who practice servant leadership comfort individuals who are hurting.[42] These leaders notice when individuals are experiencing low moments—like not receiving an expected promotion—and provide them with support and encouragement. To function as a healer in your organization, you must have a vested interest in the people you serve—yes, this is a common theme in servant leadership. Get to know your team members as much as the team member will allow. Ask them how they are doing and what support you can provide them. Address acrimony and discord between individuals on your team as soon as you observe it and do your best to make sure discord does not fester. Encourage restorative justice by asking individuals in conflict to work together to resolve their conflict.[43] Pay attention

---

[40] Peter Northouse, *Leadership: Theory and Practice*, 7th ed., (Thousand Oaks, CA: SAGE, 2016), 227.

[41] "How to be Empathetic," https://www.psychologytoday.com/us/eblog/what-would-aristotle-do/201505/how-be-empathetic (last accessed July 19, 2020).

[42] Spears, "Character and Servant Leadership," 10.

[43] Deborah L Kidder, "Restorative Justice: Not "Rights" But the Right Way to Heal Relationships at Work," *International Journal of Conflict Management* 18, no. 1 (2007): 9–10.

to the health of your relationships as well. Forgiveness—a spiritual act—is a core component of maintaining healthy relationships. Practice forgiveness.

Healing also takes the form of fostering a "just culture" in the organization. A just culture acknowledges that people make mistakes and strives to distinguish between mistakes and reckless behavior with appropriate accountability so that learning still occurs when mistakes occur.[44] Unfortunately, many leaders default to punitive measures when something wrong happens. When things go wrong, these leaders starting by asking "who." These leaders are looking for who to blame and for the proverbial "throat to choke." For example, when clients identify a defect in production, the first question these leaders ask is, "who tested this?" And so, the organizational culture promotes blame and fear with fingerpointing and scapegoating. Restorative justice instead focuses on repairing the relationship and addressing the damage that has occurred. To bring healing to your organization means that you do not default to blaming people when things go wrong. Instead, you assume that individuals had good intentions and that whatever occurred is more likely due to a failure in the process than it is due to someone acting maliciously. Work with teams to improve their processes and then provide emotional support to individuals who might experience shame or disappointment from the incident.

Awareness

Having a high degree of self-awareness is essential for leading from a place of service. Self-aware people know who they are and recognize the effect their actions have on their followers.[45] Many people who care about self-awareness focus primarily on internal or inward self-awareness. However, people must pay attention to external or outward, upward (spiritual), and onward (time) self-awareness to achieve holistic self-awareness.[46] You do not only need internal self-awareness, but you also need to remain aware of what people think of you. Leaders lose sight of peoples' perceptions of them and fall in love with their self-image. Unfortunately, the leader's image often differs significantly from how others see them.

Self-awareness needs to result in a desire to improve oneself and their surrounding conditions.[47] To increase your self-awareness, reflect on your behavior in the workplace. Journaling is a simple approach you can use to keep track of your interactions during the day. Every interaction creates a learning

---

[44] Sidney W. A. Dekker and Hugh Breakey, "'Just Culture': Improving Safety by Achieving Substantiative, Procedural and Restorative Justice," *Safety Science* 85, (2016): 187–188.

[45] Northouse, *Leadership: Theory and Practice*, 228.

[46] Jiying Song, "Leading Through Awareness and Healing: A Servant-Leadership Model," *The International Journal of Servant-Leader* 12, no. 1 (2018): 262.

[47] Spears, "Character and Servant Leadership: Ten Characteristics of Effective, Caring Leaders," 27.

opportunity, but only if you pay attention and subsequently reflect on what occurred. I try to spend time each day reflecting on my interactions with people. I think through what went well and what did not go so well. Increase your external awareness by requesting specific feedback from people you trust and who care for you. Awareness requires that you pay attention to your environment. Greenleaf says, "Awareness is not a giver of solace—it is just the opposite. It is a disturber and an awakener. Able leaders are usually sharply awake and reasonably disturbed. They are not seekers after solace. They have inner serenity."[48] Pay attention to changes in the workplace, your industry, and society more broadly. As we will see in the upcoming chapter on adaptation, awareness is a precursor to seeing the options available to you.

Persuasion

As we saw in Chapter 1, leaders influence followers within the context of the leadership system. It is not uncommon for leaders to rely on coercion when they need to influence those they lead. Many leaders resort to their formal authority and use statements such as "you have to do this because I said so" whenever they face any form of resistance. Often, these statements come with veiled threats and a reminder of the leader's positional power. Servant leadership, on the other hand, values persuasion as a means of influence. Leaders with a heart for service patiently convince followers to change their feelings or behaviors in service of something greater than them.[49] Robert Cialdini identified through research that effective persuaders apply the following persuasion principles:

- Reciprocity
- Scarcity
- Authority
- Consistency
- Liking
- Consensus (or social proof)[50]

Persuasion based on the Reciprocity Principle occurs when people do things for you because you supported them in the past. For example, a team member helps you with a task because they recall when you helped them. The Scarcity Principle clarifies to team members potential opportunities they will miss out on if they do not act. For example, after a series of software outages, a

[48] Greenleaf, *The Servant as Leader*, 15.
[49] Ibid.
[50] Robert B. Cialdini, *Influence: Science and Practice* 5th ed., (Boston, MA: Pearson Education Inc., 2008).

manager made it clear to her team that their brand reputation would suffer if they did not improve system uptime. It is also easier to persuade people when they view you as an expert in a specific area and trust your judgment—the Authority Principle. You use the Consistency Principle when you challenge team members to act according to their values. When team members like you and allow you to persuade them, the Liking Principle is at work. Finally, you can persuade team members by highlighting the positive actions of other individuals or groups you would like them to emulate—the Consensus Principle. A Product Management Director put this principle to use when she asked her team members to capture product analytics because other product managers had used metrics to improve their products.

Using these persuasion principles can help you become more effective at using persuasion as part of your influence tactics. And yet, persuasion can be weaponized and used to get people to do things that are both unethical and immoral. Destructive leaders are also skilled at persuading their followers—history has many examples of this. Use these persuasion principles for the benefit of your team and the organization. Examine your motives and ensure they are ethical and moral.

Conceptualization (Conceptual Thinking)

Servant leadership requires that your current situation does not constrain you. Conceptualization requires that leaders look beyond their day-to-day operations and have a futuristic outlook.[51] Day-to-day organizational pressures can prevent you from spending time thinking about the future. While you need to stay on top of your organization's day-to-day operations, you also need to make time to imagine what your organization could become. To effectively lead your organization requires that you spend time connecting disparate ideas and developing novel solutions. Some of these ideas might come off as strange to your teams because they cannot imagine a future that you envision. I block off time Friday afternoons to imagine and daydream about how my organization could operate differently. Do not ask for permission to reserve time for conceptual thinking. Make it part of your standard practice. Ask yourself what options might exist if your team does things a bit differently. Conceptual thinking requires creativity, and while you might not be the most creative person, you can develop creativity skills with time and practice. You do not want to focus all your attention on the here and now. Think about what you want the future to look like as a service to your team members, your organization, and the benefit of your team members.

---

[51] Spears, "Character and Servant Leadership," 28.

Foresight

Foresight and conceptualization are similar but not the same. Servant leaders use data from the past (which includes experience) and present to anticipate what might happen in the future, and then they prepare team members for these events as an act of service. As Henri Poincaré astutely observed, "It is far better to foresee even without certainty than not to foresee at all." I am not asking you to become a fortune teller or to get into the prediction game. Instead, I recommend that you adopt practices that help you anticipate what might happen in the future. Many leaders only focus on what is happening right now and miss the leading indicators that foreshadow what is likely to occur. Some people buy into the notion that there is little wisdom in anticipating what might happen because the future is uncertain. Failing to consider what might happen in the future is an abdication of leadership responsibility.[52] Paying attention to your firm's financials (month over month) can help you anticipate what might happen, and it does not take much effort. Foresight can help you prevent a negative situation from occurring or improve your response to the negative situation if it does happen. Do not forget that the best way to predict the future is to create it.[53] With foresight, you can avoid being caught off-guard. Invest in learning foresight techniques such as Wardley Mapping, scenario planning, backcasting, and horizon scanning.

Stewardship

Another characteristic of a leader who serves their organization is stewardship. Stewards take care of the entity placed in their trust, and leaders, who see themselves as stewards, feel a tremendous sense of responsibility for people, their organization, and society. Such leaders treat their leadership responsibility with a great deal of seriousness because they recognize that their actions positively or negatively impact their organization. Stewards do not look the other way when they observe inappropriate behavior—they speak up and address the situation. Ethical stewards also take care of organizational resources. Because you are a steward, you will not mismanage the budget and spend organizational funds on frivolous activities. An example of good stewardship is that if a team member suggests that a specific process is not helping the team, you work with the team member to change the process. Many leaders are only interested in taking care of themselves and their image. They punish team members who "speak truth to power." Servant leaders care for their organization, and so they welcome information that can help their organization improve. Stewardship leads one to consider their leadership role more than a job for which they get paid. Leadership becomes more than an

---

[52] Greenleaf, *The Servant as Leader*, 13–14.
[53] This saying is attributed to both Abraham Lincoln and Peter Drucker.

occupation and instead becomes a profession that deserves your best efforts.[54] Leading people is not a hobby or something to be taken lightly. I consider leading others a sacred duty.

Commitment to People Development

Leaders with a heart of service care deeply about the development of those they lead. They identify methods to help team members improve their abilities and make resources available for their team members' development. There are many ways to support peoples' development. Start by asking them how you could support them. There is no one-size-fits-all approach to how you can help team members develop. However, you must be intentional about working with the people in your care to identify the appropriate development opportunities for them. In my experience, many leaders reserve these opportunities for "high potential" team members, but the organization requires everyone's contribution for it to excel. Servant leaders provide developmental opportunities to everyone who desires them. As Spears notes, "the servant-leader recognizes the tremendous responsibility to do everything in his or her power to nurture the personal and professional growth of employees and colleagues."[55] So, make available different forms of training, provide educational material to read, create book clubs, assign stretch assignments, and recommend mentorship programs. You cannot force team members to use the development opportunities you provide. However, this should not deter you from providing the right opportunities to your team members because it is part of serving those you lead.

Building Community

The last characteristic of leaders who practice servant leadership is that they focus on building community with other people. A community in this context refers to more than a group of people living or occupying a single space. People experience community when they have shared interests and goals with other people. Servant leaders are passionate about unifying individuals around a cause that is greater than any one individual. To foster community, routinely ask yourself the question, "how can I nurture a sense of togetherness for my teams and within my organization?" and "how can the work we are doing bring us together?" The virtual workplace has made community even more crucial and challenging because people are no longer together in person. I know leaders who instituted happy hours, ice cream socials, and office hours to bring people together and keep the community intact during the COVID-19 pandemic. In-person activities like

---

[54] Barbara Kellerman, *Professionalizing Leadership*, (New York, NY: Oxford University Press, 2018), 7.
[55] Spears, "Character and Servant Leadership," 29.

potlucks, team outings, and community service are also good for fostering community within your organization. Use your authority (formal and informal) to break down walls between teams and departments. Create bridges where you can. Remember that many people want to feel that they belong to something larger than themselves. A critical role of your job is to encourage an environment where people feel belonging. Community building requires that you connect with people and teams throughout your organization, so spend time developing and investing in relationships with people throughout your organization.

Characteristics Worth Developing

These ten characteristics might seem overwhelming to you at first glance. It is a humbling list, especially if you are honest about the areas you need to develop. The truth is that consistently building community, providing emotional healing, deep listening, etc., are challenging for any leader. Leaders are human, will make mistakes, and will not demonstrate these characteristics all the time. However, as we discussed in Chapter 1, leadership is a profession where we continue developing our knowledge, skills, and abilities. The desire to lead from a place of service causes you to commit to developing and strengthening the characteristics found in servant leaders. The motivation to develop these characteristics stems from your overwhelming desire to ensure team members have increased autonomy—with the requisite support—as they tackle organizational challenges. Do not become despondent when, for example, you do not show empathy or fail to influence team members through persuasion. Consider it a development opportunity for you as a leader. Work on these characteristics every day, and they will become part of your leadership approach. Now that we have looked at the characteristics of leaders who serve, let us look at their behaviors.

Behaviors of Leaders Who Serve Others

People know we are servant leaders based on how we interact with them. What we do—our behaviors—determine whether we lead with a focus on meeting the needs of the people we work with or whether we have some other focus. Bruce Winston and Dail Fields identified the following ten essential behaviors of "servant leaders":[56]

- Practices what they preach
- Serves people without regard to their nationality, gender, or race

---

[56] Bruce Winston and Dail Fields, "Seeking and Measuring the Essential Behaviors of Servant Leadership," *Leadership & Organization Development Journal* 36, no. 4 (2015): 413–434.

- Sees serving as a mission of responsibility to others

- Genuinely interested in employees as people

- Understands that serving others is most important

- Willing to make sacrifices to help others

- Seeks to instill trust rather than fear or insecurity

- Is always honest

- It is driven by a sense of higher calling

- Promotes values that transcend self-interest and material success

Would your teams say that you consistently demonstrate these behaviors? If the answer is yes, then you might just be a servant leader. The Servant Leadership Survey is an example of a validated servant leadership instrument you could have your teams complete to assess your servant leader behaviors.[57] The survey asks questions like

- "My manager gives me the information I need to do my work well."

- "My manager takes risks even when he/she is not certain of the support from his/her own manager."

The next chapter will provide examples of these behaviors in practice; however, it is safe to say that the ten essential servant leadership behaviors reinforce the point that serving others and attending to their needs is at the core of servant leadership. Servant leaders recognize that their job is to address individual and group needs—inside and outside the organization. They make sure people have the resources they require to achieve organizational objectives. Attending to people's needs does not mean that you do whatever people want. It means you provide people with the resources they need to achieve organizational goals because you genuinely believe that organizational excellence occurs when people excel in their jobs. Sometimes that means telling people "No" because "Yes" is not in their (and the organization's) best interest.

There is nothing mushy or soft about servant leadership. Servant leadership poses a significant challenge to many leaders because it differs from their strongly held leadership paradigm. It challenges you to put the interests of others before your interests, which is easier said than done.

---

[57] Dirk van Dierendonck and Inge Nuijten, "The Servant Leadership Survey: Development and Validation of a Multidimensional Measure," *Journal of Business Psychology* 26, no. 3 (2011): 249–267.

Servant Leadership's Dark Side

The positive commentary on servant leadership makes it seem like servant leadership solves all leadership challenges, i.e., if you adopt a servant leadership approach, all will be well, and there will be no challenges. So let me remind you that there are no leadership panaceas nor silver bullets. Servant leadership is not without its challenges and limitations. Unfortunately, a lot of the literature on servant leadership does not speak to its adverse effects.[58] That popular press books do not talk about limitations and side-effects of certain practices is not uncommon. For example, much leadership literature now encourages leaders to become more empathetic but fails to warn leaders of the emotional toll empathy can have on them. Failing to recognize and guard against servant leadership challenges may leave you with blind spots you could have avoided. It can also leave you struggling for answers when team members do not respond as you expected they would. So, you should familiarize yourself with servant leadership limitations.

One of the challenges servant leadership faces is that it has many definitions, so people misinterpret servant leadership. An example of such a misinterpretation is that servant leadership requires leaders to give up their organizational power and authority to serve people.[59] Many organizations struggle with establishing a shared understanding of servant leadership. A team member's understanding (based on previous experience) of servant leadership may not align with yours. Misalignment can lead the team member to have expectations of you that you are unaware of. Because servant leadership is a paradox—serving and leading at the same time—servant leadership is ultimately defined by both the leader and the follower, i.e., servant leadership is socially constructed. Socially constructed means that your team members also determine whether your actions constitute service.

National cultural background also influences how people respond to servant leadership. As outlined in Chapter 3, not all cultures respond positively to leaders who have chosen to serve. Some cultures expect their leaders to lead with a more directive style and might reject or resist the notion of service. Servant leadership may face resistance or yield limited positive outcomes in cultures where power distance and collectivism are high because people in these societies do not expect this type of leadership from leaders.[60] People in these societies may feel uncomfortable with the notion of their leader serving them.

---

[58] Rocco Palumbo, "Challenging Servant Leadership in the Nonprofit Sector: The Side Effects of Servant Leadership," *Journal of Nonprofit Education and Leadership* 6, no. 2: 87.

[59] Wong, "Not Just Simply Looking forward," 90.

[60] Yucheng, Zhang, Yuyan Zheng, Long Zhang, Shan Xu, Xin Liu, and Wansi Chen, "A Meta-Analytic Review of the Consequences of Servant Leadership: The Moderating Roles of Cultural Factors," *Asia Pacific Journal of Management*, (2019): 1–30.

The opposite problem exists in Western societies. Many people struggle with the word "servant." I have spoken to many leaders who find the idea of "servant" distasteful. For them, the word "servant" conjures negative images that make them uncomfortable—even when service is central to how they approach leadership. As a result, they reject the leadership theory in its entirety. While I understand this response, I believe it is a mistake and short-sighted. I believe that Greenleaf was intentionally provocative in choosing the word "servant" to challenge the default posture of leaders in his time (and even today). He wanted leaders to shift their focus from being primarily concerned with their needs to the needs of those they led. Make sure you pay attention to how culture, race, gender, etc., influence how people in your work circle respond to the concept of servant leadership.

And yet, even when there is shared understanding and receptivity to servant leadership, leaders can still take the approach too far. Rocco Palumbo observed several unintended consequences of servant leadership while studying servant leaders in a charitable organization in Tanzania. They are

- Followers' disempowerment

- Followers' reliance on the leader

- Followers' negligence

- Leaders' paternalism

- Leaders' protective behavior[61]

These unintended consequences of servant leadership can negatively impact organizational success if not adequately mitigated. Therefore, I share them here so that you can make sure you avoid these adverse side effects.

Followers' Disempowerment

Followers' disempowerment occurs when team members cannot function because the leader is not available.[62] Team members have become accustomed to you acting on their behalf, so that team members do not know what to do (or do not desire to take actions on their own) when you are not available. Followers' disempowerment also results from leaders performing team member tasks. You might have good intentions for doing these tasks; however, in doing so, you are preventing team members from doing their job. It does not take much for follower disempowerment to occur. Several

---

[61] Palumbo, "Challenging Servant Leadership," 81–98.
[62] Ibid., 92.

times in my career, I inadvertently disempowered teams in the interest of serving them. In one instance, I made it my responsibility to get feedback on our software releases from our operations team even our team had a process for getting this feedback. In my mind, I was helping the team out. I did not realize how this action negatively impacted the team until I went on a trip and was not around for a significant software release. No one on the team asked for feedback from the operations departments. They did not consider it their job. Because I was not around, we ended up missing feedback that would have improved our next release. Let your team members do their tasks.

Followers' Reliance on the Leader

Whenever team members cannot make any decisions without first hearing what the leader has to say, they have an unhealthy reliance on the leader for direction.[63] You need your team members to engage in critical thinking when faced with situations that require decision-making—especially when it is within the scope of their authority. If you make all the decisions, team members will not feel comfortable making decisions when you are not around—especially if you have expert authority. Early on in my career, I developed the reputation of being an "Agile expert" because people frequently came to me for Agile-related advice. After a while, people began to rely on me for answers for anything related to Agile, and no one would make an Agile-related decision without seeking to know what I would do. Team members would sit on decisions for days if I were not in the office because they believed they should not make any decisions without me. Initially, I felt good about being the trusted expert, but I quickly realized that I was holding the team back. This situation was unhealthy for the organization. This reliance can occur when you do not challenge your team to solve their problems by themselves. Hence, you must make sure your team knows that you trust their decision-making and that they have your support even if they make a poor decision.

Followers' Negligence

Followers' negligence is a subtle variation of followers' disempowerment even though the consequences are similar. With followers' disempowerment, the team member does not develop the skills or knowledge required to address the challenges even though their job requires them. In the case of followers' negligence, team members have the skills to address challenges but do not

---

[63] Ibid.

because they consider it their leader's responsibility.[64] Stated differently, when team members see something that is not right in the organization, they respond with, "not my circus." They sit back and wait for their leader to address issues even though they could—followers' negligence. I have seen this side effect many times in organizations where team members consider it the leader's responsibility to step in and fix problems that the team or teams can address. I once worked with a team that would not address process gaps because they wanted their leader to do it for them. Serving your team does not mean solving their problems for them. You want to encourage your teams to take ownership of the problems they can address.

Leader's Paternalism

Protecting followers from organizational challenges in the workplace is leader paternalism.[65] Just like many parents will, by default, shield their children from events that may lead to negative feelings, leaders often prevent their team members from having unpleasant experiences. Several times in my career, I have delayed (or even avoided) discussing upcoming changes (such as a new reporting structure, new product direction, or new staffing strategy) because I wanted to protect my team members from unpleasant news. I have also prevented my managers from providing my team feedback because I did not want to hurt their feelings. I took on a paternalistic role that I thought was in the best interest of my teams. In doing so, I unknowingly denied my team member's developmental opportunities because I shielded them from certain information that they needed to hear. My actions limited the team's ability to adapt to organizational challenges and take on more ownership. You need to avoid preventing your team from receiving bad news. Recognize that they are adults just like you are and can handle difficult news. When you have difficult news to share, make yourself available to provide support and create a safe space for team members to share their feedback.

Leader's Protective Behavior

Effective leaders hold themselves accountable and responsible when things go wrong in the organization. A consequence of protective behaviors is failing to recognize and acknowledge when team members might be responsible for organizational errors. Protective behavior occurs when the servant leader believes any of their followers' mistakes result from the leader failing to provide the followers with the resources they needed to succeed.[66] While workplace processes are often responsible for failures, it is also true that

---

[64] Ibid.
[65] Ibid.
[66] Ibid.

sometimes people do not do their job or make mistakes. After all, we are only human. Leaders who take full responsibility for team members' mistakes or negligence rather than addressing these situations head-on with the team demonstrate protective behavior. If you are a servant leader in an organization with a "blame culture," you might find yourself practicing protective behavior as a defensive response for your teams. I remember once leading a software engineering department that continually received blame from another department. They received so much blame that team members operated from a place of fear. I decided to protect my team by placing myself between my team and the other department. While my intentions might have been noble, I missed opportunities to provide team members with feedback that would have helped them improve because my focus was solely on protecting them. There are times when pointing out team members' (or team's) mistakes to them is an act of service—it is part of fostering a "just culture." By kindly pointing out mistakes, you allow their team members to learn and develop.

I have highlighted these challenges with servant leadership because you must be aware of them as you lead. Despite a sense of higher calling and a genuine interest in people, servant leadership requires effort and commitment. Servant leadership is not for the faint of heart as it requires a willingness to pour your energy into serving others. Remember that effective servant leadership provides team members with what they need to excel at their jobs. Just because you care about people does not mean you lower the standards for the team and organization. Servant leadership expectations are that team members continue developing and performing better than they have in the past in service to the organization. Servant leadership must result in your organization doing its best to achieve its goals.

Let me end this chapter by saying that I believe you have no business leading people if leading through service is not what you try to do every day. No business whatsoever. Tragically, we have too many leaders who primarily care about serving themselves (and even at the expense of the people they lead). Self-centered leaders make the workplace a miserable place leading to low employee morale and disengagement. Servant leadership places taking care of the people you lead at the heart of the leadership process. Become a leader who thrives from attending to follower needs. Significant joy comes from leading with a heart of service. The next chapter will show servant leadership in action in the product development context.

Takeaways

- Servant leadership is an other-centered leadership philosophy where meeting team members' needs is a central concern for the leader.

- Servant leadership is not an "anything goes" form of leadership. Instead, it is a leadership approach that challenges you to provide team members with the resources they need to succeed in their roles.

- It is hard to serve others if your focus is primarily on your specific needs.

- Attending to people's needs requires that you develop the skills of listening, empathy, healing, awareness, persuasion, conceptualization, foresight, stewardship, commitment to people's growth, and building community.

- Avoid the dark side of servant leadership. Do not foster an unhealthy reliance on you to address organizational challenges, and make sure you do not disempower followers.

- The ultimate servant leader test is whether those you lead through service also choose to lead others through service.

Leading Through Service in Practice

Life is an exciting business and most exciting when lived for others.

—Helen Keller[1]

We are much more likely to act our way into a new way of thinking than think our way into a new way of acting.

—Richard Pascale and Anne Miller[2]

In the previous chapter, I described servant leadership's strategic and operational aspects, servant leader characteristics and behaviors, and servant leadership limitations. I shared that servant leaders attend to others' needs by

---

[1] Hellen Keller was an American author, political activist, and lecturer.
[2] Richard Pascale and Anne Miller, "Acting Your Way Into a New Way of Thinking, "Leader to leader 1998, no. 9 (1998): 36–43.

© Ebenezer C. Ikonne 2021
E. C. Ikonne, *Becoming a Leader in Product Development*,
https://doi.org/10.1007/978-1-4842-7298-5_6

practicing various behaviors using a combination of ten characteristics unique to servant leaders. As Bruce Winston and Dail Fields observed, servant leadership requires having the desire to serve others.[3] And yet, it is not enough to know what constitutes servant leadership—you also need to practice it. Thus, you need to go from head knowledge to hands-on application.

So how can you become an impactful servant leader? How can service shine ever brighter through your leadership approach? Well, here is a little secret—we become by doing. Herminia Ibarra tells us that people become more effective leaders through a commitment to practicing new leader behaviors.[4] In this chapter, I share stories of various leaders who attended to their people's needs, fostered healthy interactions, built community, increased motivation, trust, and support, and took actions to prevent burnout on their teams. Each story provides you with practical tips and ideas on how to lead through service. The stories do not have every detail outlined; however, I have shared the essential points. Hopefully, these practical stories become a source of inspiration and help you uncover what you can do to meet people's needs more effectively in your organization.

Addressing Needs and Fostering Healthy Interactions

We start by reliving Ijeoma's story. Ijeoma became the managerial leader for a product development team that was in disarray. Their previous manager had left with some team members for a new job. The interim manager paid the team little attention because he knew it was a temporary assignment. It was not long before the remaining team members became disillusioned and began to look for new opportunities outside of the company even though the team was responsible for a critical product. Commitment to the team and the firm began to spiral downward. Each software release had many defects. Team meetings became blame sessions. In short, the team was struggling, and the firm needed to do something about it if they were going to achieve their business goals. Finding a new dedicated Software Engineering Manager was vital. So, after a long candidate search, Ijeoma was hired to lead the team. Ijeoma had the authority to make whatever changes (including hiring and firing changes) she felt were best for the team as long as they did not violate any company policies.

On Ijeoma's first day, she set up a meeting with the team. She started the meeting by telling them she was there to help them succeed. Team members

---

[3] Bruce Winston and Dail Fields, "Seeking and Measuring the Essential Behaviors of Servant Leadership," *Leadership & Organization Development Journal* 36, no. 4 (2015): 413–434.

[4] Herminia Ibarra, *Act Like a Leader, Think Like a Leader*, (Boston, MA: Harvard Business Review Press, 2015): 117–158.

were surprised to hear Ijeoma say this. Ijeoma surprised them even further when she said she was there to *listen* to what they had to say about their challenges and how they thought they could address them. You see, the team expected Ijeoma to begin with a list of changes that she would make because of their current challenges. They did not expect their new leader to ask them for their thoughts. After all, she was the leader brought in to fix things.

However, Ijeoma sincerely desired to hear their suggestions and thoughts on how the team could get back to providing elegant solutions for their customers. So over the next few days, Ijeoma met with each team member for about an hour. She closed her office door, put her phone on silent, and placed it face down so they would not be interrupted. In each meeting, she asked the team member to share what was working well, what was not working well, and what ideas the team member had for improvement. She captured their comments and suggestions and asked questions to make sure she understood their thoughts fully.

Each meeting also provided Ijeoma with an opportunity to get to know her team members. She asked each one to share something about themselves because she wanted to learn more about each individual. She learned that many of the team members had worked for the firm for a long time. They had enjoyed most of their time as employees and appreciated the benefits the firm had to offer them. Many of them were original members of the team that had developed the firm's flagship product and were proud of how well it had done in the market. However, the product's current status in the market concerned many team members. Product revenue was in steep decline, and many team members had begun to wonder if layoffs would happen because of revenue loss. Job security Layoff concerns negatively impacted team member intrinsic motivation, and even though they physically showed up to work every day, their minds were not there.

As Ijeoma listened to the team members, she *empathized* with them. She tried to see things from their perspective as they shared their stories. She patiently listened as people shared with her how their job was no longer what it once was. She did not rush them as they shared their experiences; instead, she encouraged them to share as much as they felt comfortable sharing. Some team members expressed that they felt leaving the firm was in their best interest. Ijeoma worked with them to identify their unmet needs using a "needs inventory."[5] Ijeoma noted their unmet needs and committed to helping them meet their needs to the best of her ability. She showed a genuine interest in understanding why some people wanted to leave the firm and repeatedly shared her desire for everyone to enjoy belonging to the firm.

---

[5] "Needs Inventory," https://www.cnvc.org/training/resource/needs-inventory (last accessed July 19, 2020).

Ijeoma also invested time learning about the career aspirations of each team member. Because she was *committed to people's development, she worked with team members to create a development plan that* supported their career goals. Some team members wanted to transition from their current role to another role in the organization. For example, Emeka, a software test engineer who had only worked with test automation frameworks such as Selenium, wanted to become a software engineer. Biola, another team member, was interested in transitioning from her software developer role into a software development manager role. Ijeoma worked with Emeka and Biola to craft individual development plans that would prepare them to transition into new roles. Emeka, for example, would begin programming classes while Biola would join a leader development cohort.

Ijeoma did not only meet with the team members individually; she frequently met with the entire team to learn what had (and had not) worked well in the past. She recognized that a team is more than a group of individuals—it is the individuals, the interactions between the individuals, and the team's interactions with people outside of the team. Her first team meeting was quiet as team members did not have a lot to say because they did not feel safe sharing in the team setting. In subsequent meetings, when team members did speak, she noticed that they were rude to each other, and there was a certain amount of bullying. In addition, the team had little psychological safety as people did not feel safe taking interpersonal risks.[6] Team members considered it risky to speak up and share their thoughts.

The difficulties of the preceding few months had led to significant distrust on the team, so the team needed to *heal.* Ijeoma invited an external facilitator to come into the office and work with the team to rebuild trust. Ijeoma addressed the team's lack of psychological safety by clarifying that no one would experience any negative repercussions for respectfully speaking up. She also established that ridiculing or demeaning team members in any context immediately would not be acceptable. There would be zero tolerance for such behavior. Ijeoma knew how critical it was for team members to feel safe expressing their observations. Open communication was essential if the team was to improve.

Ijeoma's software engineering team consisted of people with different cultural heritage. She had six people from the United States, three people from India, one person from China, and one from Nigeria. While each team member had lived in the United States for at least over ten years, they still identified strongly with their country of origin. The team also had three men and four women. It was a diverse team. Ijeoma knew the importance of serving all the team members regardless of their background. Recognizing the different

---

[6] Amy C. Edmondson, "Psychological Safety and Learning Behavior in Work Teams," *Administrative Science Quarterly* 44, no. 2 (1999): 350–383.

cultural backgrounds and gender differences on the team and having a desire to *build community* on the team, Ijeoma asked the team members what activities they thought would build community. After many conversations, the team decided they would have monthly potlucks. Once a month, individuals brought in a special dish. It could only be a dish from their homeland or a dish from a colleague's homeland. The team would then gather around lunchtime to exchange stories about their backgrounds and experiences while they ate. The potlucks helped to strengthen the bond between team members.

Some team members did not appreciate the new environment that Ijeoma was attempting to foster. The new environment made them less powerful. Change often results in a feeling of loss for some individuals. These team members—unfortunately, all of whom were men—became particularly disruptive. They challenged Ijeoma in meetings whenever the opportunity presented itself. They did not show up for the team potluck and barely engaged with people outside of their clique. They skipped out on the trust workshops and had nothing positive to say about the team's progress. Their behavior was hurting the team. While Ijeoma empathized with them—their situation had changed—she knew better than to affirm these team members' behavior. She also recognized that overlooking these team members' behavior was a disservice to all the other team members, i.e., to serve everyone, she must look out for the whole. When specific individuals make it challenging to meet the needs of the whole, changes need to occur.

Ijeoma deserves a ton of credit because she spent a significant amount of time working with these disruptive team members. She wanted to help these individuals as much as possible, so she tried hard to find other opportunities for them in the firm. However, it was clear that the team's new direction was not for them, and they needed to find new positions outside the organization. In the end, there were no other positions available, so these team members left the firm. Leaders with a heart of service are altruistic and demonstrate kindness, grace, and forgiveness even when the working relationship does not work out.[7] On the last day of their employment with the firm, Ijeoma met with each individual, thanked them for their contribution, and wished them the best in the next endeavor.

While we are talking about people leaving Ijeoma's firm, we need to talk about Akachi. Akachi was a talented software developer on Ijeoma's team who desired a position that Ijeoma could not provide. Many managers would have focused on giving Akachi reasons to stay with the team because it benefited the team and the manager (at the expense of Akachi's development). But Ijeoma was a leader *committed to the development of individuals* and saw it as her mission to serve others even if it inconvenienced her and her team. Ijeoma was

---

[7] Peter Mulinge, "Altruism and Altruistic Love: Intrinsic Motivation For Servant-Leadership," *The International Journal of Servant-Leadership* 12, no. 1 (2018): 337-370.

transparent with Akachi about the lack of opportunities within her group. However, she did not end there; instead, she committed to helping him find the right opportunity, even if the opportunity was outside their firm. She reviewed internal and external opportunities with Akachi. Eventually, Akachi decided to take an opportunity outside of their firm. Even though Ijeoma was sad to see Akachi go, she delighted in the fact that he had found a position that met his needs. Ijeoma's desire to attend to team member needs guided her actions.

Building Community Across Departments

Servant leaders work to build community wherever they find themselves. Impactful product development requires that different groups with different skills work well together. Unfortunately, many groups within companies find collaboration hard to do. One of the reasons it is hard is because groups that need to collaborate disagree on how to do so. The groups do not speak the same collaboration language, do not have the same incentives and rewards systems, and do not appreciate how each department contributes to organizational success. I saw this exact problem with a product development team and auditors. The product development team had the task of developing internal-use software for the auditors; however, the teams had difficulty working together. That the groups had difficulty working together should no longer surprise you because you know that the differentiation perspective of culture states that organizations have multiple cultures. Here is a story of how I helped teams from different departments improve their collaboration, leading to improved organizational outcomes.[8]

Money Recovery[9] specialized in auditing claims for large institutions. The company identified overpayments—when the institutions owed the payer money—and underpayments—when the payer owed the institution money. Money Recovery received a commission from whatever Money Recovery recovered on behalf of the payers. Money Recovery had a team of tenured auditors that audited claims to identify overpayments and underpayments. Unfortunately, the software the auditors used was outdated, buggy, and slow. Instead of enabling them to do their jobs well, the system made their job difficult. The company's leaders decided to have one of the internal product development teams work with the healthcare provider to develop a new system that met their needs.

I was hired six months after product development had started to lead the product development team because progress was not happening as fast as people wanted it to happen. While everyone acknowledged that there was

---

[8] At the time this happened, I did not know that community building was a servant leader characteristic.
[9] Not the name of the company

some tension between the product development team and the auditors, it was considered a minor issue. However, after a few conversations with my team and some auditors, I quickly realized that the tension was anything but minor; it was a major issue. The need for healing the relationship between my team and the auditors was evident. The relationship was so strained that neither group wanted to speak with each other in person; instead, the groups relied on e-mails and documents in a shared folder to communicate. My team wanted every bit of detail for each new feature captured in a requirements document. They also wanted every new feature to go through multiple sign-offs before adding the feature to the system because if anything went wrong with the change, it was critical to know which group had introduced the problem. Trust was nearly non-existent between the groups, and it was impacting software delivery.

Bringing healing to a situation requires that a leader understand why people are hurting and the cause(s) of the broken relationship. Because I led the product development team, I knew it was vital to develop trust with the auditors. Initially, the auditors considered me an outsider because I was part of the enemy—an IT department team member (as they put it). Also, it did not help that I had no auditing experience. To become more of an insider, I scheduled lunch with various auditors to learn more about their relationship with my team. They shared how the relationship with my team had deteriorated over the past year. Through these conversations, I identified that a source of the auditors' frustrations with my team was that they felt disrespected by the software developers. Auditors also expressed frustration that the software developers failed to respect their expertise. Most of the auditors had worked for many decades in hospitals. Some of them had many years of experience working in other recovery audit firms and knew what features a recovery audit system needed. Unfortunately, they did not believe that the software developers considered them competent.

Auditors also found it hard to understand the software developers. The software developers used technical jargon that the auditors did not understand when explaining the difficulties of implementing specific features. They also did not believe the software developers had empathy for how the current system's limitations made it difficult for auditors to do their job. In their minds, the software development team did not appreciate the urgency for a new system. They had overheard some software developers laugh at their limited technical skills and their inability to solve technical problems.

When I spoke with my team, I discovered they shared similar feelings with the auditors. My team desired respect for the work that they did. They wanted the auditors to be more empathetic, especially when they gave them feedback on the system. This was the first time many team members had worked in this domain, which meant that many of the terms used during conversations were unfamiliar. Translating these concepts into the software system required dialogue. The software developers were having to learn the business of recovery auditing while at the same time developing a new system for the auditors to use. The auditors also did not understand the inherent challenges of product development. It was clear that both groups did not have a healthy respect for each other's expertise. There was also little to no empathy regarding the challenges each group faced. And what was the result? Little progress on developing a new system the firm desperately required.

After my discovery, I asked the Audit Director for the auditing group to support a facilitated meeting where the auditors and the software developers would talk through their challenges as a single group. The Audit Director was supportive, so I arranged for an external facilitator to conduct a two-day working session with our combined group. (Both groups had already accused me of supporting the "other side.") The facilitator helped both groups identify the behaviors that the other group did not appreciate. For example, the auditors shared that when the software developers rolled their eyes during the conversation, it came across like the software developers were questioning their competence. On the other hand, the software developers needed the auditors to believe that they were trying their best to understand the recovery audit industry.

At the end of the two-day session, both groups had a better understanding of each other's challenges. The groups also learned what behaviors triggered negative feelings in the other group, and they acquired techniques for interacting with each other more productively. Broken or strained relationships rarely heal entirely in 48 hours, and depleted relationship trust banks take time to build back up. However, we started the healing process by understanding both groups' concerns and bringing in an expert who could start the groups on the path to restore relationships and grow trust. Two years later, the product development team and the auditors had formed such a strong bond that everyone had forgotten the challenges that had existed in the past—healing had taken place.

For people from different departments (or even different organizations) to work well together, they need to consider themselves as belonging to the same community. Leaders who serve others recognize that *building community* is key to team member satisfaction and organizational success. As I worked with my team and the auditors, I saw the opportunity to help these two groups become part of the same community—a community focused on improving the payments process in the audit industry. Belonging to the same community would mean that the product development team and the auditors would share the same purpose. It would lead to a fellowship. As is the case in many organizations, people could not see beyond their department, and power struggles dominated. Therefore, both departments needed to understand that they co-owned organizational outcomes.

Servant leaders foster an environment that allows everyone to contribute to building the community. I partnered with the Audit Director to identify external volunteering activities which our teams could do together. For example, the groups passed out food on behalf of food banks, participated in volunteer walks, and cleaned up streets in the city together. In working together to make society better, the two groups deepened their relationship with each other, and strong bonds formed between members of the groups. Not only did the groups participate in external events together, but they also did private events together. Whenever one group had an internal function or event, they would invite the other group to attend. For example, if one group had a potluck, they made sure they invited the other group.

The two groups continued to support each other and celebrate wins as one group. Whenever the product development teams delivered a major release, or the auditors exceeded their recovery targets, they would celebrate together. The groups sometimes even went off-site to a bowling alley or an arcade center to celebrate with one another. Product development team members made the area where the auditors sat their second home and often spent multiple hours learning from the auditors to understand what system changes would simplify their jobs. In response, the auditors became so fond of the product developers that they would regularly bake treats for them. Over time, even though the product development team and the auditors belonged to different departments and had different cultural elements, they came to see themselves as belonging to the same community and worked together towards organizational excellence.

Increasing Motivation, Support, and Trust

For all the glory given to leaders, organizational success requires having motivated and committed people working towards a shared goal. Product development is not exempt from this fact. In his seminal work on followership, Robert Kelley argues that despite all the focus on leaders, organizational success occurs because of the contributions of exemplary followers.[10] In the context of product development, it is team members that produce the product that meets peoples' needs. The importance of having teams of motivated individuals is core to Agile. Servant leaders do not want to rely on extrinsic motivators—external regulation— as the motivational source for individuals on the team; instead, they want team members to feel inspired to perform their functions.[11] These leaders use persuasion, conceptualization, and foresight to inspire the individuals they lead. Servant leaders avoid actions that decrease team member motivation and organizational commitment

---

[10] Robert E. Kelley, *The Power of Followership*, (New York, NY: Doubleday Business, 1992), 7–8.

[11] Karlene Kerfoot, "From Motivation to Inspiration Leadership," *Nursing Economics* 19, no. 5 (2001): 242–243.

because they know that disengaged team members do just enough to keep their jobs. Let us look at how a product development director practiced servant leadership as she focused on increasing motivation, trust, and support on her team.

Nkechi had responsibility for a product development department with a reputation for producing low-quality products. Every product release introduced new defects, and the product teams had to spend weeks post-release resolving defects and appeasing clients. Clients hesitated to install new releases even when the releases had features they desired because they knew the release would introduce problems and negatively impact their operations. No one involved with the product was delighted with anything about it. However, Nkechi believed that it did not have to be this way. She knew her department had it in them to create a delightful experience for their clients.

Nkechi brought all the teams in the department together and facilitated a visioning session. At the beginning of the session, Nkechi asked everyone to imagine a future state that they felt was attainable and different from their current state. They were to imagine that product quality was no longer an issue and that they had satisfied clients. They were not to let any of their current limitations constrain their thinking. However, many team members found it difficult to imagine a different future because of their current obstacles. But Nkechi did not give up easily. She challenged and encouraged team members to think boldly and broadly and even provided examples of a different future. Eventually, the teams crafted a vision for themselves that went something like this "Our clients desire our products, and we enjoy working here."

Team members found the vision inspirational because it gave them a different future from their current situation. At the time they crafted the vision, clients did not desire their products, and team members were demoralized and disengaged. The vision provided a direction they could head towards with intentionality. They began to do activities that would move them in the direction proposed by the vision—the vision served as a compass for team members. The teams invested themselves in adopting quality practices that enabled them to build quality into the product. Whenever there were different perspectives on how they could approach a task, team members evaluated the options based on how well each option supported a future where clients desired their product. As the quality of their product improved, the relationship with their clients improved. All of a sudden, clients no longer hesitated to adopt newer product releases. The improved client relationships improved team member morale, and team members enjoyed working in the business again. One of the benefits of the visioning exercise is that it helped strengthen the department's sense of community.

Nkechi also understood the importance of preparing her department for potential change. She knew that providing them up-to-date information on business performance kept them engaged. As she went through her week, she noted signals (internal and external) that provided insight into the future. Then on Friday, she reviewed her notes and extracted patterns and common themes that she could share with the department. Her weekly review gave her the space to develop insights on potential organizational changes. It also sharpened her overall awareness. Many of these insights led to a change in focus for her teams. Her foresight meant that she could prepare her teams ahead of time for the possibility of upcoming organizational shifts. For example, on one occasion, Nkechi sensed that the business unit she supported would soon offer new services requiring software changes. Her foresight enabled her to give her team advance notice of this. Helping her teams get ready for change before it occurred meant that when the change did occur, her team members had an easier time embracing the change because they knew it was coming and had prepared themselves for it.

Nkechi did not practice foresight by herself. Instead, she made it a group activity. Regardless of the forecasting technique, Nkechi made sure she leveraged the collective intelligence of team members as much as possible. By involving her team members in foresight activities, team members stayed informed of the broader socio-economic and technological trends. An example of foresight from collective intelligence in action was when a team leader recognized that two teams would need to understand how to mine data as part of their new business strategy. The team leader also knew that getting the team excited about this opportunity would help them become more successful. So Nkechi and the team leader arranged machine learning and artificial intelligence training for the teams. Then, when the time came for the teams to begin to mine the data, they were ready.

Leaders who practice servant leadership use foresight to serve their team members. Having a sense of what the future might hold allows leaders to make prudent decisions, hedge their bets, and be conservative when that is the right thing to do. For example, Nkechi kept an eye on company finances and the broader economy. She understood that a financial downturn or a bad financial quarter could mean she would have to look for cost-saving opportunities. One of the first places businesses look at is labor costs (even though this is rarely the best place to look), and so Nkechi slowed down hiring when business performance indicators showed they would most likely not meet their financial goals for consecutive quarters. There were also occasions when Nkechi anticipated that an upcoming change in business strategy would result in the retirement of certain systems. The retirement of these systems would mean that her department would no longer require individuals with the skills required by those systems. To prevent these individuals from experiencing the distress of losing their jobs, Nkechi worked with them to develop transition plans to find jobs in other parts of the business before their current job was no longer available. Team members were confident that Nkechi would always try to do what was in their best interest and trusted her because of this. Their sense of security and safety meant that they could focus on team goals while remaining confident that their leader, Nkechi, would do her best to anticipate upcoming changes that could impact them.

Nkechi also understood that conceptualization is not a one-and-done type of activity. As a leader with a heart for service, it was crucial she regularly assessed her teams' progress and direction and also took time to imagine with them the potential futures. She routinely revisited the vision in her staff and department meetings. She understood that she was responsible for providing the team with inspirational and impactful goals. Nkechi's job included encouraging team members when they faced setbacks. Visions, missions, objectives, goals, priorities, or purposes serve as objects that can focus groups of people around a shared cause. However, people also have personal visions. A personal vision reflects where an individual would like to be in the future, and some people want to achieve aspects of their vision through their work opportunities.[12] By spending time with team members, Nkechi was able to help them understand how they could achieve aspects of their vision through their work.

And yet, it is not enough for you to inspire through vision. You must also make the means and methods for realizing the vision available to followers. Russell Ackoff stated that "inspiration without implementation is provocation, not leadership."[13] Failing to provide team members with the resources required to move in the direction of the vision is a demotivator, so Nkechi routinely asked team members to identify their unmet needs that inhibited progress towards the vision. Examples of unmet needs included the lack of proper equipment for their jobs, the need for software quality training, few opportunities to visit clients, and more flexible working arrangements. Once Nkechi received the feedback, she immediately went to work to address the unmet needs. She arranged for team members to get new equipment. An industry expert in software quality practices came in at Nkechi's request to teach software quality techniques teams could use to improve their product quality. Client visits began so that the managers and their teams could get to know clients and understand how they used their products. Finally, the department started a flexible work program.

However, it is essential to note that Nkechi could not address all the unmet needs simultaneously, and sometimes it took a while for a change to produce desired results. Nkechi let the team members know which obstacles she could not address due to other organizational impediments. And while people were disappointed that some obstacles would not have an immediate resolution, they appreciated Nkechi's honesty and transparency. Nkechi's

---

[12] Peter M. Senge, *The Fifth Discipline: The Art and Practice of the Learning Organization*, (New York, NY: Doubleday), 211.

[13] Russell Ackoff, "A Systemic View of Transformational Leadership," *Systemic Practice and Action Research* 11, no. 1 (1998): 23–36.

service to her team led to increased trust, intrinsic motivation, and engagement, resulting in an enjoyable workplace and teams going above and beyond to achieve department goals.

Preventing Burnout by Maintaining a Sustainable Pace

Leaders who practice servant leadership consider themselves stewards of the organization and its people. Servant leaders take care of team members (and their families), finances, time, reputation, brand, and other organizational resources. A leader with a heart of service will make it a top priority to preserve the well-being of the people in their care. They will work to keep unhealthy stress levels minimal. How can a product development leader nurture a workplace that promotes team member well-being where goal attainment is a first-order concern? The following story provides a few suggestions.

When I took over the leadership responsibilities for the software engineering division of the product company where I worked, my first observation was that team members worked excessive hours. When I arrived at work at about 7 a.m., I would find many of the software development teams already at work, and when I was leaving at 6 p.m., many of the team members would still be at work. I felt guilty because I was neither the first one nor the last one out, and I was the leader! I also observed that the organization recognized, celebrated, and rewarded team members who worked all the time. Team members who had worked long hours during the week and worked over the weekends received recognition on the company's website. It was routine practice to invade team members' private time by sending them after-work hours and weekend emails, texts, and messages. I learned that team members felt pressured to respond to these messages, and the pressure placed unhealthy stress on the team members (and their families). Unfortunately, the team members did not feel safe sharing how they felt.

It was evident that the "always working" organizational norm distressed people, and I needed to do something about it. It was my responsibility to ensure that team members were not overwhelmed by stress and experience burnout. My leadership team would need to modify their behaviors if organizational norms were going to change. The first change we made was to stop sending emails outside of regular working hours. Weekends were now considered sacrosanct and off-limits. If there were a legitimate emergency (like a production system outage), managers would call their team members instead of sending them emails or texts. It became okay for team members to go home at the end of the day during the workweek. Managers stopped recognizing team members because they participated in death marches.

Instead, they now had the challenge of recognizing teams who worked at a sustainable pace and achieved organizational goals.

Team members had felt pressure to remain at their desks all day, so it looked like they were always working. With the change in working norms, their leaders now encouraged breaks throughout the day. The breaks helped team members de-stress and clear their minds. During breaks, team members would chat with other team members in the café or play ping-pong in the game room. My leadership team organized outings where team members socialized and celebrated with each other. We worked hard to foster an organization where team members could have fun even while they worked. Over time, people learned that work did not have to be a burden and a source of stress. Instead, work could be a source of meaning, enrichment, and fulfillment. In product development settings, servant leaders will foster a workplace where people work at a sustainable pace.

One of the significant causes of death marches is the imposition of artificial deadlines and poor planning techniques. Agile frameworks take an approach where product development teams determine what they can accomplish in a given time frame. Unfortunately, the organization's market-like culture meant that the managers set deadlines for the teams, and teams had to extend themselves to meet these deadlines. To eliminate this pressure, we eliminated arbitrary deadlines, and the teams adopted Agile practices for planning and forecasting what they could accomplish in a given time frame. Managers were to clarify how their work supported the organization's objectives and why those objectives mattered. Teams would then identify what they could accomplish to support those objectives and then work hard—not continuously overextending themselves—to achieve those goals. Several managers offered stiff resistance to the process change because they felt that they would lose control of the teams if they could not set deadlines. I had to remind the managers that if our team members were motivated, they would do their best to achieve organizational objectives. It was up to the managers to provide team members with inspirational goals and support. I continued to champion the new approach by recognizing and rewarding teams and the managers who showed the ability to achieve their goals while maintaining a healthy work pace.

I also ensured that the managers understood the importance of resolving any organizational impediments that induced stressful working situations. It was not enough for us to offer mental health resources. We needed to reduce the amount of stress caused by the workplace. In some instances, team members did not have the resources needed to simplify and streamline their work processes. Managers had the responsibility of providing their teams with the necessary resources for goal achievement. For example, it took one of the teams an entire day to prepare their product releases, and because preparing a release was so time-consuming, the team released new features infrequently.

To enable the team to release frequently, their manager acquired licenses for continuous integration and continuous deployment tools, which the team used to automate software release creation. Suddenly, a process that used to take an entire day now took a few hours. The team could now release software as frequently as customers desired because releases no longer required a herculean effort. Servant leaders foster a healthy and positive workplace.

Servant Leadership and Product Development

This chapter has provided real-life stories of the application of servant leadership in a product development context. These are stories of leaders like you and me that illustrate servant leadership in practice. While the examples are neither exhaustive nor prescriptive, they provide aspiring leaders with a frame of reference for how they can serve their product development organization. If you want to adopt servant leadership, identify a set of practices that works for you, and add them to your leadership approach. Do not expect overnight success; instead, be patient and committed to the process of serving your teams. Make the workplace an environment where team members thrive. Although conflict will occur in the workplace, focus on restoring relationships between individuals, teams, and departments. Sometimes you will need to help people find opportunities outside of their organization so that the community can continue to flourish. That is service to both the individual and the organization.

Excellent product development cannot succeed without dedicated and motivated team members throughout the organization. Listen to your team members so you can help them address their unmet needs. Develop the patience needed to persuade individuals and help them understand why specific actions benefit them and the organization. Removing demotivators is a critical component of how you serve those you lead. So also is ensuring the well-being of team members in the organization. Make attending to the needs of team members part of how your organization achieves its primary task. The stories show how you can support excellent product development through a service-oriented approach. Hopefully, they get your creative juices going. Table 6-1 shows where servant leader characteristics can support the Agile value and principles.

Table 6-1. Mapping Servant Leader Characteristics to Agile Values and Principles

Servant leadership characteristics	Agile values and principles
Listening, empathy, healing, and commitment to the growth of people	Individuals and Interactions
Healing and building community	Business people and developers must work together daily throughout the project
Persuasion, conceptualization, foresight, commitment to the growth of people, and building community	Build projects around motivated individuals. Give them the environment and support they need, and trust them to get the job done.
Stewardship	Agile processes promote sustainable development. The sponsors, developers, and users should be able to maintain a constant pace indefinitely.

Reflection Questions

- What are your core values and principles?
- Have you shared them with your team?
- How well do your actions reflect your values and principles?
- What would your team say?
- How much time do you spend getting to know team members and their interests?
- How transparent are you in your decision-making?
- How often do you explain "why" you made a specific decision?
- How often do you ask your team what help or support they need from you?
- How many team members would consider you a "servant leader?"

Leading Through Change

In times of change, learners will inherit the earth while the learned will find themselves beautifully equipped to deal with a world that no longer exists.

—Eric Hoffer[1]

Change cannot be put on people. The best way to instill change is to do it with them. Create it with them.

—Lisa Bodell[2]

---

[1] Eric Hoffer was an American philosopher.
[2] Lisa Bodell is a futurist and CEO of Futurethink.

© Ebenezer C. Ikonne 2021
E. C. Ikonne, *Becoming a Leader in Product Development*,
https://doi.org/10.1007/978-1-4842-7298-5_7

Many have said that "change is the only constant."[3] Organizations and the individuals that comprise them are not immune to change. In fact, the leadership context for many (if not most) leaders often includes a healthy amount of change. Leaders need to understand their leadership system context so that they lead appropriately.[4] The product development context experiences constant change in at least three ways. First, product development organizations regularly need to change organizational structures and improve the current ways of working. Second, product development organizations need to keep up with a rapidly changing technology landscape, e.g., moving software solutions from onsite and local datacenters to a cloud-based computing platform or change their offerings (and supporting systems) to remain competitive in the marketplace. For example, many brick-and-mortar retailers have responded to the rise of e-commerce by creating an online presence as buyer preferences shifted from physically visiting a store to buy goods to sitting at the computer and ordering new merchandise. Lastly, businesses often need to reinvent themselves and develop new business strategies that require adopting new values, attitudes, and norms. These changes are developmental (minor improvement), transitional (major improvement), and transformational (radical improvement).[5] Organizations usually have all three forms of change occurring at the same time. The outcome of an effective leadership process is successful developmental, transitional, and transformational change.

Organizational adaptation (transformational change) is the most difficult of these changes to facilitate. And the mantra "adapt or die" remains a reality for many organizations. Jerry Glover, Harris Friedman, and Gordon Jones suggest that the most critical challenge leaders face today is ensuring their organizations adapt to their surrounding environment successfully.[6] Your value as a leader comes from how well you can guide your organization through periods of adaptation. Unfortunately, the leadership process in many organizations results in a never-ending cycle of change programs, with none of the change programs producing the desired results. There are several reasons for this outcome, but a significant contributor to failed change is that leaders struggle to facilitate their groups through all types of change. Product development leaders can improve the change experience and increase their organization's chances of success by practicing adaptive leadership. This chapter discusses what adaptive leadership is, why leaders need to understand adaptive leadership, maladaptive responses, and the limitations of adaptive leadership. In the next chapter, I present adaptive leadership in action.

---

[3] Some will add death and taxes as the only constants.

[4] Barbara Kellerman, *Professionalizing Leadership*, (New York, NY: Oxford University Press, 2018), 133–136.

[5] Linda Anderson, "Organization Development and Transformation," in *Practicing Organizational Development: Leading Transformation and Change*, ed. William J. Rothwell, Jacqueline M. Stavros, and Roland L. Sullivan (USA: Wiley, 2016), 62–66.

[6] Glover and Friedman, "When Change is Not Enough," 15–32.

What Is Adaptive Leadership

Adaptive leadership is a leadership approach developed by Ron Heifetz and Marty Linksy that describes how leaders and followers can tackle complex challenges requiring meaningful change.[7] It is a leadership approach that stresses both leaders' and followers' importance in the leadership processs. The leader facilitates the adaptation process but is not separate from the process. In his review of adaptive leadership, Peter Northouse notes that an adaptive leader is not the savior with the answers to the challenges.[8] Northouse's observation challenges popular leader definitions, which position leaders as experts who have prepackaged answers for all organizational issues. Many leaders believe that they will come across as incompetent if they do not act like they have all the answers. The reality is that many organizational challenges are beyond the mental capacity of any single leader (or any individual) in the organization.[9] For example, in the product development context, anticipating, understanding, and meeting the needs of customers, clients, and team members is something that no leader can do on their own.

Adaptive leadership incorporates aspects of systems, biology, service orientation, and psychotherapy.[10] The leadership theory recognizes that organizational challenges occur within a complex adaptive system. The biological aspect of adaptive leadership stresses the need for adaptation through a change in beliefs, values, and mindset.[11] Adaptation encourages the modification of our existing worldviews. Instead of defaulting to providing answers through commands and directives, adaptive leadership theory encourages a service orientation stance and reinforces servant leadership. Adaptive leadership theory also incorporates aspects of psychotherapy because change is ultimately personal. Everyone has unconscious processes that influence their behavior, including their defensive mechanisms when faced with the need to change.[12] Leaders who practice adaptive leadership understand unconscious processes play a role in organizational life. Psychotherapy incorporates listening and communication, facilitating conversations, and providing individuals with the support they need during

---

[7] Ronald Hefeitz, *Leadership Without Easy Answers*, (Cambridge, MA: Belknap Press of Harvard University Press, 1994).

[8] Peter G. Northouse, *Leadership: Theory and Practice* 7th ed, (Thousand Oaks, CA: Sage Publications, 2016), 257–294.

[9] Brian W. Head and John Alford, "Wicked Problems: Implications for Public Policy and Management," *Administration & Society* 47, no. 6 (2015): 711–739.

[10] Hefeitz, *Leadership Without Easy Answers*, 2–5.

[11] Gabrielle Ka Wai and Diana L. H. Chan, "Adaptive Leadership in Academic Libraries," *Library Management* 39, no. 1/2 (2018): 108.

[12] Manfred Kets de Vries, "Organizations on the Couch: A Clinical Perspective on Organizational Dynamics," *European Management Journal* 22, no. 2 (2004): 187–188.

the adaptive process.[13] Change endeavors struggle when leaders ignore the people aspects involved.

The need for adaptive leadership results from the reality that many of the problems individuals, teams, organizations face do not have known and apparent answers. In making this point, Heifetz distinguished between technical challenges and adaptive challenges by noting that technical challenges have clearly defined problems and solutions, whereas adaptive challenges do not.[14] Unfortunately, many leaders incorrectly characterize adaptive challenges as technical challenges. The consequences of this mischaracterization can be dire, mainly because it leads to organizations failing to adapt to the new conditions which surround it appropriately or introducing solutions that cause even more problems. Hence, leadership researchers Mary Uhl-Bien and Michael Arena note that organizational viability depends on leadership that facilitates successful adaptation.[15] As such, adaptive leadership could be considered an element of Complexity Leadership Theory (CLT).[16] To facilitate successful adaptation, you must be able to distinguish between technical and adaptive challenges. Table 7-1 outlines the difference between technical and adaptive challenges.

Table 7-1 Technical and Adaptive Challenge Descriptions. Source: Ronald Heifetz, Marty Linsky, and Alexander Grashow, The Practice of Adaptive Leadership, (Boston, MA: Harvard Business Press), 20

Type of challenge	Problem definition	Solution	Locus of work
Technical	Clear	Clear	Leader
Adaptive	Requires adaptation	Requires adaptation	Group more than Leader
Technical and Adaptive	Clear	Requires adaptation	Leader and Group

Technical Challenges

It is essential to know that not all change requires or results in adaptation.[17] That is, not all change requires us to modify our values, attitudes, or mindset. Some change is limited to modifications to current operating procedures, e.g., going from multiple VPN solutions to a single VPN solution or upgrading to

---

[13] Alaina Doyle, "Adaptive Challenges Require Adaptive Leaders," *Performance Improvement* 56, no. 9 (2017): 18–26.

[14] Hefeitz, *Leadership Without Easy Answers*, 73–76.

[15] Mary Uhl-Bien and Michael Arena, "Complexity Leadership: Enabling People and Organizations for Adaptability," *Organizational Dynamics* 46, no.1 (2017): 16–19.

[16] Ibid: 10–11.

[17] Jerry Glover and Harris Friedman, "Adaptive Leadership: When Change is not Enough (Part One)," *Organization Development Journal* 20, no. 2 (2002): 18–19.

the latest version of a software program. Challenges that do not require paradigm shifts are technical challenges within adaptive leadership. Leaders can use their formal authority to address technical challenges. For example, if a team member's laptop keeps crashing, then you have a technical challenge because the problem—a crashing laptop—is clear and defined. The solution—replacing the laptop—is also clear and defined. All that needs to occur is the implementation of the known solution. Technical challenges are not necessarily simple, even if they might be straightforward. Solving a 10,000-piece jigsaw puzzle is hard work; however, it is a technical challenge because there is a pre-defined solution. It is also important to note that even though technical challenges have known solutions, the leader may not solve a technical challenge due to the lack of resources.[18] Imagine that you want to approve a team member's request for a new laptop, but you do not have the budget. The solution is straightforward but unattainable until funds become available. Sometimes people, bureaucracy, or processes prevents the resolution of a technical challenge. Nonetheless, technical challenges have a known solution, and implementing the solution requires the right expertise, authority, and resources.

Many leadership theories imply that leaders have the solutions, and everyone else implements the solutions. These theories have you singlehandedly establish the vision, define the strategy and develop the tactics. After you have done all that, you can then hand off work to the team. You are supposed to do this while inspiring employees day in and day out. Firms have layers arranged in hierarchical structures, with each layer in the hierarchy responsible for solving the problems of the layer below it.[19] These leadership perspectives make organizational success completely dependent on your ability to problem-solve. You better be good at it.

In fairness, I have found that many leaders love technical challenges because it allows them to show off their competence and exercise their formal authority. Technical challenges reinforce their position and make them feel valuable to the organization. But let us not put the love of technical challenges solely on leaders. As we saw with the dark side of servant leadership, team members can develop unhealthy expectations of their leaders, like expecting their leaders to have answers to all questions. I once had a team member question my ability to lead because I asked for their opinion on an non-technical organizational situation. To this individual, I needed to have the answers.

---

[18] Wai and Chan, "Adaptive Leadership in Academic Libraries," 107.
[19] Jean-Marc C. Haeusler, "Medicine Needs Adaptive Leadership," 12–13.

Adaptive Challenges

Unlike technical challenges, where you (or a delegate) can solve the challenge due to your knowledge and expertise, you cannot solve adaptive challenges. Adaptive challenges lack a clear problem definition and solution. They are not solved; instead, they are managed and continuously addressed. Adaptive challenges require team participation in addressing the challenge through the leadership process. For example, satisfying stakeholder needs through product development is an adaptive challenge as solution discovery occurs during the product development process. All stakeholders need to work together to identify a solution to their adaptive challenges.

Organizations tackle adaptive challenges through adaptive work. Adaptive work results in shifts in leader and followers' values, priorities, and roles while addressing the adaptive challenge.[20] Adopting or modifying our values is often uncomfortable, and people may give up on adaptive work without the proper support. Leaders must also continuously test their beliefs and assumptions, which is easier said than done.[21] The depth of the changes required for adaptive work is one reason why many leaders treat adaptive challenges as if they are technical challenges—they do not want to go through the difficulty that accompanies adaptive work. However, to address adaptive challenges, everyone needs to take on adaptive work.

Technical and Adaptive Challenges

It is most likely that your organizational challenges will consist of a combination of technical and adaptive elements. The business problem might have a clear definition; however, a single known solution does not exist.[22] An example of a technical-adaptive challenge was a situation of weekly system outages that a team I led faced. While we knew we had an outage problem, I could not prescribe a single solution to address our product quality. Neither could I use my formal authority to prevent outages. Addressing the system outages required that the team changed their attitude towards quality. It also required that the team adopt new practices that none of the team members had used before. Even though aspects of this challenge were technical, figuring out the solution was adaptive. And even when the team thought it had solved the immediate quality problems, they would need to continue to address quality if they were responsible for that system. Part of your job is to understand the nature of the challenge you are dealing with and then mobilize the appropriate response in your organization. Challenges that consist of adaptive aspects will require a change in attitudes and norms in addition to potential changes in processes and tools.

---

[20] Northouse, *Leadership: Theory and Practice*, 273–274.
[21] Glover and Friedman, "When Change is Not Enough," 15–32.
[22] Northouse, *Leadership: Theory and Practice*, 262.

Types of Responses to Adaptive Challenges

How well your organization responds to an adaptive challenge reflects its adaptive capacity. Remember, an organization is not limited to the firm. It could be the department, function, or team you lead. I have already noted that many leaders treat adaptive challenges like they are technical and, as a result, the requisite adaptation does not occur. But how does this happen? Organizational adaptation occurs through the equilibration—holding in balance—of assimilation and accommodation.[23] Assimilation is acquiring new information, i.e., recognizing an adaptive challenge, while accommodation is change in attitudes, behaviors, and processes. Failing to hold assimilation and accommodation in balance leads to a maladaptive response.[24] Organizational adaptation is the result of making the right changes based on insights. There are four possible ways in which a leader (and their organization) can respond to adaptive situations:

- Cultural trap

- Natural selection

- Serendipity

- Maximum adaptive capacity[25]

Three of these responses are maladaptive, and you need to make sure your organization avoids them. Figure 7-1 shows the different adaptive responses.

---

[23] Glover and Friedman, "When Change is Not Enough," 23–24.
[24] Ibid, 24–28.
[25] Ibid.

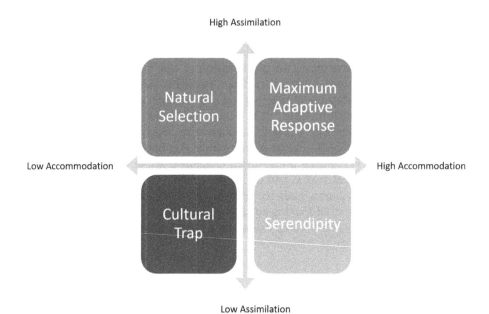

Figure 7-1. Adaptation responses. Jerry Glover, Harris Friedman, and Gordon Jones, "Adaptive Leadership: When Change Is Not Enough (Part One)," Organization Development Journal 20, no. 2 (2002), 15–32

We Have Always Done It This Way (Cultural Traps)

If existing values and beliefs prevent you from considering new information that requires changes to your current approach, you are stuck in a "cultural trap." In these situations, assimilation and accommodation are low. You intentionally ignore new information and do not encourage any change in behavior or process from yourself or anyone else in your organization. The cultural trap response maintains the status quo even though new information in the environment suggests that a change is needed. "We have always done it this way" signals that the cultural trap is at work. Your past success prevents you from paying attention to the changes in your environment. Unfortunately, it is only in hindsight or after we eventually make changes to recognize that we had been in a trap. The demise of many businesses is in large part due to cultural traps which have held them back. Hubris leads to individual and organizational downfall.

A personal example of how previous success can trap us is when I failed to modify my leadership approach in a new department and engage individuals from departments outside of mine in particular conversations. My past successes in leading different organizations meant that I assumed that a similar approach in the new organization would work just as well. I was wrong. People interpreted my actions as an attempt to exclude other groups, and people were quick to tell me that my actions violated existing cultural norms. Unfortunately, I was proud and not in the mood to receive this feedback. My previous success had trapped me. As I edit this chapter, many organizations face "return to the office" decisions. It will be interesting to see how many become victims of the cultural trap. You need to ensure that prior success does not obscure your organization from recognizing when to act differently.

We Will Get Lucky (Natural Selection)

The second maladaptive response is natural selection. Natural selection occurs when leaders recognize the value of new information but fail to use it. There is high assimilation but low accommodation with leaders leaving adaptation to chance or fortune.[26] Why do we, despite having information that will help us, often decide not to act on this information? It is because we want to save face, protect our political status, or simply not do the hard work involved with the change.[27] Sometimes, acting on new information is politically more dangerous than doing nothing. Acting on new information may require that we tell people we were wrong or made a mistake, and this can be difficult for people to do—especially people in assigned leader roles. With natural selection, you wait long enough to let the situation potentially handle itself. And sometimes it does.

Continuing with my success trap example, if the organization had experienced turnover, and suddenly, people who complained about being excluded from specific conversations were no longer in the organization, adaptation would have occurred without any changes. In my case, however, these people did not leave, and so it became a waiting game. If you do not initiate change in response to information from your environment, you have left adaptation entirely up to variables outside of your control. Many firms take this approach, and it works out at times; however, it rarely yields the best results in the long run and causes firms to leave transformational opportunities on the table.

Flavor of the Month (Serendipity)

The serendipity response is taking a copycat approach to adaptation. Serendipity is characterized by low assimilation and high accommodation, with leaders making changes because they believe that people want to see change.[28] In this case, you are making changes because everyone else is doing

---

[26] Jerry Glover, Kelly Rainwater, Gordon Jones, and Harris Friedman, "Adaptive Leadership (Part Two): Four Principles for Being Adaptive," *Organization Development Journal* 20, no. 4: 20–23.

[27] Ronald Heifetz, Marty Linsky, and Alexander Grashow, *The Practice of Adaptive Leadership*, (Boston, MA: Harvard Business Press), 89–100.

[28] Ibid.

it. You do not assess whether the changes have a high likelihood of positively impacting your organization. Any feedback (positive or negative) generated from the change process is ignored or discarded. While the organization may—due to luck—see some immediate benefit from the change, the benefits will not last because there is little or no learning. Adaptation requires more than copying what others are doing. You need to understand the information that serves as an impetus for the change. You need to understand why you would make the change first, and then after the change is in place, you need to process feedback from the change. It is quite common for leaders to copy successful approaches of other organizations without understanding the thinking behind the approaches.

The widespread adoption of the "Spotify model" since 2010 is an excellent example of this. I worked in an organization where I (and several other leaders) tried hard to replicate Spotify's guilds, communities of practice, and management structure before understanding why Spotify came up with its model in the first place. We spent no time trying to learn what challenges Spotify was attempting to address with their approach. Unfortunately, we could not sustain the Spotify model, and eventually, it crashed and burned. You may have seen leaders copy DevOps, architectural, and product practices without understanding how those practices make a difference. Copying in the short-term may provide some value, but it is not a healthy long-term adaptive approach.

Getting It Just Right (Maximum Adaptive Potential)

Maximum adaptive capacity occurs when both assimilation and accommodation are high in the organization. Maximum adaptation happens because leaders absorb new information and then use what they learn as the basis of changes—even if the new information and the changes it causes challenge current beliefs and values.[29] For example, let us imagine that you just received uncomfortable feedback that your teams no longer meet stakeholder needs, e.g., the product is difficult to use. What could an adaptive response look like? It would start with validating the feedback. After validating that the feedback has some substance to it, you could present the challenge of making the software easier to use. The team could then take on the challenge and make changes, e.g., modify their product development process to make their software easier to use—all with your support. These changes would require a potentially disruptive change in attitudes and norms. Then, stakeholders would express their delight because the software is easier to use, and they are more effective at their jobs because the team made some changes. Maintaining this level of stakeholder satisfaction will require constant attention to stakeholder needs.

---

[29] Ibid.

Maximum adaptation starts with you—you need to set an example. People must see that you are willing to receive feedback and make personal changes. Once you do this, you can then encourage the same response from others. Working with your teams to make progress on adaptive challenges through a collective maximum adaptive response is the essence of adaptive leadership.

Adaptive Leadership Means Living Dangerously

At its core, adaptive leadership mobilizes and persuades people to take on challenges. In many cases, people prefer the status quo because addressing challenges will require changes. These changes often involve a form of personal loss like giving up a preferred working style, sharing power so that others can participate more fully in a process, or even changing teams and relationships for a more effective organization. In other words, adaptive leadership introduces discomfort. People often resist change when the change requires that they let go of an idea, value, attitude, resource, or norm that matters a lot.[30] Remember, you are asking people to let go of what has served them well in the past. Why should they give up ideas or attitudes that were instrumental in achieving previous success? People will actively resist adaptive work. Ronald Heifetz and Marty Linksy remind leaders engaged in adaptive change that, "You appear dangerous to people when you question their values, beliefs, or habits of a lifetime."[31] People might even try to remove you from the situation if they consider you too dangerous to the status quo. You probably know of an executive who lost their job because people considered them too disruptive, i.e., they had gone too far in challenging the status quo. These executives thought they were leading change; however, the proposed changes signaled impending and unacceptable loss to the people around them. And so, these people orchestrated their removal.

If you think that only executives face dangers while encouraging adaptation, you are wrong. Leaders at all levels "live dangerously" as they navigate the treacherous landscape of transformational (and unpopular) change. I experienced living dangerously when, as a manager, I changed team composition for improved organizational effectiveness. I intended that the moves would decrease silos and spread knowledge within the teams. The change would result in multiple teams being able to work on multiple solutions. I thought a change like this would go on without any resistance with the goal of improved organizational effectiveness. I was wrong. I did not consider that the new team structure would end well-established relationships forged over many years. Also, I did not appreciate that several team members did not have a burning desire to learn new solutions, which these changes would require

---

[30] Heifetz, Linsky, and Grashow, *The Practice of Adaptive Leadership,* 89–100.
[31] Ronald Heifetz and Marty Linsky, *Leadership on the Line: Staying Alive Through the Dangers of Change,* (Boston, MA: Harvard Business Review Press, 2017), 12.

them to do. They were going to lose the prestige that came with being an expert and become novices.

Unfortunately, this was early in my career, and I did not recognize that I had created an adaptive challenge which involved adaptive work. This change required a change in attitudes and norms. It would also mean that some team members would experience loss. I did not address any of these things and paid dearly for it. People leave organizations because of changes like the ones I made. They also leave unpleasant feedback during their exit interviews. A seemingly innocuous change has ended up derailing many a manager's career. Indeed, leading through adaptive work is a risky business. Therefore, you must know how to lead such that your organization maximizes its adaptive responses. Shortly, we will discuss competencies that will help you succeed with adaptive leadership, but a few thoughts on the importance of informal authority before we do that.

Informal Authority in Adaptive Leadership

While many leadership approaches rely on formal authority as the sole means to lead, adaptive leadership stresses the importance of informal authority. As discussed in Chapter 1, informal authority is the authority conferred on you by others because they trust you, respect you, and believe that you have their best interest at heart. Unlike formal authority, determined by your role or given to you by an authorizer, the scope of your informal authority does not exist in official documents.[32] When you challenge people to take on adaptive challenges, you quickly learn how much informal authority you have. Informal authority is crucial for engaging people in the difficult work of modifying their beliefs and behaviors. While you might be able to use your formal authority to initiate change, it is improbable that formal authority will be enough to sustain the effort required to address adaptive challenges. People commit to difficult change because they believe in their leader (and not necessarily their position). In addition, formal authority has a fixed scope because it depends on your position in the organization. On the other hand, you can increase your informal authority by strengthening your relationships, scoring early wins, addressing interests unconnected to the adaptive challenge, and selling small parts of your idea.[33] The more extensive your informal authority, the more likely it is that people will choose to address the adaptive challenge regardless of how difficult it is.

The notion of expanding informal authority might cause you to bristle and feel that such behavior is "playing politics" in the workplace. The reality, however,

---

[32] Ronald Heifetz, Marty Linsky, and Alexander Grashow, *The Practice of Adaptive Leadership: Tools and Tactics for Changing Your Organization and the World*, 23–28.
[33] Ibid, 133–136.

is that whenever we participate in any actions in support of a cause that we believe improves our situation, we are involved in politics. Politics is a part of organizational life because organizations are political entities. For example, suppose you felt that your entire team needed computer upgrades immediately, but the next scheduled upgrade was a quarter away. If you went to your supervisor and convinced her to approve the off-schedule upgrade, that would be politics. It is using your power to make something happen.

The question is this: what is the primary driver for how you use power for politics? Do you primarily use politics in service of the organization's greater good or primarily use politics to attend to your needs? If you want to expand your informal authority, you will take the time to develop relationships with key individuals whom the adaptive challenge will impact. Key individuals can include your leader(s), peers, team members, boundary partners, and a host of other stakeholders in the organization. It is good practice to identify who will be most impacted by the change and make them allies. Also, understand the expectations of the individuals who might have authorized you to lead the change. You must keep them abreast of what is happening and make sure expectations remain aligned.

Showing competence by achieving some early wins helps to increase personal and organizational confidence in the change. It can be tempting to impress people by taking on significant challenges or making sweeping and broad-scale changes, especially when starting a new job. However, do not try to boil the ocean—even if people on your team suggest you should. In many cases, these approaches fail and cause people to lose faith in your ability to lead.

I once took on a new job where I was supposed to lead an "Agile transformation." Coming into the role, the hiring manager had debriefed me on several things the organization was doing incorrectly, so I decided that I would come in, press the reset button, and start from scratch. I challenged every single behavior that I felt was wrong. I developed a roadmap of massive change that would ultimately turn the organization around. I did have a few allies in the organization, including my boss, but that was about it. No one else was in my corner, and most of the organization passively resisted the work I was trying to do. Finally, after months of frustration, I was ready to throw in the towel and move on to something else. Fortunately, I received unsolicited advice from another leader in the organization who possessed considerable informal authority. She said, "Eb, create a small but impactful win that you can build on. Do that, and you will be okay." Those two sentences are some of the best advice I have received in my entire career.

Leader Competencies for Adaptive Leadership

Several competencies are essential for you to facilitate organizational adaptation. Competencies, like active listening and clear communication, are competencies effective leaders need to possess in almost any context. However, additional competencies are required when leaders need to lead their organizations through adaptive change. The competencies are that you need to deeply understand your organization, embrace uncertainty and ambiguity, and demonstrate humility.

Know Your Organization

Every organization has tacit and explicit knowledge. Leaders who successfully guide their organization through change need to acquire this knowledge. One way to get this knowledge is through talking to people who have this knowledge. You also need to identify the norms that have helped the organization succeed over the years, especially when these norms will need to change as part of an adaptive challenge. Do not begin adaptive work without first understanding the existing power structures and relationships. Connect with organizational influencers who need to help you with adaptive work. Identify the loyalties in the organization, recognize the losses that people will experience as a result of the upcoming changes, and actively work to respect loyalties while gently handling losses.[34] For example, the evolution of a product development organization from a "feature factory"[35] to one that co-creates value with other departments will mean that those department leaders will need to change their perception of the product development organization. You will need to help these departmental leaders cope with what they perceive as a loss of authority and responsibility. Not understanding your organization will lead to struggles with adaptive work.

Embrace Uncertainty and Ambiguity

I do not believe it is possible to successfully guide an organization through adaptation without a high level of comfort with uncertainty and ambiguity. Unfortunately, it is not uncommon for leaders to assume and expect the high certainty and clarity with technical challenges to exist with adaptive challenges. Embracing uncertainty and ambiguity means maintaining composure and leading with grace while navigating adaptive problems. Additionally, adaptive challenges consist of paradoxes. Paradoxes are contradictions that you need to manage. An example of a paradox would be managing individual needs and

---

[34] Heifetz, Linsky, and Grashow, *The Practice of Adaptive Leadership,* 89–100.
[35] A feature factory is an organization obsessed with churning out features over solving problems.

organizational needs, giving teams autonomy while maintaining the right level of control, or acting locally and globally. You might also have the paradox of exploring new, unproven opportunities while at the same time exploiting proven opportunities that benefit the business. You must balance paradoxes in response to your environment and desired organizational outcomes.

Accomplishing adaptive work also requires that you balance multiple perspectives and ideas within the organization. There is often the desire to identify a single truth; however, various assertions can be accurate in many cases, i.e., situations can be ambiguous and generate multiple interpretations.[36] Because multiple interpretations are valid, do not hold on too tightly to your opinions. Suppose you insist that your analysis of an adaptive challenge is the only viable interpretation. In that case, you might miss opportunities to generate solutions that result from the combination of various ideas and perspectives. Many leaders want to come across as confident and knowledgeable in all situations. A lack of confidence, they believe, signals weakness. However, when dealing with an adaptive challenge, rarely (if at all) does a single person have the solution. Remain comfortable with the uncertainty and ambiguity that are inherent in adaptive situations.

Stay Humble with Deep Conviction

Adaptive leadership is not for the faint of heart. Mobilizing your organization to take on and persist in adaptive work requires your commitment to change in the face of resistance and even personal attack. When dealing with adaptive challenges, you must remain committed to the cause even when progress is slow. Hold the firm belief that change is required for your organization to thrive and lead this change with humility. Experimentation is critical during adaptation because experiments tell us when we need to improve our hypothesis and make different choices.[37] To learn means that you will make mistakes. And yet, many leaders place so many controls in place to prevent mistakes. They fail to realize that in doing so, they prevent organizational learning. I am not endorsing going through with silly ideas like touching a hot stove with your hand. Instead, it is fostering an experimental mindset within the organization.[38] Not every decision made during adaptive work will work out as originally intended. Humble leaders understand this and do not let mistakes make them afraid to try out new ideas. Instead, they encourage people to learn from experiments by making it safe to discuss how the results did not match expectations. They also do not go around saying "I told you so" and claiming credit for ideas that work out. You must focus on facilitating successful adaptation and not becoming the center of attention. Remember

---

[36] Ibid., 113–124.
[37] Uhl-Bien and Arena, "Enabling People and Organizations for Adaptability," 18.
[38] Wai and Chan, "Adaptive leadership in academic libraries," 108.

that successful adaptation is due to the hard work of many people. Humility is a critical competency that leaders who want to facilitate adaptation within their organization need to have.

Leader Behaviors That Foster Organizational Adaptation

You need to set the example for adaptation in individuals, teams, and the entire organization. Unfortunately, individuals, teams, and organizations routinely have maladaptive responses. While adaptive leadership involves leaders and followers, leaders set the stage for adaptive change to occur even though leaders cannot manage the change by themselves.[39] An example of adaptive change, at the individual level, is a manager (maybe after reading this book) modifying their leadership approach to become service-oriented while giving up their directive and transactional approach. Another example might be a product development team adopting a brand new set of product development practices, which require new attitudes and beliefs on developing products.

I need to repeat the following point because it is crucial. You cannot successfully address adaptive challenges alone. And yet, the responsibility of mobilizing team members to face organizational challenges largely rests on your shoulders. Ronald Heifetz observed the following behaviors from leaders who facilitate maximum adaptive responses to adaptive challenges—these leaders:

- Get on the Balcony
- Identify Adaptive Challenges
- Regulate Distress
- Maintain Disciplined Attention
- Give the Work Back to the People
- Protect Leadership Voices from Below[40]

Let us look at what it means to practice each of these leader behaviors.

---

[39] Benyamin B. Lichtenstein et al., "Complexity Leadership Theory: An Interactive Perspective on Leading in Complex Adaptive Systems," *E:CO* 8, no. 4 (2006): 3.
[40] Hefeitz, *Leadership Without Easy Answers*.

Get on the Balcony

For you to "get on the balcony" means you can create separation between you and the challenge so that you can make some sense of the problem. Heifetz et al. compare attaining distance to going to the balcony and watching people on the dance floor.[41] Distancing yourself from a situation allows you to see the interactions between the different people involved while not leaving the situation.[42] Doing this helps you take on a systemic view of the situation by understanding the perspective of different groups. For example, if you have two teams struggling to collaborate, taking a step back to view the relationship from each team's perspective allows you to see some of the relationship dynamics between the two teams. You would alternate between addressing collaboration problems and observing how the teams collaborate. Alternating between perspectives is why the ability to handle uncertainty and ambiguity is vital.

Viewing situations through multiple frames is a superpower for this behavior. Learn and hone your skills in using different frames to study challenges so you can gain multiple perspectives when facing novel situations. For example, using Morgan's organizational images[43], leaders can adopt frames that provide different perspectives on two teams struggling to collaborate. A political frame might reveal issues of power and different interests. A cultural or symbolic frame would ask whether each team has cultural norms and values that conflict with each other? What is it about the teams' structures that could be causing this conflict would be a question a structural or machine-like frame would pose? These are examples of how various frames can help you make sense of what is happening inside and outside their organization.

A couple of suggestions are essential here because it is not difficult to conclude that you are outside of the challenge because you are on the balcony. Nothing could be further from the truth—you are still in the room. And because you are in the room, you do not want to lose sight of the fact that your view is also subjective and that you have blind spots. Gary Klein observes that our flawed beliefs and passivity can act as obstacles to gaining insight.[44] Therefore, I encourage you to ask other trusted individuals to join you on the balcony. Have them share what their observations are and what stands out to them in the current situation. Run challenges through multiple frames as group exercises to generate learning and insight on what might be happening at that moment. Your job is to make sure that the right people get on the balcony to make sense of the situation.

---

[41] Heifetz, Linsky, and Grashow, *The Practice of Adaptive Leadership*, 7–8.

[42] Wai and Chan, "Adaptive Leadership in Academic Libraries," 108.

[43] Gareth Morgan, *Images of Organization*, (Thousand Oaks, CA: Sage Publications, Inc., 2006).

[44] Gary Klein, *Seeing What Others Don't: The Remarkable Ways We Gain Insights*, (New York, NY: Public Affairs, 2013).

Identify Adaptive Challenges

Hopefully, you now recognize that many of the challenges your organization faces are adaptive challenges. Becoming adept at recognizing adaptive challenges is a critical aspect of adaptive leadership. You do not want to foster maladaptive solutions and put your organization at risk.[45] So how can you tell that a challenge is adaptive? Ronald Heifetz, Marty Linsky, and Alexander Grashow provide the following archetypes for adaptive challenges:

- A gap between espoused values and behaviors
- Competing commitments
- The need to speak the unspeakable
- Work avoidance[46]

At the core of these situations is the need for individuals to alter their current values, beliefs, or behaviors. An example of a gap between espoused values and behaviors could be that a leader espouses the value of being open, honest, and direct but punishes team members who provide respectful yet candid feedback. Many organizations faced competing commitments during the coronavirus pandemic. They had to take care of their employees and stay financially viable at the same time. This situation was difficult for many leaders as it presented a paradox. Any attempt to discuss the undiscussable—sacred cows—can also be career-limiting, and so many employees do not speak up if it might hurt their career interests. Many of us have experienced occasions where we avoided adopting new ways of working—work avoidance—because making a change would involve significant discomfort.

For successful adaptation to happen, you need to nurture an environment that allows adaptive challenges to rise to the surface.[47] Let us revisit the situation with the team that had software quality issues. The challenge presented (at least) two archetypes that indicated we had adaptive work. One archetype was work avoidance because the team members did not want to adopt new practices that would improve quality. The other archetype was a gap between espoused values and behaviors. The team espoused producing a high-quality solution, but their behaviors did not reflect a commitment to quality. The team had to improve the quality of their product, or customers would switch over to the competition, thereby impacting company revenue. A continued drop in revenue would eventually negatively impact the team. It was clear that changes that would improve the product's quality were required. These changes would require modifications to the team's product development practices. Some of these practices—like mob programming and test-driven

---

[45] Ibid., 264.
[46] Heifetz, Linsky, and Grashow, *The Practice of Adaptive Leadership*, 77–86.
[47] Uhl-Bien and Arena, "Enabling People and Organizations for Adaptability," 17–19.

development—were not popular with the team and required a change in attitude. Adopting new practices did not come easy. Many team members did not like the idea of mob programming because they had been solo programmers for most of their careers. Unfortunately, I (initially) misdiagnosed the issue as a technical challenge as I thought I could use my authority to mandate the adoption of technical practices. I did not recognize the signs indicating that improving quality was an adaptive challenge for this team and delayed adaptation. It is essential to correctly identify challenges as adaptive when that is what they are.

Regulate Distress

Let me be honest with you. That adaptation process is stressful because it requires a change in beliefs, values, attitudes, and behaviors, which is not easy. Paradigm shifts do not happen overnight, and change is personal. Hence, stress exists for the duration of adaptive work because there is movement from comfort to discomfort. Therefore, the stress is prolonged, i.e., it is distress. For successful adaptation to occur, you need to do your part to ensure that the degree of stress people feel during the adaptation does not rise to the level where it discourages commitment to the adaptation process. Starting with yourself, help people keep their stress in a healthy balance as much as is possible. In Chapter 9, we explore the importance of leader self-care. Manage the stress caused by adaptive change by creating a holding environment, continually providing direction, protecting people involved in change, orienting people to new roles and responsibilities, addressing conflict quickly, and ensuring teams have productive working norms.[48] These leader actions are all necessary, but I want to focus on "creating a holding environment" because it is foundational to adaptive work success.

You must nurture an environment where adaptation can take place successfully. First, your workplace must be safe for individuals and groups to make the changes the adaptive challenge requires.[49] A sign that the workplace is safe is that mistakes do not lead to negative consequences; instead, they lead to learning, i.e., you preserve a "just culture." Second, your holding environment needs to be a container—any structure, physical or virtual space—where people engage in adaptive work through self-organization—the process through which complex adaptive systems identify new patterns of working.[50] As a leader, use your formal authority to maintain a healthy workplace for self-organization. Another way to maintain a healthy holding environment is

---

[48] Northouse, *Leadership: Theory and Practice*, 266–269.

[49] Alaina Doyle, "Adaptive Challenges Require Adaptive Leaders," 20.

[50] Edwin E. Olson and Glenda H. Eoyang, *Facilitating Organization Change: Lessons from Complexity Science*, (San Francisco, CA: Jossey-Bass/Pfeiffer, 2001), 11–13.

to manage the rate of change in the workplace.[51] Too much change will overwhelm people, and too little change will lead to inaction, so you want to make sure the rate of change is appropriate. Unfortunately, many organizations have too much change happening at the same time. The amount of change impedes adaptive work. Limit the amount of change and focus on the vital few. Stress is unavoidable when there is meaningful change; however, as the leader, you must make sure you do your best to regulate distress in your organization.

Maintain Disciplined Attention

Having people stay focused on adaptive work can prove challenging because, as mentioned previously, adaptive work is complex, cannot be solved (in a traditional sense), and involves loss. How can you recognize when people are not paying attention to the work at hand? First, look for certain avoidance behaviors. Avoidance behaviors include blaming others, focusing on areas that are not as important, and completely ignoring the adaptive challenge.[52] When people do not want to discuss critical change topics, it is a sign that they prefer the status quo. Adaptive work is hard. The discomfort created by adaptive work causes people to turn their attention away from the work they need to do. Getting the timing right for initiating change cannot be overstated. The situation must be ripe, and people must see that failure to change is not in the best interest of their community.

Tackling an adaptive challenge requires focus and discipline. If the conditions are ripe for change, ensuring the people remain focused on the adaptive work becomes paramount. While people quickly state that they value responding to change, that only seems to hold up when they are not the ones who have to make meaningful changes. Doing the work that maximizes the adaptive response is easier said than done. While avoidance may be appropriate when an issue is not ripe, you need to avoid the mistake that many leaders make of taking their eyes off the adaptive situation and assuming that the situation will resolve itself. If you have not made this mistake (yet), good for you—I have not been so fortunate. I have assumed that group issues would resolve themselves independently—a natural selection response if you have been paying attention. Unfortunately, I failed to recognize the lack of desire in individuals to do the adaptive work. It was my responsibility to keep the adaptive work front and center of the group. It is, however, vital that you make sure that maintaining disciplined attention does not cause you to become an overbearing leader. Finding this balance is more art than science, so consistently evaluate your engagement with your teams and get their feedback on your methods of maintaining disciplined attention.

---

[51] Ibid., 34.
[52] Northouse, *Leadership: Theory and Practice*, 269–270.

Give the Work Back to the People

Adaptive leadership requires that leaders "give the work back to the people." Whereas many leader descriptions position the leader as responsible for doing the work or having the work done according to the leader's instruction, adaptive leadership recognizes that the people in the organization must determine and do adaptive work. As Northouse puts it, "...giving work back to the people means empowering people to decide what to do..."[53] I am not a fan of the corporate-speak usage of the word "empowerment" because I believe it avoids the real issue. Many organizations do not need to empower their people; instead, they need to liberate or free their people to handle adaptive work. Regardless of your perspective on empowerment, adaptive leadership states that it is crucial that the people who need to do adaptive work also have the autonomy for the adaptive work. You need to make sure that team members participate in solving the problems they own. Giving the work back to the team might be the most critical step you will take as part of adaptive leadership. It ensures that leadership is dispersed and shared by the group. However, this behavior presupposes that the team can do the adaptive work. Giving people a challenge they cannot handle (even with your support) is an abdication of your leadership responsibility.

In the product development setting, "giving the work back" to the team could mean working with the team to determine how they will meet stakeholder needs. Depending on the context, you might specify an initial challenge and why the challenge matters and then let the team focus on how they will tackle the challenge. While you will need to clarify desired outcomes and any constraints that might exist, you do not spend time outlining how you would address the problem. That is not valuable because, as we have discussed, adaptive challenges do not have clear-cut solutions. If they did, they would not be adaptive challenges. To quote Mary Parker Follett, "...orders come from the work, not work from the orders."[54] Leaders often have a hard time leaving the implementation approach to the team because they view themselves as "chief problem solvers." This a trap many leaders (including myself) get caught in—especially when it feels like progress is slow. It is vital that once you identify the work as adaptive, you give it back to the team and then support them.

There are various approaches to giving the work back to the people. Many of the most effective methods to give the work back to the people require that leaders bring "the whole system into the room." Bringing the whole system into the room means that the leader presents the challenge to as many of the stakeholders required to address the challenge as is possible. The size of the

---

[53] Ibid., 271.
[54] Mary Parker Follett, *The Giving of Orders*, ed. Pauline Graham (USA: Harvard Business School Press Classic, 1995), 137.

system will depend on the nature of the challenge and the primary stakeholders. Sometimes, an executive team might need to address a challenge, and bringing the whole system into the room would mean presenting the challenge to the executive team. In other cases, an entire organizational unit needs to engage in adaptive work, and in those situations, bringing the organizational unit into the room is the appropriate action. Barbara Bunker and Billie Alban present approaches like future search, real-time strategic change; participative design; work-out; and open space technology that leaders can use as part of giving the work back to the people.[55] Do not discount the value of having a team meeting to discuss the best way to handle adaptive work.

Protect Leadership Voices from Below

Many leaders claim they want people to express their opinions. However, these leaders do not add that they only want the opinion expressed if it agrees with their opinion. Fortunately, every organization has a Taiwo and Kehinde who will ask uncomfortable and awkward questions during town halls and other large organizational meetings. These are the individuals, for example, that call attention to your behaviors that do not match the espoused values. Ensure these individuals do not become marginalized because they are often emergent leaders. Protect individuals with unpopular opinions so that they feel free to speak up.[56] Protecting these voices does not mean that you will agree with their perspective; instead, it means you will make sure that every individual in the group has an opportunity to have their views considered. Protecting team members with unpopular views signals to the group your commitment to having everyone participate in adaptive work. People are watching to see how you respond to unpopular opinions. How you respond in these situations may carry more weight than anything else you might say.

Protecting unpopular voices allows leaders to get perspectives that they might not have obtained from the popular voices on the team. In many cases, "voices from below" say what others in the room are afraid to say. These unpopular perspectives generate insights that would otherwise go unnoticed. However, unpopular ideas and perspectives can also create chaos, and the leader will need to make sure the group remains stable.[57] Your formal authority allows you to protect the "voices from below" during adaptive work. Appreciating, recognizing, and rewarding individuals who share unpopular opinions is one way that you can encourage team members to speak up. A word of caution is needed here, however. Ensure you maintain the trust of other team members

---

[55] Barbara Benedict Bunker and Billie T. Alban, *Large Group Interventions: Engaging the Whole System for Rapid Change*, (San Francisco, CA: Jossey-Bass, 1996).
[56] Heifetz, Linsky, and Grashow, *The Practice of Adaptive Leadership*, 145–148.
[57] Peter G. Northouse, *Leadership: Theory and Practice*, 271–272.

while protecting the unpopular views of specific team members. You want to keep your team together.

Table 7-2 provides a quick recap of adaptive leader behaviors.

Table 7-2. Adaptive Leader Behavior Descriptions

Adaptive leader behaviors	Description
Get on the balcony	Stepping away from the challenge to see what is happening more clearly.
Identify adaptive challenges	Using adaptive challenge archetypes to distinguish technical challenges from adaptive challenges.
Regulate distress	Keeping stress at healthy levels so that people can still do the work.
Maintain disciplined attention	Making sure team members remain focused on adaptive work.
Give the work back to the people	Providing the team with the autonomy, authority, accountability, and resources required to do adaptive work.
Protect leadership voices from below	Making it safe for people to express unpopular opinions.

Limitations of Adaptive Leadership Theory

It would not be unreasonable to expect that a leadership approach focused on facilitating adaptation in response to complex issues would also have many critiques of the theory. Interestingly, this is not the case. The lack of criticism is a possible indicator of the lack of awareness of adaptive leadership as an approach to leadership in the workplace. Because adaptive leadership does not seem to receive the same attention as other leadership theories such as servant leadership, transformational leadership, and authentic leadership, it does not have the same level of critique as those theories. I believe that adaptive leadership theory would benefit from additional practitioner adoption and critique. The lack of practitioner adoption in product development is why I decided to share this approach to leadership with you. You face adaptive challenges, and the adaptive leadership approach can help you become a more effective leader.

Even though adaptive leadership has not received as much critique as other leadership theories, it is not free of criticism. Northouse identified four areas for improving adaptive leadership theory: more empirical research, additional theory refinement, reducing its scope, and explicitly including a moral dimension.[58] Furthermore, several researchers have suggested that adaptive

---

[58] Ibid., 276–277

leadership would benefit from additional complexity science concepts.[59] Indeed, complexity leadership theory and adaptive leadership theory overlap, and investigating complexity leadership can only help you become more effective at facilitating adaptation in your organization. Unfortunately, because of the lack of extensive empirical evidence on adaptive leadership, there is a lack of resources on adaptive leadership that you can reference. Fortunately, you now have this book.

Another limitation of adaptive leadership lies in its strength. Because it focuses on responding to change, it provides little guidance for maintaining a steady state. Adaptive leadership theory implies that maintaining a steady-state by ensuring operations continue without a hitch using authority, power, and influence is not leadership.[60] I beg to differ. Responding to change is not your only concern as an organizational leader. You also need to make sure that your organization can continue to offer its existing products and services. Uhl-Bien and Arena observed that organizations first start as entrepreneurial, and then success leads to an operational focus on consistency, stability, and order.[61] A significant amount of the bureaucracy and hierarchy that exists in organizations exists to maintain order and stability. Complex adaptive leadership will provide you with further guidance on managing the steady-state and adaptative paradox.[62] Organizations need to establish a consistent and reliable way of delivering their products and services at high levels of quality while meeting customers' demands. For example, the customer service department of a telecom firm needs to respond to customer inquiries within service level agreements. You have probably experienced poor and inconsistent customer service, which left you unhappy and reconsidering whether you would continue to do business with the company. The goal of operational leadership is to make sure that the company continues to satisfy customers. Therefore, adaptive work cannot negatively impact current organizational excellence.

Adaptive leadership assumes that individuals and teams possess the knowledge, skills, and ability to face challenges—this is not always the case. In some situations, an individual or a team may not have the skills required to tackle the challenge, and giving the work back to them would be the incorrect step to take. It is crucial to honestly assess your team's capabilities before deciding whether you take a hands-on or a hands-off approach. Adaptive leadership, like most leadership theories, focuses on what you, as the leader, need to do

---

[59] Marcus Thygeson, Lawrence Morrisey, and Val Ulstad, "Adaptive Leadership and the Practice of Medicine: A Complexity-Based Approach to Reframing the Doctor-Patient Relationship," *Journal of Evaluation in Clinical Practice* 16, no. 5 (2010): 1014.

[60] Heifetz, Linsky, and Grashow, *The Practice of Adaptive Leadership*, 23–27.

[61] Uhl-Bien and Arena, "Complexity Leadership: Enabling People and Organizations for Adaptability," *Organizational Dynamics* 46, no. 1 (2016): 9–20.

[62] For a good overview of complex adaptive leadership, see Nick Obolensky's book of the same title, *Complex Adaptive Leadership*.

to facilitate maximum adaptive capacity. The theory is leader-oriented even though it acknowledges that success with adaptive work depends on followers. Remember that you are part of the adaptive process and do not work outside of it.[63] Fight the temptation to see yourself as a hero. Instead, recognize your role as responsible for mobilizing and facilitating the leadership process to tackle adaptive challenges.

Takeaways

- Addressing adaptive situations requires a change in mindset, attitude, and behaviors—adaptive work. Adaptive work is ongoing.

- You need the competencies of organizational knowledge, comfort with uncertainty and ambiguity, and deep conviction with humility.

- Your primary responsibility in adaptive leadership is to foster conditions in which adaptive work can thrive.

- Practice the behaviors of "getting on the balcony," "identifying adaptive challenges," "regulating distress," "maintaining disciplined attention," "giving the work back to the people," and "protecting leadership voices from below."

- The bulk of adaptive work is in the hands of the people you lead. You cannot address adaptive situations on your own. Team members need to understand that you do not have the answers.

- Do not underestimate the importance of your informal authority during adaptive work.

---

[63] Dennis Tourish, "Is Complexity Leadership Theory Complex Enough? A Critical Appraisal, Some Modifications and Suggestions for Further Research," http://sro.sussex.ac.uk/id/eprint/76349/ (last accessed July 19, 2020).

Adaptive Leadership in Practice

What people resist is not change per se, but loss.

—Ronald Heifetz[1]

Change starts with you, but it doesn't start until you do.

—Tom Ziglar[2]

As I began writing this chapter in March 2020, the coronavirus (COVID-19) pandemic took the world by storm. The pandemic shut down countries as leaders everywhere tried to control the spread of the disease. While the COVID-19 pandemic is not the first pandemic the world has faced, it had been

---

[1] Ronald Heifetz, Marty Linsky, and Alexander Grashow, *The Practice of Adaptive Leadership: Tools and Tactics for Changing Your Organization and the World,* (Boston, MA: Harvard Business Press, 2009), 22.

[2] Zig Ziglar and Tom Ziglar, *Born to Win: Find Your Success,* (Issaquach, WA: Made For Success Publishing, 2017).

© Ebenezer C. Ikonne 2021
E. C. Ikonne, *Becoming a Leader in Product Development,*
https://doi.org/10.1007/978-1-4842-7298-5_8

over 100 years since society had faced a health challenge of such global proportions. The pandemic presented an adaptive challenge because the problems and solutions of the pandemic did not have pre-determined answers. Infectious disease experts knew there was a disease but did not initially understand how the virus was transmitted. Experts did not also know the best way to treat it. Containing the spread of the virus depended on people adopting behaviors such as hand washing, self-quarantining, mask-wearing, and social distancing. However, many people (including elected officials) resisted adopting or discouraged these practices. Thus, containment was out of the hands of leaders. Getting the pandemic under control required more than the experts' exercise of authority. Adaptation would require that individuals, organizations, and even governments change their attitudes, norms, and behaviors.

Businesses also had to operate differently to prevent the spread of the disease. Many companies asked their employees to work from home if they could perform their role from home. Many school buildings closed, and employees had to take care of their parents, children, and pets, all while working from home. For many parents, this was a brand-new situation they had not had to deal with before. As many people observed, individuals were not trying to work from home; they were at home trying to work. The working situation was an adaptive challenge because there was no defined solution for how teams function in this new work situation. Also, it was clear that organizations would have to adopt new values and behaviors if they were going to function effectively in the new normal. Finally, successful organizational adaptation would require everyone in the organization to contribute—leaders did not have the answers. Leaders needed to practice adaptive leadership to mobilize their organizations to face this challenge.

Leaders need to practice the adaptive leadership behaviors of getting on the balcony, identifying adaptive challenges, regulating distress, maintaining disciplined attention, giving the work back to the people, and protecting leadership voices from below in the face of adaptive challenges. These behaviors do not have to occur sequentially. For example, the leader might start by spending some time on the balcony, then protect leadership voices from below, and find ways to give work back to people on their team while helping the team regulate their distress. Regardless of how you go about practicing adaptive leadership, do not forget that it is your responsibility to foster a workplace where people feel safe to learn how to address the challenges in front of them. Unfortunately, too many leaders do not practice these behaviors. Instead, they treat situations like the remote work situation like a technical challenge and try to use their authority and expertise to solve the problem to the organization's detriment. In this chapter, we will see adaptive leadership in action through two stories. The first story is about Ada[3], a product development team manager who encouraged her team to deal with the adaptive challenge of remote work during the coronavirus pandemic. The second story is a personal one.

---

[3] All names in the stories have been changed to protect the innocent.

Gaining Perspective

Adaptive leadership starts with the leader assessing what is happening inside and outside their organization—this is assimilation. When the news of coronavirus infections and deaths in Italy began to make the headlines in the United States, Ada realized she needed to "get on the balcony" and observe her team's response to the news. Her initial observations revealed that most team members were not paying much attention to what was happening in Italy. However, as media coverage of the coronavirus deaths increased and cases began to appear in the United States, she noticed team members spending a few minutes each day discussing the government's response to the increase in known cases in the US before starting their workday.

Ada's team members began to pay even more attention to the pandemic once their state health department confirmed cases in the state. As neighboring states instituted social distancing, closed schools, and prohibited public gatherings, Ada noticed increased anxiety in her team members. The tone of water cooler conversations changed as team members spent more time discussing the spread of the virus in the country. Ada could see the concern growing and distress increasing. She also noticed, from the balcony, that team members wanted to know how the pandemic would impact their work and livelihoods. As other firms in the community stopped travel, limited large gatherings, and asked their employees to work from home, Ada knew it would only be a matter of time before her organization would take the same actions. She knew she needed to prepare in advance for upcoming changes.

Adaptive leadership requires transitioning between paying attention to specific details and paying attention to larger patterns. You need to alternate between the dance floor and the balcony continually. Even though Ada stepped away from her team to gain perspective on how the coronavirus might impact them, she never lost sight of the fact that she was part of the team. She could not be an absent leader, so focused on the big picture that she did not connect with her team members to understand how they felt in those moments. The truth be told, attaining distance was difficult for Ada as her teams had several critical product releases planned for the quarter. She had to establish a routine that provided her space to get on the balcony to assess the current situation regularly. She used her team meetings as an opportunity to listen to what her team members were (and were not) saying, i.e., the song beneath the words.[4] Ada excelled at asking powerful and open-end questions that encouraged dialogue, allowing her to gain insight into team members' concerns regarding the coronavirus. Their answers helped Ada understand how team members felt the pandemic might impact them.

---

[4] Heifetz, Linsky, and Grashow, *The Practice of Adaptive Leadership*, 76.

Getting on the balcony was never more critical than when the firm's executives told Ada and her peers that teams would need to work from home to help "flatten the curve."[5] Ada knew the remote work situation would impact her team even though she did not know how it would. She met with the team to talk about their new and upcoming work situation. In the meeting, Ada shared with the team that they would all start working from home the following week, and then she opened the floor for team members to provide feedback and ask questions. The team's response to this change was mixed. While team members understood the rationale for working from home, there was a lot of concern regarding how they could make this work; especially considering that schools had also closed, and team members would now have to take care of their children while working. The pandemic and the circumstances it had created were new to everyone, and it was clear that the team was facing an adaptive challenge.

Where Is Learning Required?

A critical aspect of adaptive leadership is ensuring that adaptive challenges rise to the level where people can begin to work on them. Tackling the COVID-19 pandemic required the participation of individuals in society. Many state governments shut down schools to flatten the curve, and many corporations—including Ada's—instructed their employees to work from home until the outbreak was under control. While working from home was not entirely new to Ada's team, this was still a brand-new situation because they had no idea when they would be back in the office. Also, many team members would need to help their children with their online schoolwork with school buildings closed—a brand-new experience for many parents and children. The company's response to the coronavirus pandemic's adaptive challenge had created a challenge for the team—an adaptive challenge.[6]

Adaptive challenges require that stakeholders go through the learning process to discover potential solutions to their challenges.[7] In many cases, learning is also necessary to understand the problem. Whatever the situation is, you cannot solve the adaptive challenge on behalf of your organization. Adaptive challenges require the full participation of everyone impacted by the situation. In the remote work situation, full participation meant that everyone on the team would need to figure out how they would work from home and navigate their unique personal situations. Team members would also have to figure out how to work together in this new situation. Even though some team members would have liked for Ada to provide them with the answers to this challenge,

---

[5] "Flatten the curve" meant slowing down the spread of the SARS-CoV-2 virus.

[6] Be prepared for new adaptive challenges to emerge while addressing adaptive challenges.

[7] Heifetz, Linsky, and Grashow, *The Practice of Adaptive Leadership*, 105–108.

Ada could not provide a manual or playbook for team members to reference because she did not have one. She could not take on the learning challenge for her team members. Besides, she was going through the same experience with them.

Even though Ada could not address the adaptive challenge for her team, she was responsible for ensuring the team tackled the adaptive challenge. It is not enough that you identify an adaptive challenge. You must make sure that the people you lead understand they have a problem for which an answer does not exist. You also need to ensure that individuals know that they are responsible for doing the work required to address the challenge with your support. Ada used her next team meeting to ensure the team understood they had an adaptive challenge they had to overcome. While Ada did not use the technical term "adaptive challenge," she emphasized the novelty of the situation for the team. She clarified to the team that changes would have to occur at the individual and team levels. Ada quickly dispelled the notion that she had the authority to address the problem(s) on their behalf. Addressing the adaptive challenge meant the team would have to take on the adaptive work.

Giving the Work Back to the People

Giving the work back to the team is one of the more unique aspects of adaptive leader behavior. Unlike many other leadership theories that implicitly or explicitly prescribe that the leader provides the team with instructions on accomplishing the work, adaptive leadership stresses that team members must perform the adaptive work themselves. For example, in the "work from home" situation, the adaptive work that the team had to do was figure out how they were going to work together during a pandemic while juggling the unplanned domestic duties of supporting their elderly parents, children, pets, and other dependents. Adaptive work involves changing ideas, beliefs, values, and even behaviors. Everyone would have to determine the personal adjustments they would make. The team would also have to learn how to work together effectively for an undefined period with everyone at home.

Even though Ada could not do the work on behalf of the team, she could use her formal authority to nurture a *holding environment* where the team could talk about how they would work together going forward. Adaptive work requires that you foster a positive workplace where people can tackle complex issues. Failing to foster such an environment is an abdication of your duty as a leader. You also need to actively participate in adaptive work because disengaging from the adaptive work signals to others that it is not critical. There is a fine line between taking over adaptive work and letting the team own the adaptive work. Walk this line carefully.

Ada gave herself and her team members a few days to settle into their new routines at home once the "work from home" began. Like Ada, many team members had school-age children who would require care and support during this time. Many of the schools had set up e-learning programs for their students while they were at home. Recognizing that her team members would have to go through adjustments on the home front, Ada made it a point not to burden her team members with work-related activities, except the activity supported a critical business function. After a week, Ada brought the team together to discuss how they could work while at home. Ada kicked off the meeting by recognizing the unprecedented nature of this new work experience. She stressed that they needed to place taking care of their family members above any work commitments. Ada also asked team members to let her know if they had a personal situation that would impact their ability to complete their work. Then she turned it over to the team to discuss how they would work together in their new normal.

Leaders who facilitate successful adaptation tap into the power of self-organization when faced with complex challenges. Because they recognize that their organization (be it a single team or a collection of teams) is a complex adaptive system, they also understand that their organization can develop new patterns and structures in response to changes in their environment. The process of coming up with these new structures and patterns is known as self-organization.[8] Another way of describing giving the work back to the people is to say that the leader needs to provide the right conditions for effective self-organization. Edwin Olson and Glenda Eoyang identified containers, significant differences, and transforming exchanges as the conditions that influence self-organization.[9] The container refers to the entity (like a team) that needs to self-organize. Any gap between individuals in the system or between individuals and other aspects of the system can serve as a significant difference the system will need to address. Last but equally as important are transforming exchanges. Transforming exchanges are the interactions between individuals that eventually lead to system changes.

For successful adaptation to occur, you need to ensure that the appropriate conditions for self-organization exist. As discussed previously, you are part of the system and not an actor residing outside the system. Olson and Eoyang provide leaders with the three responsibilities of setting containers, focusing on significant differences, and foster transforming exchanges for self-organization to occur.[10] Ensure these conditions exist at the proper levels. If any of the conditions is under-constrained or over-constrained, it negatively impacts self-organization. Hence, your responsibility is to assess and modify

---

[8] Edwin E. Olson and Glenda H. Eoyang, *Facilitating Organization Change: Lessons from Complexity Science*, (San Francisco, CA: Jossey-Bass/Pfeiffer, 2001), 10.
[9] Ibid., 11–15.
[10] Ibid., 33–37.

the conditions continuously. The "effectively work from home" goal was the container for Ada's team. They needed to create new working patterns and structures to support this goal. The significant difference for the team is remote work during a pandemic, and the team needed to focus on resolving this difference.

Ada set up the online team meeting as the medium for creating transforming exchanges between team members. The meeting was a psychologically safe holding environment where team members could openly share their ideas on developing products and supporting the business despite the challenging work situation. After extensive dialogue, they identified some new team norms they would adopt. Here are some examples of new team norms:

- Team members agreed to have a huddle to check in with each other at the end of the day.

- Team members agreed to publish their schedules on the team communication platform to know where everyone was. For example, some team members would need to step away from the team to help their children with their e-learning schoolwork, and other team members needed to know when this would happen during the day.

- Also, team members always agreed to use video during team meetings to improve communication with each other. However, video meetings would only occur if they were the most effective means of getting work done.[11]

- Each team member handled an amount of personal change because of the pandemic, so the team agreed to show each other tremendous amounts of grace.

Throughout the self-organization process, Ada made sure to focus the team on how they could cope (and potentially thrive) (both as individuals and a team) in their new circumstances. She asked leading questions such as, "how will we respond if one of us has our child come on the screen while we are in the middle of a meeting?" Ada's responsibility was to keep the self-organization conditions in a healthy balance with one another. While she participated in the self-organization process, Ada did not decide the new team norms; instead, she reminded the team that determining the team norms was up to them. It would be on them to follow through on behaviors that supported these norms. These were team norms, not Ada's norms. As we will see next, a vital part of defining team norms included giving voice to the less vocal people on the team.

---

[11] As the pandemic lasted longer, the team modified how they used video as a response to video meeting fatigue. Their response is another example of adaptive leadership.

Listening to Everyone's Voice

One of the biggest obstacles to successful adaptive leadership is not allowing everyone to have their voice heard. There are always people in a group who are the center of attention. Their peers consider them the de facto leaders of the group and look to these individuals for guidance and direction. Team members often support the thoughts and ideas of these individuals without reservation because they hold these people in high regard. These individuals are usually technically competent, experienced, have charisma and expert power. Unfortunately, these individuals often prevent the voices of those with lesser status from being heard. As already alluded to in Chapter 1, authority, power, and influence are not distributed evenly within teams and organizations. Some team members will have more power and influence, even among peers at the same level on the same team. Hence, it is crucial to ensure that those with lesser social status can express themselves during adaptive situations.[12]

On Ada's team of 10 people, two individuals did not speak up that much. Moji and Chigozie were both team members who went about quietly getting their work done. Their quietness was not an indicator of poor performance, as both individuals made impactful contributions to the team. They were easygoing individuals who routinely decided to go with the flow and follow whatever others on the team decided. Some might describe them as "low maintenance" team members. As long as the decisions were not disruptive, they would support them. Left to themselves, Moji and Chigozie had no problem keeping their peace as the team worked out new norms, but adaptive challenges are not the time for silence. Ada made it a point to encourage everyone to speak up and share their concerns by going around the room and asking everyone to share their thoughts. It was important that everyone— including Moji and Chigozie—spoke up as the team identified their new working norms.

Protecting voices, however, goes further than making sure everyone has an opportunity to speak up. It also encourages those who have unpopular opinions to speak up. We all know that one person who sees something wrong in every decision. These are individuals who want to go left when everyone else wants to go right. If you are honest with yourself, you do not enjoy working with individuals who consistently voice dissent.[13] And yet, you still need to make sure that these voices can share what is on their minds. Their thoughts and ideas need the group's attention because they can lead to profound insight. Diversity in thought and approach—requisite variety—helps groups address adaptive challenges. So-called "unpopular voices" can increase a group's requisite variety.

---

[12] It is vital to make it safe for people to speak at all times, but vitally important when facing complex changes.

[13] Heifetz, Linsky, and Grashow, *The Practice of Adaptive Leadership*, 145–148.

Ada, like any other leader under the sun, had a few perpetual dissenters on her team. These individuals challenged most of the ideas that their teammates presented during the team meeting on norms. For example, when Chinaza suggested that everyone post their status on Slack so that others would know where they were, Segun (one of the team's most vocal dissenters) noted that doing so was a violation of individual privacy. While many leaders might have just shut Segun down at that moment, Ada realized the importance of having a dialogue on unpopular opinions. Ada asked Segun to explain why he thought posting statuses was an invasion of individual privacy and encouraged the rest of the team to explore the issue of individual privacy. It became clear that Segun (and others who had not spoken up) has some personal situations that he preferred to share privately through conversation (and not publicly on the board). So, the team agreed to a predefined and finite list of statuses, e.g., kid time, fresh air time, and lunch, etc., that the team could use to share what they had going on while at the same time maintaining some level of privacy.

Another example of how a dissenting and unpopular voice positively impacted team norms was the team dress code. Several team members believed the office dress code needed to apply while working from home. However, Maryam strongly disagreed with this recommendation. Maryam was often in the minority when it came to team decisions, and many of her peers considered her views extremely unpopular and divisive. Their natural inclination was to ignore her ideas or thoughts. However, because Ada recognized the importance of providing the "voices from below" with a platform, she encouraged Maryam to share why she opposed mandating the office dress code while people worked from home. Maryam shared that these were unique times and requiring conformance to the office dress code was a bit too much. Maryam felt that people could wear baseball caps or sports jerseys while they were on video calls and that the dress code stipulations were too strict for the new working situation. Maryam pointed out that many people were dealing with several stressors in their lives and requiring a dress code at this time was not the best use of anyone's time. After careful consideration, many people shifted from their original position—transforming exchanges occurred—and the team decided to relax the dress code by requiring that people dress respectfully for video calls.

As these examples show, you can use your formal authority to provide those with unpopular opinions a safe space to express themselves. Adaptive work requires contributions from everyone on the team—not just the most experienced, well-spoken, or most-liked. Make sure everyone has their voice heard. And yet, having their voice heard does not mean that every idea will see the light of day or that the group will follow every idea suggested. Giving everyone a voice is not a commitment to doing what each person wants. It is a commitment to allowing everyone to participate in the dialogue fully. No idea—except if it is outright offensive—gets shut down before a conversation. Good ideas come from all sorts of places. However, you may also need to use your formal authority to make sure dissenters do not derail adaptive work. Ada understood the importance of creating space for everyone on her team to express their thoughts on the remote work norms. While no individual might have gotten everything they desired (and maybe some did not get anything they desired), Ada made sure that everyone could contribute to team norm development regardless of their status on the team. She did this by (a) managing the contributions of the popular team members; (b) encouraging the less vocal team members to speak up; (c) protecting the team members who presented dissenting views.

Keeping Your Eyes on the Prize

Adaptive work is not for the faint of heart. It requires that people accept that they will need to make meaningful changes in what they believe and how they act. These changes often cause a feeling of loss and discomfort. To avoid these feelings, people will try to focus on other work and avoid the adaptive work confronting them. You are not immune to this struggle, yet you have the responsibility of keeping adaptive work in front of the group and helping them remain focused on the challenging work they need to do. The coronavirus pandemic made this especially difficult for Ada because these were unusual times that no one had experienced before. She had to find the balance between keeping the team focused on how they worked together while dealing with the stressors of the pandemic. While it might be easy for outsiders to suggest that Ada had no business trying to get the team to focus on how they were working together, the reality is that the world had not come to a complete halt. Clients depended on Ada's team to provide them with product changes so that these clients could keep their businesses afloat during the rough economic times brought on by the pandemic.

So, how did Ada keep her team members focused on the adaptive work? At first, Ada checked in with each team member every day to see how things were going. Then, as the weeks progressed, she went from every day to a couple of times a week. Her check-in, while not scripted, followed a general format that looked like this:

- Ada first asked the team member how they were doing as an individual, then she would ask how the team member's family was doing, and then she would finally ask the team member if there was anything she could do to support them and their family.

- Once Ada had checked in on the team member's personal affairs and made sure they were doing well, she then checked in with them on how well they felt the team was performing in their new work situation.

- She then asked for feedback on team norms as she wanted to know which norms team members found the most challenging to practice. For example, Moji, found the number of chat messages overwhelming and distracting, making it difficult for her to focus. Ada suggested that Moji set her status to "Deep Work" and block all incoming messages as agreed to by the team.

By talking with her team members about the team norms, Ada was able to keep that part of the adaptive work front and center.

The right metrics provide teams with insights on how well they are working. With all the stressors that team members were dealing with, Ada knew it was not the time for the team to hyper-focus on their productivity metrics. At the same time, ignoring metrics was foolhardy. Clients expected the team to provide solutions that enabled their operations even during the pandemic. The team monitored the following metrics: deployment frequency, lead time for changes, mean time to recover, and change failure rate.[14] Systems needed to remain functional and available so that client operations proceeded without a hitch. Any dip in performance in "mean time to recover" (the time it took to restore the system) and "change failure rate" (the number of unsuccessful releases) would negatively impact clients. The metrics review kept the team focused on how they could continue to provide stellar service in the "new normal."

The team had a bi-weekly cadence, where they reflected on how they could improve their overall effectiveness—a retrospective. As part of this meeting, the team would reflect on how their new norms were helping them succeed at providing value to their clients. Focusing on the new norms during their retrospectives also helped the team remain focused on this adaptive work. The retrospective provided the team with the opportunity to continue the adaptive work refining their norms. For example, the team began to practice asynchronous communication as a communication style. Asynchronous communication was not an easy change because the team had relied on synchronous communication for a long time. On the surface, it seemed like a technical challenge, but it was not. Asynchronous communication required a paradigm shift in how team members approached communication. Adaptive situations are improved, not solved.

Keeping the significant difference, i.e., the adaptive work in front of team members is critical for you to do. Remember that your participation in the adaptive work signals to team members that it is critical. Ada signaled the importance of adaptive work by talking with team members, reviewing

---

[14] See *Accelerate: Building and Scaling High Performing Technology Organizations* for more information of software development metrics.

metrics, and developing team norms as part of team retrospectives and futurespectives. The passion and focus she brought mobilized and encouraged the team. Avoiding the adaptive work was not an option, regardless of how uncomfortable the changes were. However, Ada also knew that the adaptive work caused a certain amount of distress for her team members and that she had an obligation to help the team manage distress.

Keep Calm and Stress Less

Changing mindset, behavior, and attitudes while feeling a sense of loss causes distress. The pandemic was already stressful for everyone as it had altered everyone's life. Many team members had new additional responsibilities such as homeschooling. Figuring out how to do remote work well by defining new team norms was just another source of stress for everyone on the team. Effective adaptive leadership requires leaders who are sensitive to the fact that adaptation is not stress-free. Disequilibrium is almost always part of the learning process, and it is up to the leader to help the team regulate the distress that comes from the learning and adaptation process. Unfortunately, too few leaders work to reduce the stress levels in their organization. As a leader, it is a bit disingenuous to recommend stress management programs if you are not working hard every day to create a workplace where stress levels are manageable. A few leaders make the opposite mistake of thinking that their job is to eliminate stress. Trying to eliminate stress will create unnecessary stress for you. Your objective is to do whatever you can to keep stress levels within a healthy range while change is ongoing. Each individual is also responsible for their stress levels. To help team members manage their stress, you need to manage yours first. It is hard for someone who is stressed out to help others experiencing stress. As the saying goes, "physician heal thyself." Ada knew that stress management had to start with her.

Ada recognized that a source of frustration and stress for many team members was that they did not know how long they would be working from home, and when they spoke out of frustration, it was due to their home confinement. Ada listened daily to team members as they adjusted to the new normal and tried to adopt and practice the new team norms. Ada tried not to overreact when she received information that upset her. Instead, she tried to keep her cool as the team worked through their challenges together. As William James said, "the art of being wise is the art of knowing what to overlook."[15] No one is perfect, and sometimes Ada lost her cool. But for the most part, Ada remained calm as they took on adaptive work.

---

[15] William James, *The Principles of Psychology*, (NY, New York: Dover Publications, 1950).

Anticipating the frustrations and negative comments that might come up when she spoke to the team about the adaptive work meant that Ada went into many of these conversations prepared. She made out time to think through the challenges team members might experience. She also put herself in their shoes and imagined what kinds of questions she might ask if in their position. Because Ada knew her team member's tendencies, she did not have to walk into conversations blind. For example, if she anticipated that a team member might paint a doomsday scenario, e.g., everyone on the team would eventually lose their jobs, she would have a proper response for the team member in front of the group. Ada often caught herself smiling when team members expressed their frustrations because she knew what they would say ahead of time. Preparation allowed Ada to calmly respond to challenges and redirect conversations when that was the appropriate response. And in the scenarios where Ada received a question she did not have an answer for, she told the team as much.

People study how you, as their leader, cope with the stress caused by adaptive work. If you come across as overwhelmed and anxious, and it seems that you cannot adequately perform your duties, people will begin to look to other places for a leader. I am not suggesting that you should not experience distress, as doing so would be to deny that you are human. Everyone experiences fear, uncertainty, and doubt—even people in leader roles. And yet, if you are a leader, you need to regulate your stress. If you cannot effectively manage your stress, it is probably best to hand over the reins to someone else because you will be ineffective, and your ineffectiveness will negatively impact those you lead. Because Ada knew that the current work situation would stress everyone, she also knew she needed to manage her stress before helping team members with theirs. If her teams saw her managing her stress, they would be more inclined to do the same. On the other hand, if she always seemed stressed, then it could lead to their stress. Stress can be contagious.

Effective leaders are honest and vulnerable with their team members, and so was Ada. When team members asked her if she experienced any stress, she would answer honestly and share her concerns. How a leader shares what is bothering them matters a great deal. Some leaders believe they need to say precisely how they feel in the name of transparency. However, the lack of a filter can backfire if people are not ready for the answer you have for them. There is no question that leaders should not lie or spin information.[16] However, you also need to know what, when, and with who to share information. Making these decisions is more of an art than it is a science. Ada walked the fine line of making sure she did not send her team into a tailspin with the information she provided them while at the same time remaining honest

---

[16] Ian P. McCarthy, David Hannah, Leyland F. Pitt, and Jane M. McCarthy, "Confronting indifference towards truths: Dealing with workplace bullshit," *Business Horizons* (2020): 253–263.

about what was going on and how she was handling all the changes. More importantly, Ada generously shared her techniques for regulating her stress with her team. As we will see in the next chapter, self-care is vital, especially for leaders faced with adaptive work.

Conflict management is an essential aspect of distress regulation. Conflict (healthy and unhealthy) is practically unavoidable when people must adopt new ways of thinking and acting. Keep conflict under control because it will cause stress for all parties involved and possibly derail adaptive work if it boils over. Teams can to reduce unhealthy friction by avoiding unacceptable behaviors. Ada's team defined acceptable and unacceptable behaviors and everyone was clear on the consequences of unacceptable behavior. While team members could challenge ideas (cognitive conflict), they could not attack people (affective conflict). For example, when Sola suggested the team modify their pull request process to reduce the chances of releasing a defect into the production environment, Emeka responded with, "Sola thinks she is the smartest person on this team and can change our process; if she wants to." Ada stepped in right away and reminded Emeka that his response did not meet the standards set by the team norms. If Emeka had concerns with Sola's suggestion, he needed to address it directly (and not speak about Sola). Emeka apologized to Sola then the team went on to discuss Sola's suggestion. Do not be a leader who does not want to talk about consequences or prefer they remain implicit; the entire team needs to understand them to avoid surprises. Ada modeled the behaviors the team agreed to. She reminded the team that healthy conflict provided opportunities for team development. When the team disagreed on what to do next, Ada would encourage experimentation.

It was important that the team felt safe to take on a playful and creative approach to tackling the adaptive challenge. Taking themselves too seriously would create additional stress for everyone. A playful approach was vital because the new working situation was new to the team. The team scheduled virtual lunches and happy hours for team bonding. These events played a role in keeping stress levels manageable. If the team was going to face the adaptive challenge successfully, the team had to accept that they would make mistakes. They would also have to show much grace towards each other as they learned together. Navigating the pandemic was stressful enough; Ada wanted to make sure the team did not create any additional and unnecessary stress for themselves. They needed to face this challenge together.

Working from Home—Recap

The previous section highlighted how Ada facilitated adaptation when her team transitioned from working in the office to working from home during the coronavirus pandemic using a set of behaviors. However, this was not the only time that Ada and her team faced adaptive situations. Adaptive work continued for months as the team refined their practices in response to what worked well (and what did not work well) as they worked from home. At the core of adaptive leadership is the recognition that adaptation is continuous. Throughout the pandemic, Ada's team faced challenges that required adaptation not covered in this chapter. For example, the team had to modify its product development approach to support its new business strategy. While the team used Agile methods to determine the most valuable item to work on at any given time at a micro-level, now they had to pivot at a macro-level to accommodate the new business climate that surrounded their company.

As I edit this chapter in June 2021, life is returning to some semblance of normal in the United States. Interestingly, many organizations are now grappling with the "return to the office" challenge. The situation is whether (or not) people need to return to work in the office. Unfortunately, many leaders have approached this challenge like it is a technical challenge that they can address with their authority and expertise when the situation has all the characteristics of an adaptive challenge. It is a challenge that requires another shift in attitudes and values formed over the preceding 15 months when many people worked from home exclusively. The situation matches more than one of the adaptive challenge archetypes.[17] The path forward will require that people in the organization do the adaptive work, regardless of what it is.

While Ada's story occurs in the context of the coronavirus pandemic—an extreme situation (a pandemic does not happen every day)—the fact is that you, as a leader, routinely must grapple with adaptive challenges. Adaptive challenges are part of organizational life, and failing to recognize and address these challenges means that your organization is not functioning optimally. Attempting to address adaptive challenges with your expertise and authority will lead to significant disappointment. On the other hand, you need to embrace the opportunity that adaptive challenges provide. Consider adaptive situations a development opportunity. Remember that you are part of the adaptive process even though your team members do most of the adaptive work. You mobilize your organization to exploit change when you commit to adaptive leadership. However, mobilizing others to overcome adaptive challenges means that you are willing to go through personal changes. Indeed, adaptive leadership requires that you become comfortable with making changes to yourself.

Becoming an Adaptive Leader—My Story

Many people step into assigned leader positions thinking it is now their job to solve their team's problems. Some of these people excelled in individual contributor roles, and when there was a technical problem to solve, everyone

---

[17] See Chapter 7 for list of archetypes.

went to them. Their expert power gave them meaning and significance, and because they excel as technical experts, promotion into a leader role eventually occurs. You may be familiar with a story like this. In fact, this might be your story. It is my story.

The Promotion

I had become one of the best software engineers in my organization. I had built a reputation as the resident expert for several software systems. If you wanted to know anything about those systems, all you had to do was ask me. My stellar performance resulted in a promotion to a managerial leadership position. Honestly, while I was happy about the promotion, I believed it was long overdue. I went into my new role thinking to myself, "this promotion is long overdue; now that I am in this new role, I am going to make the most out of it." I was finally in a position to fix many of our organizational problems. The team I would lead had some unhappy customers, and I excelled at addressing software problems. How hard could it be to fix the software issues and have our customers happy again? I intended to make sure that my leaders regretted waiting this long to promote me.

I decided we were going to address our customer problems by adopting a new software development approach. The new software development approach—Agile—had become popular in several user groups I belonged to. I believed that this approach would change things for my software development organization. We were still spending countless hours writing business requirement specifications only to get to the end of the development cycle and discover what we produced looked nothing like what we had documented. There were radical (at least to me) programming techniques like test-driven development and emergent architecture that Extreme Programming (XP) encouraged. Agile made sense to me, and at long last, I was in a position—I had the formal authority—where I could make my teams adopt this new software development approach. If people thought that I was a top-notch problem-solver in my previous role, they had not seen anything yet; I was about to take software development to the next level in the organization.

The Imposition

I gathered my team together for our first meeting and expressed my excitement at becoming their manager. Even though I did not say it aloud, I was thrilled to have the opportunity to fix the team's problem. What I did tell them, though, was that I had identified solutions to all their problems. The solution was in this new software development approach—Agile. Agile was the approach that would make sure they identified what stakeholders needed, developed good software, and wasted less time in meetings debating requirements. So, I needed everyone to get on board with the new approach. I had already decided that we would adopt many of the Extreme Programming practices. Beginning the following week, we would begin using these practices, and there would be no exceptions. Everyone would need to learn these practices on their own. I shared a list of websites where people could educate themselves on Agile and XP, told people to go and study, and then ended the meeting.

The Resistance

I was ready to begin our new way of work the following Monday. I brought everyone together for our first stand-up and asked them to share what they intended to work on for the day. Expecting people to respond with excitement, I was surprised that no one wanted to speak. After some prodding, I was able to get some people to share what they intended to do, but the energy in the room was low, and no one was paying much attention to me. I chalked up the overall response to nervousness with trying something new. After stand-up, I told the team they would now use index cards to capture what their stakeholders needed. But that was not it. Not only were we changing how the team gathered requirements, but we were also going to change how they developed software. Pair programming and test-driven development were now software development practices the team had to adopt as quickly as possible. I wanted team members to learn these technical practices as quickly as they could, starting from that moment.

I believed it was my responsibility (as manager of the team) to tell the team how it would address its challenges, and not doing so was not doing my job. So, I was completely surprised by the lack of engagement from the team. No one wanted to take the initiative to learn more about XP or learn the new technical practices. Team members resisted change by sticking to their current ways of working. They would act like they were trying to work differently on the surface, but immediately I looked away, they discarded the new practices. As the weeks passed on, team members said even less at the stand-up. Apathy set in with team members, and I could see that they no longer cared much about achieving team goals. The whole team had rejected my solutions. I now had a situation where my attempt to solve the team's problems had backfired and had created a brand-new set of challenges. Team members had started complaining to my manager about me. They wanted me reassigned. I had not planned for my first managerial role to go this way, and if I did not make some changes quickly, this opportunity might be my last.

The Awakening

I was at a loss for what to do. Throughout my career, I had excelled at problem-solving and helping people with their technical problems. I had invested a lot of effort into achieving technical mastery. Because I was still an effective software developer, I contemplated going back to my old role. Maybe leading software engineering teams was not the ideal role for me. Afterall, it is not uncommon for organizations to make the mistake of promoting people into managerial positions due to their technical excellence. And yet, I remained convinced that adopting Agile could benefit my team because it encouraged producing small chunks of value and getting feedback from stakeholders as quickly as possible. Agile discouraged developing year-long detailed plans with multi-page requirement documents and multiple sign-offs between phases of the development process. What excited me the most was that the Agile approach (specifically XP) encouraged some new technical practices. I believed that these practices would help the team reduce the number of bugs in our software and make it easier to modify the system when responding to customer requests. So, I was at a complete loss on why I could not get the team to adopt an approach that would benefit them and the organization. Nonetheless, I told myself that I was probably in the wrong role, so out of frustration, I decided to speak to my manager, Tumi, and ask her to consider moving me back into my old role.

I met with Tumi and shared the challenges I was facing with the team. I even suggested that the organization might be better off with me in my old role—solving technical problems as I had done in the past—as the current situation was not working for anyone. After I finished complaining about the team's reluctance to engage and support the Agile approach, Tumi looked at me and said, "Let me remind you, your job is not to solve the team's problems for them. The team needs to own solving its problems. Your job is to help them see those problems and provide the support and resources they need to tackle their problems." This was not the first time that Tumi had provided me with this wise advice. In fact, in our first meeting after my promotion, Tumi told me that my new role was different from the old role. Success in my previous role depended on my technical expertise; however, I would need to rely on others to succeed in my new role. I would address problems by ensuring the team had all it needed to do excellent work. Tumi affirmed her confidence in me and reminded me that I had her support; however, it was up to me to make the necessary changes to how I showed up to lead.

It was clear. My new role required a different mindset, approach, and set of behaviors. In my previous role, I had found solutions to problems and then implemented those solutions. In my new role as a manager, I would need to help the team (a) see the problem, (b) identify potential solutions, and (c) implement the solution(s). If the team was going to overcome a challenging problem, they would need to own it. The team would have to identify opportunities for improvement and then commit to doing the activities that would eventually result in team improvement. As their leader, I would need to provide the team the resources—time, budget, education, training, information, etc.—required to do a good job. I began to understand that I was supposed to serve as a catalyst; however, my current actions had me acting as an inhibitor. Instead of fostering conditions for excellence, I was getting in the way. For someone who had spent his entire career, up till that point, tackling problems directly, this was a significant change. And yet, if I were to succeed in this new role, I would need to take in the information I had received from the team and Tumi (assimilation) and make significant changes to how I led (accommodation). I would have to adapt and adapt quickly. It was time for another team meeting.

The Adaptation

In my next team meeting, I apologized to the team for imposing Agile on them. I was transparent with the team that I would need to make some changes in how I led if we were going to succeed. I was also honest that it would take time to make all the necessary changes required for my new role. I asked that the team extend grace as I worked on becoming a better leader for them. I encouraged them to let me know when they felt like my approach hurt them more than it helped them. From now on, everyone would work together to identify the best way to achieve team goals and objectives. I committed to providing the team with the resources they needed to achieve these goals. I let the team know that I did not have all the answers, but I was confident we could overcome our challenges as long as we worked together.

I will confess that changing my paradigm was not easy. Fortunately, I had a team with a lot of patience that showed me much grace because they knew I was trying hard. Slowly but surely, I changed how I interacted with my team. I made clear what goodness looked like from an organizational perspective. I started asking more questions and exhibiting genuine curiosity. I also provided the team with the support and resources they needed to improve how they worked. As a result, the team embraced Agile, which became a critical part of developing products for our clients. Our transition was not without its bumps and bruises; however, we took on the adaptive work of supporting our clients as a team. I adapted as a leader and started my journey practicing adaptive leadership.[18]

---

[18] It would be nearly 2 decades later that I would discover that what had occurred was adaptive leadership.

Reflection Questions

- What personal change(s) do you need to make to become a more effective adaptive leader?

- What challenges are adaptive, but you are approaching them like technical challenges?

- How do you give work back to your teams and foster conditions for self-organization?

- What are you doing to ensure you hear the "unpopular voices" in the organization?

Follow Well, Lead Well

Some of us are leaders, but we are all followers.

—Lynn Offermann[1]

He who cannot be a good follower cannot be a good leader.

—Aristotle[2]

I sat at the lunch table in shock. I could not believe what the senior executive I was having lunch with was telling me. I had gone to lunch thinking this executive would recognize my excellent work and tell me how well I was doing. But I could not have been more wrong. The executive let me know that my newly appointed leader, Chidibere, found it challenging to work with me. Chidiebere complained that I responded with much hesitation and reluctance whenever he asked me to provide information or follow up on a task. Chidiebere had begun to wonder if the firm was still the right place for me. I could not believe that Chidibere had come to this conclusion. How did I get here?

---

[1] Lynn Offerman, "When Followers Become Toxic," *Harvard Business Review* 82, no. 1 (2004): 55.

[2] Aristotle was a Greek philosopher.

© Ebenezer C. Ikonne 2021
E. C. Ikonne, *Becoming a Leader in Product Development*,
https://doi.org/10.1007/978-1-4842-7298-5_9

First, other leaders, many of my peers, and the teams I supported trusted and respected me. Second, I had a track record of getting things done, and I rarely caused any trouble. Third, even though I often had strong opinions on how we could improve as a business, I found (most of the time) respectful and non-disruptive ways to share my opinions. Finally, many people in the firm looked up to me. And yet, despite my stellar reputation and work history, I now found myself on the proverbial chopping block. What had gone wrong?

Let me tell you what had gone wrong. I had lost sight of the fact that it was not enough that I was an effective leader. I was no longer an effective follower—at least to Chidiebere. Even though I was a leader in my own right—I had team members who willingly allowed me to influence them—my actions indicated that I was not willing to follow my manager. I had forgotten that I was not just a leader; I was also a follower. Leaders, regardless of organizational rank, follow others in their organization.[3] For example, the CEO of an organization follows the board or the owners of the organization.

I have intentionally limited using the term "follower" in previous chapters (except for Chapter 1) because of the negative connotations associated with the term in some circles. However, I think it is time to talk about what it means to function as a follower in an organization. If we are to have leaders, then we must have followers. Leading cannot exist without following. To do away with the concept of followers is to do away with the concept of leaders. Effective leadership cannot occur without effective followership that complements it.[4] In this chapter, we discuss followership, its importance to leadership, and how you can become a better follower even as you lead in your organization. Leading well depends on following well.

Understanding Followership

Before diving into how you can become a more effective follower, we need to clear up some of the misunderstandings surrounding the notion of followership and followers. Leadership literature is full of material on how leaders can become more effective in their roles. I am aware that I am adding to the ever-growing collection of leadership material focused on this topic. And yet, think about all the people involved in the successful endeavors that you have experienced. If your experience is anything like mine, you will quickly notice that many people did not have formal leadership responsibility for the group. They were not primarily accountable for ensuring the group went from Point

[3] Pat Townsend and Joan E. Gebhardt, "For Service to Work Right, Skilled Leaders Need Skills in Followership," *Managing Service Quality* 7, no. 3 (1997): 136–137.
[4] Marc Hurwitz and Samantha Hurwitz, "The Romance of the Follower: Part 2," *Industrial and Commercial Training* 41, no. 4 (2009): 199–201.

A to Point B. Yet, when I think back to successful product releases or organizational transformations that I had to manage, I recall the massive contributions of many team members. Indeed, success has many mothers and fathers.

As I shared in Chapter 6, Robert Kelley argues that group success is primarily due to exemplary followers doing their jobs well.[5] I cannot disagree with this position because I know from first-hand experience that it is true. While assigned leaders have formal authority and positional power in the organization, many others do the work that results in success and excellence. In the product development context, team members are responsible for performing the critical tasks that create a product that meets people's needs. The Vice President of Product Development in a large organization probably does not write a line of code or test the product. She does not directly determine code quality despite all the tools she might provide their team—she trusts the team to produce a high-quality product. If the team members decide they will not aspire to write defect-free code, then quality will suffer (and it could be years before she finds out about certain product defects). Effective followership is vital for organizational success.

So, what is followership? John McCallum says that followership is "the ability to take direction well, to get in line behind a program, to be part of a team, and to deliver on what is expected of you."[6] Followership is concerned with how people in follower roles can contribute in a way that helps their organization achieve its desired outcomes and what organizations must do to establish a workplace where followers thrive. Followership complements leadership in achieving organizational outcomes. While you must develop effective leader competencies, you also need to develop effective follower competencies. Like the story I told at the beginning of this chapter shows, failing as a follower can have consequences. For decades, scholars have suggested that organizations need to recognize the importance of followers and pay more attention to followership.[7] Even though I have begun to see a shift in organizational discourse, I believe we still have a long way to go.

There are several reasons why followership is not more prevalent in both academic and popular circles. One of the most cited reasons is that the term follower has too much baggage associated with it. When I bring up the term "follower" on social media, I always have people express disappointment with my use of the term. Some leadership experts have suggested using other terms like "constituent" instead of "follower" to avoid the stigma associated with

---

[5] Robert E. Kelley, *The Power of Followership*, (New York, NY: Doubleday Business, 1992), 8.
[6] John S. McCallum, "Followership: The Other Side of Leadership," *Ivey Business Journal (Online)*, (September/October 2013): 1.
[7] Stephen C. Lundin and Lynne C. Lancaster, "Beyond Leadership…The Importance of Followership," *The Futurist* 24, no.3 (1990): 18–22.

"follower."[8] For others, the term follower evokes an image of passive people who follow instructions without ever questioning or challenging them.[9] While there are people who possibly demonstrate those characteristics as followers, using a particular type of behavior as the definition for "follower" would be like saying all leaders are destructive because Hitler or Stalin were leaders who did terrible things. No one does this for the definition(s) of "leader," and it does not make sense that we do it for the definition of "follower."

And yet, some individuals—to avoid using the term "follower" in the context of group leadership—have promoted concepts such as shared leadership and the leader-leader model. These leadership concepts overtly suggest that leaders need to turn their followers into leaders—subtly implying (maybe unintentionally) that followership and the follower are inferior.[10] This approach ignores the fact that groups produce leadership (and followership). Leadership is not a process solely reserved for people in assigned leader roles—effective leadership is shared because multiple people participate in the process. It also ignores the fact that there are nearly always individuals, in the group, with more social influence than other group members, even when all group members might be peers.[11] These individuals are often the assigned leaders of the group and are accountable for facilitating and mobilizing the leadership process. While a desire may exist for everyone in the organization to have equal power, equal influence, and equal access to resources, the reality is that this is rarely the case. In fact, research suggests that organizations prefer to have a hierarchy and unequal distribution of authority and power.[12] Specific people have the explicit and direct responsibility of leading the group in a particular direction. They are accountable for ensuring leadership occurs.

Another criticism of followership is the lack of a single and comprehensive definition for "follower." Some researchers argue that the term "follower" in leadership discourse comes from political movements and that the term "subordinate" is adequate.[13] But, again, I see this as dancing around the issue to avoid using a word that evokes feelings of inferiority for many (particularly

---

[8] John Rost, *Leadership for the Twenty-First Century*, (Westport, CT: Praeger, 1993), 107.

[9] Barbara Kellerman, *Followership: How Followers are Creating and Changing Leaders*, (Boston, MA: Harvard Business Press, 2008), 6–9.

[10] L. David Marquet, *Turn the Ship Around!: A True Story of Turning Followers into Leaders*, (NY: New York: Penguin Group, 2012).

[11] Boas Shamir, "From Passive Recipients to Active Co-producers: Followers' Roles in the Leadership Process." in *Follower-centered Perspectives on Leadership: A Tribute to the Memory of James R. Meindl*, ed. Boas Shamir, Rajnandini Pillai, Michelle C. Bligh, and Mary Uhl-Bien, (Charlotte, NC: Information Age Publishers, 2007), xviii.

[12] Deborah H. Gruenfeld and Larissa Z. Tiedens, "*Organizational Preferences and Their Consequences*," in *Handbook of Social Psychology 5th ed.*, ed. Susan T. Fiske, Daniel T. Gilbert, and Gardner Lindzey, (USA: John Wiley & Sons Inc.), 1252–1287.

[13] Jon Aarum Andersen, "On 'Followers' and the Inability to Define,"*Leadership & Organization Development Journal* 40, no. 2 (2019): 274-284.

in Western cultures where high individualism and low power distance are prevalent). The term "leader" does not have a single agreed-on definition. Yet, we accept that some leaders are assigned while others emerge while achieving a shared goal or objective. I also do not consider the term "subordinate" superior because following someone does not inherently mean a superior-subordinate relationship exists.[14]

An individual's leader status is legitimized when people willingly choose to follow that individual and allow the individual to influence them.[15] When you allow other individuals to non-coercively influence you, you have willingly accepted to follow them—you are now a follower. There is no leader without followers. Barbara Kellerman might have said it best by noting that "followers are more important to leaders than leaders are to followers."[16] Thus, there is no need to disparage the concept of followership and the follower. Instead, understanding how followership impacts leadership and how you can be the best follower possible even while leading others is something worthy of your attention and effort.

There are at least two ways to discuss followership in the business organization setting. The first way is to approach followership through the lens of rank within an organization's structure, i.e., a leader is considered the "superior," and a follower is considered the "subordinate."[17] In the context of a software development team, an example of this view would be that the software engineering manager would be the leader because she occupies the higher rank, and the team would be followers because they occupy the lower rank. The second way to view followership is through a social constructionist perspective.[18] In this perspective, an individual takes on the follower's identity when they allow others to non-coercively influence them. Continuing with the example of a software engineering manager and their team, when a team member influences the manager, e.g., convinces the manager that the team needs to take a different approach towards some activity, the manager then becomes the follower, and the team member becomes the leader. In this example, the follower and leader roles do not tie back to rank in the organization; instead, the roles relate to the leading-following dynamic between individuals.[19] Hence, it is also valuable to also see "leader" and "follower" as fluid identities and not just as static roles tied to positions in the organization.[20] In this latter view, we see how individuals can alternate between

---

[14] Excuse the pun.

[15] Mary Uhl-Bien, Ronald E. Riggio, Kevin B. Lowe, and Melissa K. Carsten, "Followership Theory: A Review and Research Agenda," *The Leadership Quarterly* 25, no. 1 (2014): 96.

[16] Kellerman, *Followership*, 242.

[17] Uhl-Bien, Riggio, Lowe, and Carsten, "Followership Theory," 89.

[18] Ibid., 89.

[19] Ibid., 89.

[20] D. Scott DeRue and Susan J. Ashford, "Who Will Lead and Who Will Follow? A Social Process of Leadership Identity Construction in Organizations," *The Academy of Management Review* 35, no. 4 (2010): 627–647.

these identities as they interact with other people in the organization with different ranks. It also explains why the leader-follower relationship can transcend organizational relationships, i.e., people can still view you as a leader even when you do not outrank them or directly lead them.

It is essential to understand that followership does not happen in a vacuum. It results when an individual grants another individual their claim to the leader identity, and then the individual with the leader identity grants in return the follower identity to the individual requesting it.[21] The implications of this process are significant because it means that a "subordinate" is not by default a follower because they are subordinate; instead, they are a follower because they recognize and accept you as their leader. Many people in assigned leader positions assume they are leaders because they have the leader role in their organization. They (and their team) fail to recognize that it is within the team's power to determine whether they will grant them leader identity. Many individuals also do not understand that their leader must grant them their follower claim. When a leader stops considering an individual a follower, the leader-follower interaction breaks down. The leader will most likely look to end the relationship, as my story illustrates. You must understand the leader-follower dynamic in the workplace and accept that you take on a follower identity in many situations. How you show up as a follower will determine how successful you are as a leader.

Types of Followers

There have been many follower typologies developed over the past few decades. Robert Kelley's typology assesses followers based on their level of independent critical thinking and engagement.[22] Ira Chaleff categorizes followers based on the support they give to their leader and their willingness to question or challenge their leader.[23] Barbara Kellerman uses how committed the follower is to supporting or opposing their leader for her follower typology.[24] Regardless of the typology, it is clear that you can either be an effective or ineffective follower.

My observation is that ineffective followers in product development contexts exhibit behaviors that range from complete disengagement with the leader to doing everything they can to remove them, as shown in Figure 9-1.

---

[21] Ibid, 630–634.
[22] Kelley, *The Power of Followership*, 87–124.
[23] Ira Chaleff, "In Praise of Followership Style Assessments," *Journal of Leadership Studies* 10, no.3 (2017): 45–48.
[24] Kellerman, *Followership*, 75–96.

Figure 9-1. Ineffective follower spectrum

In Kelley's typology, disengaged followers are alienated.[25] Alienated followers show up to work, but they are not inclined to contribute to organizational outcomes because they are disengaged. They do the minimum required to get the job done even though they are critical thinkers. While many of us have possibly had brief periods where we felt disengaged and unmotivated, alienated followers find themselves in a prolonged state of going through the motions and feeling uninterested. Alienated followers show up to work because they have not found a new job (yet).

The causes of becoming an alienated follower include a loss of trust in your leader or co-workers.[26] If you have ever had a heated argument with your leader or another team member, which did not go your way, you may feel disrespected or unheard, leading to feelings of alienation. I know that I have had experiences where I felt like an outsider because I disagreed with the organizational direction. I have also experienced situations where I felt my leaders, peers, and other team members did not appreciate my contributions to the organization. In those moments, my level of engagement dropped significantly. It does not take much to go from an alienated follower to a passive follower. Passive followers, in addition to low engagement, do not demonstrate independent and critical thinking.[27] When I have become a passive follower, I have refused to suggest ideas. Being an alienated or passive follower is an unenjoyable work experience. It would be best if you did what you can to move out of this state by either changing your attitude or changing your environment.

On the other end of the ineffective followers' spectrum are followers who will go to any length to oppose people they do not want to follow. Kellerman describes these followers as activists working against the leader.[28] They consider the leader an obstacle to success, actively oppose this individual and look for ways to remove them from their position in the organization. The individual is not a real leader in the follower's eyes because they fail to meet follower expectations. Followers deny the leader's claim to leader identity. At best, they consider the individual a superior that must be removed from their position. It has become increasingly common in the social media age to see

[25] Kelley, *The Power of Followership*, 99–107.
[26] Ibid.
[27] Ibid., 121–124.
[28] Kellerman, *Followership*, 151–178.

leaders ousted out of their positions based on complaints from followers in the organization. I have now witnessed several situations where followers were primarily responsible for the removal of their manager. They complained to the manager's manager (and anyone who would listen). They actively revolted and challenged their manager in public. The firm had no choice but to relieve this manager of their position. Follower power continues to increase in organizational settings.

Like identifying what might have led you to become a passive follower, you also need to explore what has caused you to become an activist motivated to remove your superior from their office. Is there anything you could do that would change how you feel about them, or is it a lost cause? If there are changes you expect from your leader, consider providing them feedback and seeing if they make changes based on your feedback. If it is a lost cause, then understand that trying to remove your leader is a risky business and may not work out to your advantage. As I have shared, I have watched team members orchestrate the removal of a leader. I have also seen situations where such plans backfired on team members. Instead of the leader's removal, the team members were reassigned or found themselves out in the cold, looking for other jobs. If you are going to campaign actively against your leader, make sure it is because the leader's behaviors violate company policy or negatively impact organizational performance. But what if the source of conflict is just a matter of different personal preferences? In that case, it might be better to look for other opportunities in the organization with a different leader if that is possible. Again, you genuinely want to avoid finding yourself in a situation where you are plotting against your leader(s) if you can help it.

There is one last type of ineffective follower that I would like to highlight: the toxic follower. The toxic follower is most likely to perform actions that benefit their self-interest at the expense of those around them.[29] In a nutshell, it is all about them. These followers are challenging to work with because they must have their way no matter the situation. In my experience, these followers are often incredibly talented and knowledgeable—they are brilliant jerks. Their brilliance is why leaders allow them to remain in the organization. However, few people want to work with them because they consistently make the workplace difficult for people. If they have been with the firm for a long time, they use their tenure and knowledge to bully people. They talk about people behind their backs, demean people in person, and consistently criticize other people's work. Yet, people do not disagree with these individuals for fear of verbal abuse.

Few people would consider themselves a toxic follower, and yet the toxic follower test is quite simple. If a critical mass of people (including leaders,

---

[29] Ted A. Thomas, Kevin Gentzler, and Robert Salvatorelli, "What is Toxic Followership," *Journal of Leadership Studies* 10, no. 3 (2017): 62–65.

peers, and subordinates) would prefer not to work with you, you are most likely a toxic follower. It is time to look at yourself in the mirror and consider making changes. Individuals I have worked with say they exhibit toxic behaviors because they feel disrespected. They believe that when people disagree with them, they do not respect their knowledge and experience. Disagreement becomes a sign of invalidation. Learning how to engage in healthy conflict will help you in this case. In other cases, you need to be honest with yourself and recognize that you are not a fit for the organization and that this conflict is the source of your toxic behavior.

Many organizations seem to have less tolerance for toxic workers now than they did 15 or 20 years ago. People no longer want to work with an individual who makes the workplace miserable or difficult for everyone else. People often overlooked brilliant jerks' toxic behavior; however, this is changing, regardless of the jerks' rank. It is no longer enough to be the most intelligent person in the room—how you treat others matters a great deal. If you are a toxic follower, you will need to change your behaviors or find another organization that is a better fit for you. I do not intend to get deep into psychodynamics, but I will point out that many toxic followers act out behaviors formed over a long time. As Manfred Kets de Vries notes, we are prisoners of our past, often stuck in vicious and dysfunctional behavioral patterns.[30] You may need professional help to escape these behavioral patterns.

I have stressed throughout this book that organizational success does not occur without followers who do their jobs effectively. These followers are highly engaged in organizational endeavors and apply critical thinking to their work.[31] Effective followers understand that their leader (and the organization more broadly) needs their expertise, perspective, and commitment to attain organizational goals. Even though you are an leader in your organization, you are also a follower. The organizational hierarchy places you as a subordinate of another leader in the organization you need to follow. In addition to following your superior, you will also benefit from following your peers and your subordinates. There are situations where we must allow our peers and subordinates to influence us as they take on a leader identity, and we take on a follower identity. In these scenarios, effective followership is required from us if effective leadership is going to take place. Practicing effective followership increases organization commitment and job satisfaction.[32] When you are a

---

[30] Manfred Kets de Vries, "Organizations on the Couch: A Clinical Perspective on Organizational Dynamics," *European Management Journal* 22, no. 2 (2004): 187–188.

[31] Robert E. Kelley, *The Power of Followership*, 125–147.

[32] Anita L. Blanchard, Jennifer Welbourne, David Gilmore, and Angela Bullock, "Followership Styles and Employee Attachment to the Organization," *The Psychologist-Manager Journal* 12, no.2 (2009): 111–131.

engaged follower, you are more likely to enjoy working in your organization. You will also be a better leader. In the next section, we will look at how you can effectively follow your leader, peers, and followers.

Effectively Following Your Leader

Most organizations have some form of hierarchy in place. Hierarchy creates a structure where some individuals have more positional authority, power, and influence than others. Even though I have held executive-level roles in my career, I still had people who had more formal authority, power, and influence than I did. As mentioned, the superior-subordinate dynamic sets up a leader-follower dynamic, where the follower (who might be an assigned leader in their own right) allows the leader (who is superior from a hierarchical perspective) to non-coercively influence them in the workplace. For example, influence might come from suggested changes to a presentation or a passionate plea to avoid system failures over an important sales weekend. Whatever the non-coercive influence approach entails, the subordinate (follower) follows the lead of the superior (leader) to pursue a goal that the leader presents to the follower. Suppose the goals are to hire diverse candidates into the organization or reduce system outages. In these cases, the leader depends on the follower to enact strategies to achieve these goals. Therefore, leaders need the contribution of effective followers. Here are five effective followership behaviors you can practice with your superiors.

Embrace and Champion Organizational Goals

As a leader, I will assume that you understand your organization's goals (if you do not: address the lack of understanding immediately). However, while understanding your organization's goals is necessary for functioning as an effective follower, it is not enough. You also need to embrace and champion those goals. You need to support the organization's shared goals. Effective followers contribute to achieving organizational goals as set out by their leader.[33] The goals championed by your leader support larger organizational goals. For example, if your leader sets a departmental goal for system uptime of 5 9's, it could support a broader customer satisfaction and revenue goal. If your leader has a continuous improvement goal, it could also support an organizational goal to produce better products and services. Understand the relationship between the goals expressed by your leader and the organization's goals. Then identify ways that help your group achieve its goals. Do not sit back and wait for your leader to give you this information. Instead, take the initiative and proactively find ways to help your group (and organization)

---

[33] William Litzinger and Thomas Schaefer, "Leadership through Followership," *Business Horizons* 25, no. 5 (1982): 78–81.

thrive. If you find that you cannot embrace and champion the organizational goals, you need to understand the source of misalignment. You do want to avoid staying put in a group or organization with goals that you cannot get behind.

Your desire to support organizational goals should lead to vertical empathy. Vertical empathy is having empathy for leaders (at least) two levels above your level in the organization.[34] Not only are you concerned with how you can help your immediate leader ensure the leadership process excels, but you are also concerned with how you can help leaders higher in rank than your leader. Think about what goals they need to accomplish, and then do whatever you can to help them achieve those goals.

One way to gain insight into the aspirations of these leaders is to meet with them. Ask them about the organizational goals and what additional support you can provide. These meetings will provide a great learning opportunity for you. For example, once a leader told me that they had observed I was influential with my peers. The leader asked if I would be willing to champion a new quality initiative on their behalf because they believed I would get people to commit to the initiative. I had not expected that the leader would ask me to help them in this way, but I was excited to get such an opportunity. It is scary speaking with leaders "higher up" in the organization. I know that I felt intimidated the first time I found myself in such a position. However, do not forget that they are also human, just like you. Prepare beforehand to have a productive dialogue with them and to avoid wasting anyone's time. Many people consider these types of conversations "going around their boss." It is only "going around your boss" if (a) you hide these conversations (including content) from your direct leader and (b) you go around them for selfish or malicious purposes.

Challenge Constructively

It is tempting to think that being an effective follower requires that you place your leader on a pedestal where they can do no wrong. Some individuals believe it is wrong to challenge their leader's actions or decisions constructively. Followers who see their leaders as people who cannot make mistakes are doing a disservice to their organization. Your leader will make mistakes—if for no other reason—because they are human. Now, this is not permission to invest all your energy in identifying your leader's shortcomings. Instead, I am just sharing that effective followers speak up when they believe an alternative course of action is valuable to the organization. These individuals "speak truth

---

[34] Michael D. Rothstein, "Great Leaders Follow First: Nine Rules for Dynamic Followership," *Air & Space Power Journal* 33, no. 2 (2019): 5–6.

to power" and appropriately challenge their leader when they need to.[35] Effective followers are not "yes people" who simply go with whatever the leader says. Neither are the individuals who support their leader in public and then disagree with them in private. These individuals constructively and respectfully express their perspectives on their leader's thoughts, decisions, and actions.

An essential aspect of challenging your leader is learning how to do it constructively. The ability to challenge constructively "or influence upward" sets effective followers apart from other types of followers. To challenge constructively means ensuring your viewpoint ties directly to organizational goals. If you cannot demonstrate the link between your perspective and organizational goals, you may want to refine your thoughts until you can. Do not make your challenge about what you want or what is in your best interest. I learned this lesson the hard way. Early on in my career, my viewpoint would solely consist of my preferences or what I wanted. Sometimes, I would challenge based on what I saw another organization doing. On other occasions, I asked my leaders to do certain things based on what I had read in a book. My approach got me nowhere. Instead, it led to some leaders marginalizing my opinions. It was not until I observed that my input was well-received when I shared how my ideas might positively impact our organizational goals that I modified how I provided feedback. Providing your perspective in the context of organizational goals requires that you have in-depth knowledge of your organization's direction. A change in approach did not lead to my leaders always agreeing with me; however, they responded more positively to me because they saw that I had the organization's best interest at heart.

Adapt Your Style

If you are not willing to adapt your follower style to complement your leader's style, you will face workplace challenges. Effective followers modify their approach based on what they observe about their leader.[36] They pay attention to their leader's preferences, likes, and dislikes. Effective followers take note of what the leader values and what the leader may not value as much. They also recognize that their leader excels in some areas and needs support in other areas. Based on all this information, effective followers adapt their follower style to support their leader. Some people might believe that adapting their style is fake or inauthentic. Believing that adapting style is inauthentic is a misunderstanding of what authenticity entails and can limit personal development.[37] Adapting your style is not giving up your core values to remain

---

[35] Ira Chaleff, "In Praise of Followership," 46.
[36] Hurwitz and Hurwitz, "The Romance of the Follower," 202–203.
[37] Herminia Ibarra, *Act Like a Leader, Think Like a Leader*, (Boston, MA: Harvard Business Review Press, 2015), 117–158.

in good standing with your leader. I am not suggesting that you tell half-truths because your leader lacks integrity or that you become a micro-manager because your leader is a micro-manager. If you find yourself in this situation, you are better off finding a new employer. Instead, I am recommending that you adapt your style to complement and support your leader. For example, I have worked with leaders who are detail-oriented and other leaders who are not. While my preference might be for less detail, I have adapted my style to match leaders I have worked with who preferred more detail. Changes like this can go a long way to improve the leader-follower dynamic even though they might be uncomfortable for you initially.

Let us look at how you could adapt your style while challenging constructively. Adapting how you challenge your leader would require paying attention to how your leader prefers to receive feedback. Do they like robust debate and dialogue in front of a bunch of people? Do they prefer that you talk with them in person if you have strong feelings about a subject that does not align with theirs? I know of leaders that struggle with being challenged in meetings, but when spoken to in a private setting, they give people all the time in the world. These same leaders who were defensive when they were challenged in public change their minds when presented with the same information in private. Now, someone will read this example and say that this leader did not demonstrate effective leader behaviors. I cannot argue with that. And yet, this chapter is not about effective leader behavior; it is about effective follower behavior that contributes to leadership success. It is about how you can contribute to organizational success by taking charge of what you can control. You will know that your changes have made a difference because now the leader consults with you on difficult decisions and thanks you for your input. Play your part, and adapt your style.

Tackle Challenges Head-On

Effective followers do their job and do it well. They are trusted to deliver excellent work consistently. They proactively communicate any challenges they face. Effective followers are proactive. Using Robert Martin's Responsibility Ladder, effective followers spend most of their time at responsibility levels 1 (make a decision) or 2 (make a recommendation).[38] At level 1, you consider options, make decisions, and subsequently inform your leader. For example, the software development manager who needs to choose between two AWS technology offerings that solve a problem works with their team to choose one of the offerings and then informs their leader of the choice they made. At level 2, instead of selecting an option, the manager presents options to their leader with a recommendation on what technology the leader should choose. In this case, the manager presents an option with recommendations because

---

[38] Roger L Martin, "The Responsibility Virus: It's Catching," *Chief Executive* (2002), 20–21.

both options are outside their budgetary approval range. Effective followers are highly responsible and can be trusted to give their all towards achieving organizational outcomes.

Effective followers do not wait for someone to tell them what to do; they take the initiative. When it is unclear what the best path forward might be, effective followers step up, act, and own their actions when they make mistakes.[39] The best followers I have worked with in my career were those team members who saw opportunities and came up with ideas for taking advantage of those opportunities. Instead of complaining about what was not working, they took the initiative to make incremental improvements within their sphere of control. In one instance, team members saw an opportunity to educate and develop an organization's servant leadership capability. So, they took the initiative to start a series of Servant Leadership workshops. In another case, some team members started a mentorship program for aspiring Scrum Masters because people had indicated an interest in such a program. These team members saw the opportunity to meet a need. While I have more examples, the sad reality in my experience is that many followers (even at the Vice President level) are more adept at pointing out what is not working well. They do not take any steps to try and make changes, even when they can. They often wait for someone else (with a higher rank) to cast a vision or pronounce a proclamation that will fix everything. As a result, they are at level 6 (ask others to solve their problem) on Robert's responsibility ladder—they take no responsibility. While there is no question that leaders play a vital role in organizational effectiveness, I want you to recognize that you can also make a world of difference in your organizations if you are willing to do so from a follower position.

Be a Role Model of Followership

Practicing all the previously mentioned follower behaviors will make you a role model of effective followership in your organization. Many leaders want followers that they can ask other followers to emulate. Excellent leaders demonstrate to others how to follow.[40] Those who follow you are learning (or not) what effective followership entails. They need to see that you are committed to complementing your leaders in achieving organizational goals even when you disagree with specific tactics or approaches. Do not speak ill of your leader behind their back. Let your followers see you providing constructive feedback to your leaders in a way that the feedback is well received and appreciated even if your leaders do not act on it. Develop a reputation for excelling at your job and being someone that leaders consult on challenging organizational issues. If you cannot be a follower role model for others in the organization, you need to identify why this is the case and address it. If you can

---

[39] Townsend and Gebhardt, "Skilled Leaders Need Skills in Followership," 138.
[40] Ibid., 136.

address it within your current organization, make those changes. If you have made changes, yet issues remain, you may have to consider leaving the organization for a different opportunity to become a better follower.

Candidly, I did not realize the magnitude of being a good follower until someone shared with me how my response to a stressful situation had positively impacted them. It is no secret that reorganizations happen all the time in businesses. Unfortunately, they happen way too often and, in my experience, consistently produce mediocre benefits. However, this reorganization was a big one—at least to the people involved who I directly supported. Most of the individuals that I had directly supported would now have new leaders in the organization. The consequence of the reorganization was that the strategy we had to improve product development effectiveness would end with the reorganization. My team was devastated, and they could not believe this was happening. No one was happy. As I think back to that day, I recall the raw emotions, people crying, and anger in the room as I informed the team of the changes that would happen that day.

As I think back to that reorganization, I recall that I was also upset with how it played out. My team had done good work up to that point. We were not always popular within the organization because we challenged the status quo, and yet, people still appreciated how we showed up and helped teams. Overall, people respected us. While I understood the rationale behind the changes, I disagreed that a new organizational structure would address some of our organization's significant challenges. I was also upset that no one had involved me in any discussions leading to the change since it impacted me directly. Lastly, I disagreed with how we were rolling out the changes in the organization and felt we could have handled the situation better. I had numerous issues with how we had approached the whole exercise. I wondered if the organization was the right place for me.

On the day that the changes were to take effect, I gathered everyone on my team to explain what would happen during the day. I acknowledged that it was going to be a tough day for everyone. I explained the rationale for the organizational changes as I best understood them, and then I allowed people to ask questions. As I painfully answered why the change was happening, celebrated the team's accomplishments, and provided insight into what this meant for people's careers, I tried to remain as honest as possible about the reorganization. I did not disparage the decision, the process, my leader(s), or the organization. Instead, I encouraged everyone to give the new organizational structure their best efforts. If things were not working after giving it a shot, I would do whatever I could to help them transition to a new opportunity (inside or outside the organization). We ended the meeting, and the events of the day unfolded.

In truth, I forgot about that day until a few years later when I ran into someone who had been on that team. They confessed that they had accepted the reorganization because of how I had addressed the team that day. My statements had shown that I would follow my leader and support the new organizational strategy that was about to be put in place, even though I had my reservations about whether these changes would genuinely help the organization achieve its goals. At that moment, years ago now, I did not fully understand what I was doing. Of course, you might conclude that I was doing what a good leader does, and there might be some truth to that. However, looking back on it now, and even though I was a leader in my own right, I now see that I demonstrated effective followership. By embracing and championing the organization's direction (even though I did not fully agree that the reorganization would improve organizational performance), I demonstrated effective followership, making a difficult transition more manageable.

Following Peers

It may be easier to understand followership through the lens of the superior-subordinate relationship because the subordinate has less authority, power, and influence than their superiors in the organization. However, as discussed previously, followership is not limited to hierarchical structures and rank. Followership also happens when you take on the follower identity while interacting with people in your organization. Even if you are the CEO of an organization, you do not lead all the time. There are times when you follow others for leadership to occur. A category of people in the workplace that you routinely need to follow is your peers. Let us talk about some ways you can effectively practice followership with your peers.

Be Supportive

Your peers will need your help in tackling organizational goals. For example, a peer might need your team to do some work that their team depends on to complete an important task. Not only do they depend on your team to complete the task, but your team also needs to do the task well so that the final product is excellent. Product development dependencies between teams are a common scenario in many product development organizations. Unfortunately, I have also observed that these dependencies lead to conflict as peers are often reluctant to take on the follower identity when interacting. Everyone wants to set the direction and have the others accommodate them. Refusing to take on the follower role leads to arguments and, in many cases, necessitates the involvement of someone with a higher rank to determine the next steps. This behavior does not help the organization achieve its goals, and it wastes everyone's time.

Effectively following your peers means that you support them when they are leading organizational initiatives. Instead of putting up roadblocks, you look for ways to help them attain the goal. It is easier to support your peers when you embrace organizational goals. There have been occasions in my career when I have not provided my peers with the support they needed because I disagreed with the organizational mission. I made it difficult for them to make progress because those who followed me could see that I did not support the organizational agenda. I also did not contribute as constructively as I could have. Not supporting them was poor followership on my part. It was not productive behavior, and I do not encourage anyone to do what I did. If you do not embrace the organizational goal, do not make it difficult for your peers. Instead, go directly to whoever defined the organizational goal and address it with that individual. Seek to understand the purpose of the goal and then lend your support to your peer in the best way you can. If there are reasons why providing support might be complex, be transparent about what will prevent you from providing your full support, and then look for ways to overcome these challenges.

If you have ever worked with a peer who always provided support and took on the follower identity once they understood the goal, you know how much difference it can make to the leadership process. Working with such individuals is satisfying. Whenever I think of peers that had no problem taking on the follower identity, I think of Chinaza. Chinaza was a peer at MoneyRecovery that always provided support whenever I needed it, even though my group was supposed to support her Operations team. She was an outstanding leader who set the direction for both the Operations and IT teams. However, it was not uncommon for her to defer to me and allow me to lead both groups when it made sense to do so. She recognized that if her team saw her take on the follower identity, they would be more likely to take on that identity with my team and me. In one instance, we ran into a problem where operational processes stopped yielding desired results, and we needed to modify these processes to improve operational effectiveness. Chinaza allowed me to take the lead in redesigning her team's workflow with the software changes that supported the new workflow. Not only did she allow me to take the lead, but she also provided me with the support I needed by making herself and her team members available to answer questions and to provide guidance. Chinaza exhibited stellar follower behaviors even though she was my peer.

Demonstrate Competence

It is not enough to follow the lead of your peers by providing them with the support they need. It is equally important that you do an excellent job in your role. There are few things more discouraging and disappointing than having a peer produce work that is low quality. It is also frustrating having to help a peer work through an assignment they are supposed to handle independently. Exhibiting your competence as a follower with your peers is an essential part of effective followership. You need to demonstrate to your peers that you can produce work products that meet their needs. They need to trust that you will do what you said you would do and that your work product will be of high quality. Hold up your end of the bargain. Do more than talk a good game by pulling your weight.

Your peers will lose confidence in your ability (or that of your team) if the quality of the work produced is sub-par. Eventually, they will not want to work with you. Here is a quick story to illustrate this point. Chido and Alozie were two software engineering managers that were part of a software engineering organization that I provided consultation services. It was not long before I observed that whenever Chido and Alozie needed to work together to solve a business problem, Chido would always ask that he (and his team) address the business problem independently. Chido would even go as far as to recommend that his team do the work that Alozie's team was supposed to do. Furthermore, Chido would do all he could to prevent his team from working with Alozie's team. Finally, I decided to ask Chido why he did not want Alozie's help. I could not understand why he would place his team under tremendous stress when there was help available. Chido's response caught me completely off guard. He said that he did not believe Alozie was a competent engineering manager and did not believe Alozie's team would produce an excellent work product. In a nutshell, Chido did not want himself (or his team) associated with failure, so he would go to any length to avoid working with Alozie. You do not want to become the leader that your peers will not work with because they question your competence. Effective followers are competent followers.

Develop Rapport

Unlike the leader-follower dynamic with your leader, who you follow more than you lead, you continuously alternate between the leader and follower identities with peers with whom you work. Developing rapport with your peers enhances this dynamic. Rapport is establishing a vibrant working relationship with peers.[41] Rapport does not necessarily mean friendship, and yet it implies having a healthy relationship with someone else. It can prove challenging to take on the follower identity when you have a strained relationship with a peer. In my experience, strained relationships lead to power struggles and an unwillingness to allow your peer to influence you. If your career has been anything like mine, you have probably had a peer or two with whom you could never develop rapport, making your working relationship with these individuals difficult and highly transactional. Instead of working through challenges together, I would either argue with these individuals or quickly disengage without addressing the challenge because we had a poor

---

[41] Hurwitz and Hurwitz, "The Romance of the Follower: Part 2," 203.

relationship. It was a battle of wills on who was going to accept the follower identity.

There are several ways you can develop a rapport with your peers. One common technique is to set up one-on-ones with them. The one-on-ones will provide you with an opportunity to explore challenges together. For example, maybe your teams find working with each other difficult. Talking about these challenges together can help you and your peer develop a plan to help your teams. During one-on-ones, you will probably alternate between leader and follower identities as you go through the process of influencing each other. One-on-ones also provide you with an opportunity to get to know your peers better. You will get to know each other's likes, dislikes, hot buttons, and pet peeves through conversation. Establish a one-on-one cadence that works for you and your peers and stick to it. I have found that the peers I have routine one-on-ones with are the peers I have enjoyed working with the most.

Another critical aspect of developing rapport is becoming a confidante that your peers can trust. Trustworthiness is especially vital if you have one-on-ones where specific issues need to remain private. Discretion is an essential attribute of effective followership.[42] Your peers should know that they can share private work-related information with you and that you will keep it in confidence. Sharing private information—like an upcoming organizational change—betrays the trust your peers have in you. In other cases, your peer might have challenges with another peer and just need a listening ear who they know will not betray their trust. Whatever the case may be, discretion helps build rapport, which helps the leader-follower dynamic between you and your peers. Be someone your peers can trust.

Communication

The Center for Creative Leadership (CCL) suggests that communication is the most crucial competency a leader needs to develop.[43] The idea that communication matters should not surprise anyone because leaders need to set clear directions and goals. Often, leaders need to facilitate meetings and settle conflicts within the organization. As a result, communication challenges significantly hamper leader effectiveness. However, it would be a mistake to think that communication only matters when you are in the leader's identity. Communication skills matter when you are in the follower's identity because you need to influence peers. In fact, it might matter just as much. Research shows that effective followers excel at conveying their message to their

---

[42] John S. McCallum, "Followership: The Other Side of Leadership," *Ivey Business Journal* (2014) 2.

[43] 5 Most Important Leadership Competencies for Functional Leaders, https://www.ccl.org/blog/5-important-competencies-function-leaders/ (last accessed July 19, 2020).

audience.[44] It does not matter who is in the audience—superiors, subordinates, or peers—effective followers find a way to get their point across. Clear and concise communication is vital in the leader-follower dynamic between peers, especially when working with a peer who has taken on the leader identity in the workplace. I have made a mistake in the past of assuming that because someone was my peer, it did not matter how I communicated with them, and so I ignored how I communicated with them. From paying attention to a specific peer, Nkem, I learned the importance of communicating powerfully, even among peers.

Nkem and I were part of a team asked to identify software development metrics that our teams could use to monitor their improvement. Anyone who has been part of a metrics conversation knows how contentious these conversations can become. Everyone has their viewpoint on the role of metrics in software organizations. The team consisted of people who had been in software development leadership roles for an average of 10 years. It was a seasoned group with a lot of experience. So, it was no surprise that our meetings got off to a rocky start, with many individuals attempting to assert themselves as leaders in the group. The only person I recall not acting this way was Nkem. She would later tell me that she had decided she would be comfortable following. Her focus was on how she could contribute to the process. Instead of jockeying for position, Nkem let her words do the talking. And did she have a way with words. She expressed her thoughts in a precise yet straightforward manner during all our working sessions and did not beat around the bush or go down rabbit holes that added no value. She stayed focused on the topics and got her points across. Nkem was incredibly thoughtful and considerate while using her contributions to nudge the group forward. She respectfully challenged ideas while providing her views. Nkem was masterful in her communication and was able to influence our group such that we eventually developed a set of metrics that we presented to the software development organization.

Following Those You Lead

It probably comes as no surprise that you need to follow leaders with higher organizational rank. Maybe, it was a little bit of a surprise that I recommended you follow your peers as well. I do hope, however, that by now, it is not a surprise that to lead well, you must be prepared to follow those you lead. Yes, you must embrace the follower identity and grant followers the leader identity throughout the leadership process. Embracing the follower identity means that you want those you support to influence you.

---

[44] Absael Antelo, Evgenia V. Prilipko, and Margaret Sheridan-Pereira, "Assessing Effective Attributes of Followers in a Leadership Process," *Contemporary Issues in Education Research* 3, no. 9 (2010): 38.

Effectively practicing servant leadership and adaptive leadership requires you to recognize when it is time for you to follow those you lead. Both leadership approaches depend on follower engagement for a successful leadership process. Those you lead are more knowledgeable than you are on various topics in the workplace. For example, people on my product and engineering teams knew details about our products and systems that I did not know. Do not let the fact that you are the leader cause you to think that it means that you must have all the answers to all organizational challenges. Some leaders think it makes them look weak when they consult with their team members. Failing to consult with your team members makes your organization less effective. When you deny yourself access to information that can help you make more positive contributions to the leadership process, you negatively impact your organization. You are also fostering conditions that demoralize your followers and negatively impact their level of organizational commitment. Following those you support should not be beneath you.

As mentioned in Chapters 3 and 4, both national and organizational cultures will impact how comfortable people in your organization feel about leading you. In some cultures, the leader's responsibility is to lead, and any sign that the leader desires that someone else leads is not favorably received. Appropriately adapt to these cultures. When leading in national contexts where some may expect the leader to lead from the front, avoid putting people in uncomfortable positions. Look for avenues where people on your team can safely share their thoughts and ideas with you while maintaining their follower identity. In some organizations, you will need to work hard to make people comfortable with providing you with feedback. We have already seen earlier that organizations prefer the unequal distribution of power in the organization. Team members recognize that you have the power to reward or punish them and modify their actions based on how they think you will respond. Until team members routinely observe that you do not punish people when they provide feedback or constructively challenge you, they may be reluctant to provide you with feedback. You will have to give it time and send signals that you appreciate and expect feedback.

You will need to watch out for followers who influence you (even unknowingly) down wrong and ineffective paths. While you may think that this cannot happen to you, you will be surprised to learn that followers often influence leaders in the most subtle ways. For example, many leaders want their followers to like them and, as a result, make poor decisions just to receive positive affirmation and flattery from their followers.[45] Have you ever made a poor decision that you knew was poor, yet you made it to avoid upsetting your team members? Trust me, you are not the only leader who has done this. However, you need to avoid making decisions for the wrong reasons. There are times where it is the wrong decision to follow the team's lead, and

---

[45] Lynn R. Offermann, "When Followers Become Toxic," 57–59.

you need to remain firm in these situations even if it makes you unpopular in the organization. Individual interests and organizational interests are not always in harmony, and sometimes, the decisions you make will not be warmly received. Any leader who is not unpopular at times is most likely not boldly leading their organization forward. Followers have more influence (which continues to grow in organizations) than we give them credit for, and leaders follow those they lead more than they would like to admit. Hence, choose wisely when to follow the advice of your team members and when to go against their advice. Remember practical wisdom—Aristotle's master virtue— is essential for leaders who practice effective followership.

Takeaways

- Effective leaders are also effective followers. Embrace followership.

- While people think of followers as individuals who have less rank (power, authority, and influence) within the organization, in reality, whenever you allow others to non-coercively influence you, you are a follower.

- Effective followership requires you to excel at following people (regardless of their rank) in your organization.

- Follow your leaders by supporting them, constructively challenging them, and being a role model.

- Follow your peers by being supportive, doing what you say you will do, and developing healthy relationships with them.

- Follow your followers and yet recognize that you will need to make decisons (for the greater good) that will be unpopular with them.

Take Care of Yourself

It is one of the most beautiful compensations in life that no man can sincerely try to help another without helping himself.

—Ralph Waldo Emerson[1]

Self-care is never a selfish act. It is simply good stewardship of the only gift that I have, the gift I was put on earth to offer others.

—Parker Palmer[2]

I hope it is crystal clear by now that effectively leading people is not simple. Altruistically facilitating the leadership process is not for the faint of heart. Leaders must support their teams as they strive towards organizational goals while at the same time negotiating the twists and turns of a dynamic business landscape.[3] Servant and adaptive leadership replace the conventional leadership

---

[1] Ralph Waldo Emerson was an American philosopher, essayist, and poet.
[2] Parker Palmer, *Let Your Life Speak: Listening for the Voice of Vocation*, (San Francisco, CA: Jossey-Bass, 2000).
[3] Amy Jen Su, "Self-care for Leaders: Make Restoration a Part of the Job," *Leader to Leader* 2019, no. 94 (2019): 1.

© Ebenezer C. Ikonne 2021
E. C. Ikonne, *Becoming a Leader in Product Development*,
https://doi.org/10.1007/978-1-4842-7298-5_10

approach, which defaults to telling, directing, and commanding with developing, facilitating, and supporting. However, practicing servant leadership and adaptive leadership does not mean that you never provide directives—doing so would be an abdication of your leadership responsibility.

Leadership is a complex endeavor, and leading is challenging. Your job is to contribute to organizational success by fostering a positive workplace where people can do their best work within leadership process. Leadership is also stressful. Research shows that unmanaged job stress and interpersonal stress can eventually lead to burnout.[4] Burnout negatively impacts your health, the health of those you lead, and your leader effectiveness. Let us look at how caring, as part of leading, induces stress and what steps you can take to prevent job stress and interpersonal stress from negatively impacting you, your team, and your leadership practice.

Caring Is Hazardous

Leaders who care for team members do so because they know that leadership is all about people. You might not have thought about it this way; however, when you accepted the leader role, you implicitly accepted the responsibility of caring for the individuals in your organization, just like a nurse cares for patients in the hospital or a social worker cares for their clients. As the famous Maori proverb asks and answers:

> He aha te mea nui o te ao
>
> What is the most important thing in the world?
>
> He tangata, he tangata, he tangata
>
> It is the people, it is the people, it is the people.

Effective leaders do more than just ensuring their organizational unit achieves its objectives; they help people become better versions of themselves. Leadership done right is high-touch work. Having a high-touch relationship does not imply that your relationship with everyone is the same; instead, it means that the well-being of all your team members is a primary concern. However, helping people develop is fraught with danger. For many leaders, a significant source of work-related stress comes from dealing with people.[5] Thomas Skovholt, Tabitha Greer, and Matthew Hanson identified seven hazards associated with professions dedicated to assisting individuals in

---

[4] P.D. Harms, Marcus Crede, Michael Tynan, Matthew Leon, and Wonho Jeung, "Leadership and Stress: A Meta-analytic Review," *The Leadership Quarterly* 28, no. 1 (2017): 179.

[5] Marek Botek, "Cope with Stress in Manager Life," *Współczesna Ekonomia* 3, no. 1 (2009): 108–109.

improving their lives.[6] These hazards transfer into any domain where people development and well-being are core concerns. I have experienced these hazards as a leader, and you will also if you incorporate the leadership guidance outlined in this book. Let me share the hazards and my experiences dealing with them. I hope my experience will help you manage these hazards.

You Cannot Solve All Problems

Sometimes leaders get stuck trying to help individuals solve an unsolvable problem. I once tried to help a manager regain trust with a team (who had no intention of ever trusting the manager again). The team had crossed the point of no return with the manager, but I was determined to help rebuild trust between the manager and the team because I knew trust must exist if the manager and their team were to achieve their goals. However, rebuilding trust was out of my control. I could not make the team trust the manager. Sadly, I lost sight of that fact and tried to force reconciliation. In attempting to force reconciliation, I began to alienate the team, and team members stopped interacting with me. It became clear that my attempts to solve this problem were hurting my relationship with the team. Damaging my relationship with the team would make a bad situation worse, so I stepped back and reassigned the manager. Recognize when the help you can provide becomes limited and when you cannot solve the problem no matter how much you care. Avoid the "Savior Complex"—believing it is always your responsibility to rescue people from challenging situations.

Sometimes People Lack the Skills

There are situations where people lack the competency required for a particular job or role, and developing those skills will be a challenge. Failing to acknowledge this can leave you and your team member frustrated because desired progress does not occur. You can think that all that is needed is time and effort when, in actuality, the person has maximized their potential in a particular area. For example, I tried to help an individual develop their emotional skills because they wanted more responsibility in the organization. Unfortunately, this individual struggled with managing their emotions, especially during difficult circumstances. Despite how hard we tried, it was clear that (at that time) they could not develop the emotional skills required for the job. It is important to remember that individuals may not develop the talents required for an opportunity they desire. You want to make sure you recognize when this is the case, so you adjust your approach.

---

[6] Thomas M. Skovholt, Tabitha L. Grier, Matthew R. Hanson, "Career Counseling for Longevity: Self-care and Burnout Prevention Strategies for Counselor Resilience," *Journal of Career Development* 27, no. 3 (2001): 168–170.

You Are Ready, but They Are Not

Even though you might be ready to help a team member, the team member may not be ready for your help. Both parties must engage in a "readiness dance" to ensure alignment on how to move forward.[7] It is discouraging when you see an opportunity for a team member to develop their skills in an area vital for their role; however, they do not see it because they lack self-awareness or are not interested in improving. It could be that the team member lacks motivation; or they genuinely believe they do not have a development opportunity despite all the evidence to the contrary. I see this with many people in authority positions who believe they are effective leaders. They do not see the opportunity for development because their teams find a way to succeed despite them. I once had a team member that everyone knew needed to improve how they behaved in meetings, but this individual believed their behavior was excellent and made little attempt to improve. I spent many frustrating hours trying to convince this person that they needed to work on their collaboration skills—all to the detriment of other items that needed my attention. Avoid getting caught in the trap of convincing people that they need to develop because you want to help them. Allow people to chart their path.

Failing to Say "No!"

Leaders who care for others can find it hard to say no to requests for their time. Saying no to requests for help (such as mentoring requests, meetings to discuss conflict, and feedback sessions) can be awkward for any leader who takes a leadership approached based on service to others. Maybe you feel guilty about saying no to requests for your time and say yes, even when you are exhausted and have little left to give to others. Saying yes all the time is not suitable for your health. Constantly attending to an individual's needs with no breaks can overwhelm you and create stressful situations. Mentoring more people than you have the capacity for will result in some low-quality mentoring relationships. Saying "yes" all the time is hazardous. Learning to say "no" is critical.

Caring Becomes a One-Way Street

Helping others can often be a one-way endeavor, with the leader doing most of the helping and caring. However, co-dependency can derail a leader's attempt to help someone on their team. It would be best if you watched out for individuals who suffer from "victim" syndrome. People who suffer from the victim syndrome routinely blame other people for everything that goes

---

[7] Ibid.

wrong and make themselves the center of attention.[8] These individuals are generally negative and constantly expect the worst. You cannot help these people because they have no intention of changing their situation, leaving you stuck in a rescuer role. Once you recognize that the person you are trying to help has taken on a victim identity, it is probably time for you to recommend that they get professional help while you step away. Attending to other's needs requires spending significant time and energy providing support to the people you serve. You have empathy for and show sensitivity to people's feelings. You listen to their complaints about themselves, their teammates, and the organization at large. Maintaining this constant focus and attention can be emotionally draining. You can only help people who are committed to improving their situation. Caring is a two-way street.

Shifty Success Measures

It can be challenging to determine whether success has occurred when helping people improve, and success measures can be highly subjective. The results from any interventions might take a while to develop. For example, when helping two team members mend a broken relationship, it might be difficult for you to determine how much progress has occurred in the short term. You have to recognize that perceptions also take a long time to change. And it can take a long time for changes to produce different results. I know I have struggled to determine whether I am making an impact and providing help. Helping others is not as straightforward as it might seem, and the results can be a bit elusive. If you are too focused on tangible results, you can become frustrated when situations do not produce immediate and tangible results. The absence of tangible results can lead to discouragement and stress. Patience is vital in these situations.

Failure Does Happen

Leaders do not always succeed in helping team members make the changes required to excel in their roles. Failure can be challenging to accept. I have watched team members fail to make crucial behavioral changes and have to leave a department. In other cases, environmental factors have prevented teams from achieving organizational goals. In both of these cases felt like I had failed at my job because I could not help the team member or the team succeed. However, as Skovholt, Greer, and Hanson put it, "…all of our determination, work, and competence, will sometimes not be enough."[9] Unfortunately, your work and effort will not always yield positive results.

---

[8] Manfred F. R. Kets de Vries, "Are You a Victim of the Victim Syndrome," *Organizational Dynamics* 43, no.2 (2014): 130–137.
[9] Ibid.

How you deal with failure will impact your stress levels. Accepting that your efforts may not yield positive results is a reality that you must accept.

These leadership hazards can create stressful situations for you. When leaders responsible for regulating distress in their groups do not manage their stress, they cannot provide those in their care the support they need.[10] As caregivers, they experience compassion fatigue—they can no longer find the energy to continue caring for individuals on the team.[11] Signs of compassion fatigue would include avoiding one-on-one sessions or not answering phone calls because you have no emotional energy left. Uncontrolled stress also impacts a leader's decision-making ability and overall leadership approach.[12] A leader who fosters a participative and autonomous leadership approach may revert to a directive and controlling approach during stressful periods.

You must proactively avoid extended periods of distress, burnout, and compassion fatigue. A proactive stance requires that you practice self-care. Self-care is essential to help you deal with the stress of leading and caring for people in a business climate that continues to demand more and more from you. The following section describes self-care and provides you with self-care practices.

Self-Care

Self-care is exactly what it sounds like—self-care. Sara Bressi and Elizabeth Vaden suggest that "self-care is care for the self and by the self." Self-care is inward-focused and necessitates that you continuously think about caring for yourself. Philip Authier notes that self-care aims to ensure that balance exists in a person's life.[13] The goal of self-care is to keep you healthy. Caring for oneself might come across as selfish or greedy. However, research has shown that when caregivers do not care for themselves, the quality of care they provide others suffers.[14] If you do not have stress under control, leading becomes challenging because you are not emotionally available. How can you care for others if you do not care for yourself? You practice self-care when you perform activities that benefit your wellness.

---

[10] Jennifer Fencl and Deborah Grant, "Self-Care Promotes Safer Patient Care," *AORN Journal* 105, no. 5 (2017): 506–509.

[11] Kim Richards, "Wellpower: The Foundation of Innovation," *Nursing Economic$* 31, no. 2 (2013): 94.

[12] P.D. Harms, Marcus Crede, Michael Tynan, Matthew Leon, and Wonho Jeung, "Leadership and Stress," 178–194.

[13] Phillip Authier, "Quality Leadership: A Balancing Act," *Nursing Management* 32, no. 2 (2001): 14.

[14] Fencl and Grant, "Self-Care Promotes Safer Patient Care," 507.

If self-care is a prerequisite for providing others quality care, why is the topic of self-care not more prevalent in business literature, and why does it seem that so few business leaders talk about and practice self-care? Consider that the Center for Creative Leadership (CCL) reported that 88% of leaders identify work as the primary source of stress in their lives.[15] However, a subsequent CCL whitepaper on stress failed to discuss explicitly self-care as a method for managing stress.[16] One can only imagine the negative impact stressed-out leaders have on the people they are supposed to serve, support, and lead. Self-care does not get the attention it deserves despite being critical.

As I speak with leaders, two main reasons emerge for why they ignore their self-care. The first reason is "no time." Many leaders leave no room in the day to take care of themselves.[17] Instead, they fill their day with work and leave no time for self-care. Kirsty Sturman advises leaders to be intentional about self-care and to make time for it during their day.[18] Self-care will not magically happen on its own. The second reason is that they do not consider self-care that important. Again, many leaders know what self-care is and yet do not create time for self-care because they believe it takes time away from what truly matters—achieving organizational results. Placing organizational results above personal well-being is a mistake with long-term consequences. Hard work and self-care are not mutually exclusive.[19] Hard work produces excellent results when you do not have to deal with the negative side-effects of stress, such as exhaustion, poor health, and even mental breakdown.

There is nothing selfish about self-care; instead, what is selfish is when you fail to take proper care of yourself and cause the people surrounding you to suffer the effects of your stress and burnout. Selfishness is not having the capacity to give the appropriate care and support to those you lead. Selfishness is not having the mental sharpness necessary to make brave decisions. Neglecting your self-care is a moral failing that can have far-reaching consequences on the organization. Maybe you are a leader who has neglected self-care or gets to self-care only when you feel near burnout or extreme fatigue. Or you might be a leader who practices some self-care but considers those activities separate from your job. It would be best if you contemplate how to make self-care a part of your lifestyle. Organizations need to incorporate self-care into their leader and leadership development programs

---

[15] Michael Campbell, Jessica Inis Baltes, André Martin, and Kyle Meddings, "The Stress of Leadership," *Center for Creative Leadership* 10, no. 11 (2007): 6.

[16] "The Stress of Leadership,"https://www.ccl.org/articles/white-papers/stress-of-leadership/" (last accessed July 19, 2020).

[17] Robert J. Wicks and Tina C. Buck, "Riding the Dragon: Enhancing Resilient Leadership and Sensible Self-Care in the Healthcare Executive," *Frontiers of Health Services Management* 30, no. 2 (2013): 7.

[18] Kirsty Sturman, "Making some time for self-care," *Vet Record* 185, no. 10 (2019): 312.

[19] Jennifer M. Heemstra, "Self-Care is Not the Enemy of Performance," *ChemBioChem* 20, no. 17 (2019): 2203–2206.

to stress (excuse the pun) the importance of self-care.[20] The following section provides self-care practices for leaders (and, for that matter, anyone who needs to manage their stress).

Self-Care Practices

You need to care for yourself both personally and professionally. There is little separation between these aspects of self-care; what you do personally impacts you professionally and vice-versa. However, some self-care activities primarily occur outside the workplace, and other self-care activities occur inside it. We will first look at personal self-care and then professional self-care. Personal self-care practices and professional self-care practices strengthen each other.[21] So, for maximum results, you want to develop a holistic self-care plan that incorporates personal and professional self-care.

Personal Self-Care Practices

Self-care starts with caring for yourself outside of the workplace. Without a strong foundation of personal self-care, it becomes hard to succeed at professional self-care. Personal self-care focuses on balancing the physical, emotional, social, and spiritual dimensions of well-being.[22] Attending to your physical, emotional, social, and spiritual well-being will help you cope with your stress.

Attending to Physical Well-Being

It is easy to ignore our physical well-being. The personal and professional demands of life cause us to place our physical well-being behind other activities. However, physical well-being is an essential aspect of personal self-care, so you must pay attention to it. It is hard to do good work and support people when your body does not feel right. You will lack the mental acuity, alertness, vigor, and strength required to perform your duties. Practicing personal care by exercising regularly, getting enough rest and sleep, and eating right is critical.[23] Attending to basic personal care requires discipline and commitment; however, the benefits of physical well-being activities are significant.

It has become a thing of pride for some famous business leaders to boast about how effective they are despite how little sleep they get. Society idolizes successful leaders whose lore says they get no more than four hours of sleep

---

[20] Stark, Manning-Walsh, and Vliem, "Caring for Self," 266–270.
[21] Richards, "Wellpower: The Foundation of Innovation," 94–95.
[22] Skovholt, Grier, and Hanson, "Career Counseling for Longevity," 174–175.
[23] Fencl and Grant, "Self-care promotes safer patient care," 507.

every night. It seems that a good night's sleep is now overrated. Is this truly the case? Research would suggest otherwise. In his study of sleep, Matthew Walker notes that getting less than six or seven hours of sleep compromises the immune system, doubles the risk of cancer, and is a critical lifestyle factor in determining whether an individual will develop Alzheimer's disease.[24] Reduced stress, thinking more clearly, and better relationships with people are all immediate benefits of getting enough sleep.[25] Sleeping well helps you remain productive and perform well at work. Sleep may even be more important than eating right and getting regular exercise.[26] There is no shame in getting a good night's sleep.

Unfortunately, I know many individuals who struggle with getting six to seven hours of sleep. If you are one of these individuals, you need to identify the factors causing your lack of sleep so that you can address them. Constant electronic media usage, a lack of exercise, a poor diet, and the inability to disconnect from work are some factors that make it challenging for individuals to sleep well.[27] Work pressure may also make it hard to sleep at night. Sleep deprivation is a big deal that requires attention. Nick Summerton recommends individuals maintain a consistent sleep routine, organize their bedroom, avoid food and alcohol at night, and exercise for a good night's sleep.[28] Anyone with sleep challenges might need medical help when essential tips do not work.[29] A good night's rest is a necessary ingredient of personal self-care.

Exercise is a pivotal part of physical well-being. The CDC reports that regular exercise provides the immediate benefits of helping with thinking, learning, and judgment while also reducing the risk of depression and anxiety.[30] Exercise also provides some long-term benefits such as helping to keep weight off, reducing the risk of heart disease, strokes, diabetes, and even certain cancers.[31]

---

[24] Matthew Walker, *Why We Sleep*, (New York, NY: Scribner, 2017), 3.

[25] "Why is getting enough sleep important," https://health.gov/myhealthfinder/topics/everyday-healthy-living/mental-health-and-relationships/get-enough-sleep#panel-2 (last accessed July 19, 2020).

[26] Ibid.

[27] John Dean, "10 Ways to Help Staff Get a Good's Night Sleep," *Occupational Health & Wellbeing* 69, no. 10 (2017): 9.

[28] Nick Summerton, "No More Sleepless Nights," *Occupational Health & Wellbeing* 69, no. 7 (2017): 12–13

[29] Ibid.

[30] "Benefits of physical activity," https://www.cdc.gov/physicalactivity/basics/pa-health/index.htm (last accessed July 19, 2020).

[31] Ibid.

So how much exercise does a person need? The Department of Health and Human Services recommends that adults

- Spend either 150 minutes in moderate aerobic activity or 75 minutes in vigorous aerobic activity a week and

- Perform strength training for all muscle groups at least two times a week[32]

Water aerobics, brisk walking, and mowing the lawn are examples of moderate aerobic activities. Playing sports such as football (soccer) and basketball are examples of vigorous aerobic activities. It does not matter whether your exercise is moderate or vigorous; what matters is that you exercise regularly. Establishing a routine will help you remain committed to an exercise program. Resources exist for individuals who have not been physically active for a while.[33] Exercise is an essential aspect of personal care. If exercising is not part of your routine, you need to make some changes for the sake of your health. Sign up at a gym, get a fitness coach, or just start to walk around your house.

My football coaches used to say to me, "you can't outrun a bad diet." Exercise is necessary but not sufficient. Personal self-care requires a healthy diet. It would help if you had abundant energy and strength to lead through organizational challenges. A healthy diet fuels the body, helps maintain proper energy levels, and provides the mental sharpness required to get through the day.[34] It is vital to remember that what you eat impacts your mental function. You cannot afford to be sluggish or lethargic, so you need to adopt a diet that helps you perform well. Regardless of the specific diet you choose, Christopher Neck and Kenneth Cooper advise a diet with reduced fat and cholesterol, high in fiber, high in calcium, and containing antioxidants.[35] Portion control and low sugar intake are also vital for your diet. Exert self-discipline and minimize eating unhealthy foods that negatively impact your health.

Emotional Well-Being

Besides taking care of your physical needs, you must also pay attention to your emotional needs. The National Center for Emotional Wellness describes emotional wellness as the awareness, understanding, and acceptance of our

---

[32] Physical Activity Guidelines for Americans, "https://www.hhs.gov/fitness/be-active /physical-activity-guidelines-for-americans/index.html," (last accessed July 19, 2020).
[33] "Getting started with physical activity for a healthy weight," https://www.cdc.gov/ healthyweight/physical_activity/getting_started.html (last accessed July 19, 2020).
[34] Fencl and Grant, "Self-care Promotes Safer Patient Care," 507.
[35] Ibid.

emotions.[36] When you do not manage your emotions, your actions become unpredictable. I know of leaders who always had unpredictable responses. One leader would have an emotional outburst when told of some minor bad news. Her responses to situations were almost always overreactions. Team members were always scared when she was in meetings because they did not know what she would say. Her unpredictable moods created an environment of fear. Poor emotional health negatively impacts your ability to manage stress and often leads to erratic decision-making. If you continue to make poor decisions, your team will lose confidence in you. Personal self-care requires that you make sure you stay emotionally healthy.

A key component of looking after one's emotional well-being is having a purpose and working towards it, whatever that purpose might be. The many demands of leadership can cause you to lose sight of what matters most to you, and so it is vital that you routinely remind yourself of your purpose. Why did you accept a leadership role in the first place? What difference did you intend to make in this role? Many individuals become assigned leaders because it seems like the obvious next step in their career, but they do not have a purpose. While you support your organization's mission, you need to have a purpose for why you chose to become an assigned leader. For example, my purpose as a leader is to foster joy at work for the people in my organization. I strive to nurture an environment where people can experience joy while developing and doing their best work every day. There are times I fall short, but my shortcomings do not alter my purpose. Whenever I face stressful moments or need to make challenging decisions, I go back to my purpose and examine how the decision aligns (or does not align) with my purpose. Examining your purpose requires periods of reflection. In these moments of reflection, explore who you are, reflect on how you react in certain situations, learn your triggers, and adjust.

It is essential to understand your tuning so that you can manage your emotions and triggers. We all have different triggers that get us going. Our triggers are behaviors from others that aggravate and upset us. A person's tuning results from the combination of their experiences in life, culture, social groups, and other factors that make them who they are.[37] For example, early on in my career, I was conflict-averse. Ironically, I worked with a few individuals who enjoyed conflict and debate. While I could debate, I was not skilled at loud arguments and often found myself on the losing end of the argument because I could not keep up. As a result, I would spend days upset over what had transpired, which was not good for my emotional well-being. Fortunately, I had a leader who pointed out that I needed to understand my tuning and

---

[36] "Invest in Your Greatest Asset…People," https://www.nationalcenterforemotionalwell-ness.org/ (last accessed July 19, 2020).

[37] Ronald Heifetz, Marty Linsky, and Alexander Grashow, *The Practice of Adaptive Leadership: Tools and Tactics for Changing Your Organization and the World*, 195–204.

watch for triggers, especially when I noticed that I was becoming angry. She challenged me to identify the triggers that were causing my anger during those debates. After some reflection, it became clear that I became angry because I felt that my peers did not respect me (which was not true). Once I realized this, I could manage my emotions more effectively because I knew my peers respected me.

Activities such as journaling, creative writing, and other artistic endeavors can help with emotional well-being.[38] Journaling is a great way to relieve stress because it allows you to express how you feel at any given time. It also enables you to track your progress over time. I heard the story of a leader who wrote down in their journal every piece of positive feedback they had ever received, and then when they had moments of self-doubt or worry, they would open their journal and read all the positive feedback. Research shows that "bad is stronger than good."[39] Negative emotions tend to overpower positive emotions. You want to keep track of positive moments that can boost your mood whenever faced with stressful situations. Engaging in an artistic activity can also help with emotional health. For example, I enjoy playing the piano, and so whenever I feel stressed, playing the piano provides me with relief.

Every leader makes mistakes. You will inevitably hire the wrong person, fund the wrong initiative, make a bad decision, or poorly respond to a question in a meeting. When this happens, you must recognize you made a mistake, apologize for it, and then move on. It is easy to become stuck in the trap of "what-if" and imagine everything you could have done differently. Instead of wallowing in self-pity, you need to forgive yourself and remain emotionally healthy. Self-forgiveness is part of self-care.[40] Like you forgive others on your team when they make mistakes, you need to forgive yourself. Remember that you are human. And yet, the fact you will make mistakes is not an excuse for setting low expectations for yourself. Have realistic high expectations for yourself and always try to do the right thing.

You need to guard your emotions and limit stimuli that trigger negativity. Positivity plays an essential role in maintaining emotional well-being. If you find yourself in an environment that consistently brings up negative emotions, you need to change your environment as soon as possible as it is not good for your health. At one point in my career, I worked at a company where the atmosphere outside of my team was toxic. The leaders of the different departments routinely blamed each other whenever there was a problem, and I routinely found myself in heated arguments with other departmental leaders. At the time, I had a Blackberry (remember those?), and I still remember that my heart would start racing anytime my phone flashed, indicating that I had

[38] Sara K. Bressi and Elizabeth R. Vaden, "Reconsidering Self-Care," 37.
[39] Roy F. Baumeister, Ellen Bratslavsky, Catrin Finkenauer, and Kathleen D. Vohs, "Bad Is Stronger With Good," *Review of General Psychology* 5, no. 4 (2001): 323–370.
[40] Kurt April and Garth Pillay, "Stress and Self-Care of SMME Owners in South Africa," 44.

received a message. It was not a good situation for me, and I eventually decided to leave the firm because I found it impossible to remain positive at work. Sometimes the best decision you can make for your emotional well-being is to change your workplace.

Social Wellness

Social wellness focuses on the health of the relationships we have with people. Lauren J. Roscoe concluded that "social wellness is the movement toward balance and integration of the interaction between the individual, society, and nature."[41] When individuals do not have healthy social relationships, they increase their chances of falling sick because social relationships impact mental health, morbidity, and mortality.[42] Healthy relationships outside of the workplace are critical, and for many individuals, a healthy social life starts at home (if they live with other people). Having family support is a foundational aspect of social wellness and personal care for those with families.[43] When family support is missing, it can be difficult for people to bring the best version of themselves to work because the family situation is not in order. For those with children at home, the National Institutes of Health (NIH) encourages parents to bond with their children to improve their social health.[44] I have spoken with many a leader who expressed regret over not spending enough time with their family. It is not wise to ignore your family at the expense of your job.

If your routine is anything like mine, then you will be familiar with the "get home from work, possibly eat a quick dinner, and then get right back on the computer" flow. I followed this routine for many years. Immediately I got home from work, I would sit on the couch, crack open my laptop, and begin to work. If any of my children came by and wanted to play, I would tell them that I was busy and would play with them later. Later, never came. Before too long, it would be time to put them to bed. After putting them to bed, I would go right back to my laptop and continue working. In my mind, work paid the bills, and the most important thing was that I stayed on top of my work and impressed my bosses[45]. We all know that there is more work than there is time and that we could spend most of our waking hours working if we so desired. However, I ignored my family and hurt my social well-being because of work.

---

[41] Lauren J. Roscoe, "Wellness: A Review of Theory and Measurement for Counselors," *Journal of Counseling and Development* 87, no. 2 (2009): 218.

[42] Julianne Holt-Lunstad, Timothy B. Smith, and J. Bradley Layton, "Social Relationships and Mortality Risk: A Meta-Analytic Review," *PLoS Medicine* 7, no. 7 (2010): 1–20.

[43] Diane J. Chandler, "Pastoral Burnout and the Impact of Personal Spiritual Renewal, Rest-taking, and Support System Practices," *Pastoral Psychology* 58, no. 3 (2009): 273–287.

[44] "Social wellness toolkit," https://www.nih.gov/health-information/social-wellness-toolkit (last accessed 2020).

[45] Impression management affects social wellness.

Work is essential, and as a leader, you provide value only when the organization achieves its goals. That said, if work is preventing you from spending quality time with your family, you want to revisit your priorities. I was devastated when my kids told me that I did not have time for them because I was always on my computer. I learned the importance of family the hard way. It hurt me to learn that even though I was present, I was absent. Once I received that feedback from my kids, I began to change my behavior. Behavioral change is not easy and takes time, but I believe I have made improvements.

It is also vital that you model the behavior you want others in the organization to copy. Do not underestimate how your actions might impact the social wellness of team members. As I shared in an earlier chapter, I was surprised when some of my team leaders told me my number one behavior that caused them discomfort was the emails and other messages I sent early in the morning (before 7 a.m.) and late in the day (after 6 p.m.). When I explained that I did not expect them to reply immediately, everyone said they understood. However, the fact that I was sending messages at those times of the day made them feel like they should be working also. I was impacting—inadvertently albeit—the social wellness of people on my team. I have since learned that many items that seem urgent are not urgent. The world will not end because I did not address the items immediately.

Social wellness is boosted by participating in social activities. The activity might be a weekly pickup basketball game with some close friends, a girl's night out every few weeks, or social programs at your religious institution. It does not matter what it is. Participate in activities that help you develop new social connections. Volunteering is a fantastic way to meet new people while at the same time giving back to your community. Many organizations have employee resource groups that benefit social wellness. If your organization has such groups, consider joining one. If you are trying to improve your physical and social wellness simultaneously, consider joining an exercise group in your community. Many gyms offer group exercise classes, and exercising with a group is a great way to improve physical wellness while at the same time improving social wellness.

Healthy social well-being requires healthy relationships. Surround yourself with individuals who love you and accept you for who you are. Focus on developing skills that build healthy relationships as well. Good social relationships benefit from listening to others and having empathy for them. It is also essential to have a diverse set of friends that challenge us to think differently.[46] It is easy to surround ourselves with people like us; however, doing so reduces our opportunity to understand and appreciate different perspectives. We are all products of our environment and experiences. Having a diverse set of friends brings richness into our lives that we would not

---

[46] Wicks and Buck, "Riding the Dragon," 9.

otherwise experience. At the same time, it is vital to avoid individuals who consistently bring negativity.[47] We all know people who regularly and intentionally steal our joy. Do as much as you can to limit your interaction with these individuals. Having a healthy social life can make it easier to get along with people in the workplace.

Spiritual Wellness

The last aspect of personal wellness I will cover is spiritual wellness. The Laborers' Health and Safety Fund of North America defines spiritual wellness as "…being connected to something greater than yourself and having a set of values, principles, morals, and beliefs that provide a sense of purpose to life, then using those principles to guide your actions."[48] Purpose is also essential for spiritual wellness. Identifying your purpose helps you give meaning to your experiences. It is also easier to accept different views when one is at peace with oneself. When individuals lose their sense of purpose and meaning, they are more susceptible to stress, diabetes, and other diseases.[49] On the other hand, when individuals are spiritually well, they are clear on their values and principles. Their actions are often congruent with their espoused values, and people can often vouch that these individuals' actions reflect their values.

It is difficult to lead when we lose sight of our values. Decision-making often depends on values and principles, and when our moral compass is off, our ability to make sound decisions is impacted. Spiritual wellness practices can help you remain connected to your values and principles. A well-known spiritual wellness practice is meditation. An example meditation practice focuses your attention on a single item and then brings back your attention to this single item when your mind drifts. Meditation has the benefits of increased focus even when we are not meditating. It also helps people become less anxious, more compassionate, and more creative.[50] Meditation helps to clear the mind and creates a sense of peace.

---

[47] Ibid.

[48] Emily Smith, "Spiritual Wellness: What is Your Meaning and Purpose?" https://www.lhs-fna.org/index.cfm/lifelines/september-2016/spiritual-wellness-what-is-your-meaning-and-purpose/ (last accessed 2020).

[49] "Definition of Spiritual Wellness," http://www.lifemedwellcare.org/docs/spiritual-wellness-lifestyle.pdf (last accessed July 19, 2020).

[50] https://www.healthline.com/nutrition/12-benefits-of-meditation#section2 (last accessed July 19, 2020).

In addition to meditation, you can also practice mindfulness. Research has shown that mindfulness positively impacts spiritual well-being.[51] While meditation aims to tune out distractions, mindfulness helps you pay close attention to your thoughts, feelings, and everything going on around you. When you are mindful, you intentionally reflect on what is happening around you. Then, you work to make yourself present at that moment. Mindfulness also provides the opportunity for gratitude. As you pay attention to everything going on around you, take a moment to express gratitude. Gratitude eases stress and relaxes your mind. The beautiful thing about mindfulness is that you can practice it at any time and in any place. All it requires is slowing your mind down and fully absorbing all that is going on around you. Mindfully appreciating nature is a great way to practice mindfulness.

Many individuals attend to their spiritual needs through a faith-based system, while others attend to their spiritual needs through a moral code. Whatever the path an individual may choose, spiritual wellness is a continual process of refining one's purpose in life while at the same time developing values and a personal belief system.[52] My faith plays a critical role in my spiritual well-being. Fellowship with like-minded people of faith gives me the support and encouragement I need, even when dealing with difficulties at work. But, it was not always this way. There was a time, where all that mattered to me was climbing the corporate ladder, and I sacrificed my spiritual wellness at the altar of material success. My sacrifices led to deep dissatisfaction with work, and I found myself without much of a moral compass. I am not suggesting that one must belong to the faith group to have a moral compass. I am sharing my story. Once I reconnected with my faith, I connected to something greater than myself, and my purpose became clear again.

Additional spiritual wellness practices include volunteering, praying, and enjoying hobbies.[53] Philip Authier stresses the importance for individuals to perform an activity they love daily.[54] Find additional events outside of work that bring you joy. Spiritual wellness is particularly essential when leading your organization through difficult situations, crises, or impactful change. At these times, you need your morals, values, and principles to guide you.

If you paid careful attention to practices for each wellness dimension, you probably noticed that several practices help multiple dimensions. For example, belonging to a recreational soccer team addresses physical, social, and

---

[51] Monali D. Mathad, S. K. Rajesh, and Balaram Pradhan, "Spiritual Well-Being and Its Relationship with Mindfulness, Self-Compassion and Satisfaction with Life in Baccalaureate Nursing Students: A Correlation Study," *Journal of Religion Health* 58, no. 2 (2019): 554–565.

[52] Roscoe, "Wellness: A Review of Theory," 220–221.

[53] "Definition of Spiritual Wellness," http://www.lifemedwellcare.org/docs/spiritual-well-ness-lifestyle.pdf (last accessed July 19, 2020).

[54] Authier, "Quality Leadership," 14.

emotional well-being. Regularly attending a faith-based institution like a church, mosque, synagogue, or temple addresses spiritual, social, and emotional well-being. You need to identify which aspect of your health needs attention and what you will do to address those aspects. Every individual's situation is different, and what works for me might not work for you. Whatever you do, do not ignore any aspect of personal self-care. Ignoring personal self-care hurts your health and makes you a less effective leader.

Professional Self-Care Practices

Professional self-care practices are self-care practices that you engage in within the workplace. That is right. You also need to take care of yourself within the workplace context. Do not wait for others to take care of you. Own your professional self-care. Professional self-care leads to joy at work. Thomas Skovholt, Tabitha Grier, and Mathew Hanson provided five pathways through which individuals can practice professional self-care.[55] Let us look at how you can apply these pathways at work.

Maximizing Professional Success

Professional self-care comes from performing well at your job. Accomplishing tasks and meeting objectives provide a sense of fulfillment and satisfaction. When this sense of fulfillment is missing, distress and burnout can set in. So how can you get a feel for whether you are doing a good job? Leaders know they are doing a good job when they see people transform, receive recognition from the people they work with, develop expertise in the domain, and have healthy relationships.[56] These four sources of validation need to be present for you to feel successful in your role. When any of these four elements are missing, they impact your sense of professional success, and you need to take steps to address the missing element.

We have already established that you are responsible for helping the people you lead develop their competencies by providing them with developmental resources. One of the most fulfilling aspects of being a leader is seeing those you serve flourishing in new roles and opportunities regardless of their role in the organization. For example, when Onyi took over as manager for a product development team, it was clear that the team did not know how to work together despite their individual talents. So, she spent her first few weeks as manager, providing the team with collaboration resources. She also showed the team how they could use an electronic tool to make their work visual and transparent to everyone. Through her coaching and training, the individuals

---

[55] Skovholt, Grier, and Matthew R. Hanson, "Career Counseling for Longevity," 171–175.
[56] Ibid.

learned how to work together as a team and become more effective at product development. For Onyi, watching and participating in the team's transformation brought her a sense of success, positively impacting her well-being.

Everyone desires recognition and appreciation, even though the degree to which we desire them differs. Leaders who do not receive recognition from the people they work with might experience a feeling of emptiness. Recognition needs to come from the different types of relationships you have in the organization. For example, recognition is not complete if you only receive recognition from your manager and receive little to no recognition from your peers or team. If you do not receive recognition from a specific group, take the time to understand why this is the case. Exploring this might be challenging to do; however, you need to do it. Esiaba observed that his direct reports barely recognized his contribution to the team. They recognized each other (and even recognized Esiaba's manager), but they would rarely recognize (or appreciate) him. Finally, Esiaba decided to ask the team what needs they had that he was not meeting. The team shared that they would like him to stop acting defensively whenever they gave him feedback. They also wanted him to show interest in their lives and recognize their contributions. Esiaba took the feedback and made some changes to how he led the team, and the team responded by recognizing his support.

The first two elements of maximizing success as a leader—achieving goals and receiving recognition—are partially outside your control. You cannot guarantee that the leadership process will succeed or that people will recognize you. Hence, leaders need to avoid measuring professional success solely on those two aspects.[57] While ignoring these aspects of professional success would be foolhardy, it would be equally dangerous to base professional well-being on elements you do not have complete control over. Professional self-care requires an understanding of an individual's locus of control.[58] Individuals who believe that they control everything have a strong internal locus of control. Individuals who believe that they control little (or nothing) have a strong external locus of control. Many people have a locus of control that lies somewhere between these two poles. For example, you do not have complete control over how people view or respond to you. And yet, your actions do influence how people respond. An unhealthy locus of control negatively impacts your well-being.

On the other hand, you have a significant amount of control over your expertise and the effort you put into relationships. Unfortunately, many leaders in product development contexts do not actively work at becoming more effective leaders. Any improvements are mainly accidental because many leaders focus most of their energy on developing expertise in the domains

---

[57] Ibid.
[58] April and Pillay, "Stress and Self-Care of SMME Owners," 38–63.

(functional and technical) they lead. For example, if they are software engineering leaders in an accounting firm, the focus is on software engineering and accounting. If they are product management leaders in a supply chain business, the focus is on product management and supply chain. I cannot overemphasize how critical it is that you have mastery of your domain. Speaking intelligently about the domains is something you must do well. You need to understand the intricacies of the business, the work people do to support the business, and the challenges they face in their work. However, domain mastery should not come at the expense of leadership mastery. Leading is a full-time job, and you need to intentionally develop your leadership expertise to excel at it. Read and listen to the leadership literature—books, journals, blogs, and podcasts. Attend (and possibly speak at) leadership conferences. Take advantage of leader and leadership development courses provided by your organization. It is improbable that you will develop leadership expertise without doing these things. Developing your leadership expertise will build your confidence as a leader, an integral part of professional well-being. Do not wait for someone to provide you with leadership development opportunities; instead, take the initiative to develop your leadership competency. Commit to becoming the best leader you can be.

You also control what you put into organizational relationships because how you show up and interact with people is something you can control. Can you say that as a leader that you tried your best? While there are many aspects that you may not have control over, you can determine how you treat the people in your care. In many situations, you also get to choose how you do what you do. It is in these moments that the values of leaders such as Ezihe shine. Ezihe had a team member who was struggling to perform their job duties. Many of the individuals surrounding Ezihe suggested that she fire the individual; however, because Ezihe hired this individual, she considered it her responsibility to give this individual every opportunity to turn their performance around. Ezihe chose to support this individual even though this individual did not turn things around and eventually left the organization. Remaining committed to this individual and living up to her espoused values brought Ezihe personal satisfaction—a critical aspect of professional self-care. Give your best in support of team members so that when a relationship does not work out—and some relationships will not—you will know that you did your best.

Having an Individualized Development Method

Beyond reading books or listening to podcasts, you need to create a development method that suits your professional goals. The development method should encourage you to try different activities and take on new challenges in your career. For example, over six years, one leader I know had four distinct roles in an organization. Each position allowed this leader to develop themselves and increase their responsibilities in the organization. A formal learning plan is an essential aspect of professional self-care. Do not develop a precise plan of what you want to do and when you want to do it. Having a flexible plan helps you remain in control of certain aspects of your professional journey. It is essential that as you make progress in your career, you take the time to reflect on what you have accomplished up to that point. Professional reflection is an integral part of self-care and is vital for emotional and spiritual wellness.[59] Professional reflection enables you to identify what you have learned up to that point in your career and what changes will help you take on new responsibilities.

Many leaders need help creating a development plan. An executive coach can help leaders address immediate concerns while also assisting them in mapping out where the leader would like to go in their career.[60] At a point in my career, I felt stuck and uncertain about how I wanted to proceed with my career. I had begun contemplating leaving my organization because I had become frustrated with work. I asked an executive coach to help me with figuring out my next steps. An executive coach does not tell you what to do; instead, they help you explore options that may exist. In my case, the executive coach reminded me of my strengths and helped me identify the type of organization that would fit my skills and talents. She reinforced the importance of owning and taking control of my career while helping me identify blind spots. A healthy coaching relationship requires that individuals accept feedback— positive and negative—because feedback provides information that leaders can use to develop their leadership capabilities.[61] Ignoring feedback deprives you of an opportunity to address areas that negatively impact your effectiveness. If you do not have an executive coach or a mentor, this is an excellent time to find one. When you do not create a development method for yourself, you place your development and professional self-care in the hands of others.

Increasing Professional Self-Understanding

As a leader, you must continue to identify what you are good at, i.e., your talents, strengths, and gifts. Increasing professional self-understanding contributes to emotional wellness. The more self-aware you are, the more likely you will choose jobs where you can thrive. Self-awareness has two sides to it: internal self-awareness and external self-awareness.[62] Possessing the

---

[59] Georgina Barton, "Recollage as a Tool for Self-Care: Reflecting Multimodally on First Five Years in the Academy Through Schwab's Lines of Flight," *Qualitative Research Journal* 20, no.1 (2020): 49–62.

[60] Constance M. Savage, "Executive Coaching: Professional Self-Care for Nursing Leaders," *Nursing Economic$* 19, no. 4 (2001): 178–182.

[61] Skovholt, Grier, and Hanson, "Career Counseling for Longevity," 173–174.

[62] Tasha Eurich, *Insight: Why We're Not as Self-Aware as We Think, and How Seeing Ourselves Clearly Helps Us Succeed at Work and in Life*, (New York, NY: Crown Business, 2017).

correct internal and external self-awareness levels means that you are in touch with how you feel about situations and welcome feedback from those around you. For example, if you have a high need for attention, you will be dissatisfied if your role does not attract the bright lights or places you on the sidelines during critical decision-making. Ergo, your work situation will not bring joy and satisfaction, and you will probably suffer from a "fear of missing out." Hence self-awareness is a vital component of increasing professional self-understanding. Have people you trust tell you what you do well. Review your job and identify the activities that intrinsically motivate you so that you can find ways to do more of those activities (and less of those that demotivate you). Find roles and jobs that are a match for you.

Creating a Professional Greenhouse at Work

Greenhouses create ideal conditions for plants to grow. Similarly, professional self-care requires that you find organizations that provide the appropriate conditions for your career to thrive. Too often, people leave it to the organization to create these conditions. Professional self-care means making sure a professional greenhouse exists at work.[63] Establishing a professional greenhouse starts with surrounding yourself with a support system of peers and mentors. Professional self-care also requires making intelligent decisions about team composition.[64] Team composition decisions include choosing your manager(s), peers, and the people you will work with. These individuals are critical to your professional well-being because you interact with them daily. Find a mentor who can be part of your greenhouse. It may not matter how much you get paid; if you do not have a robust support system at work, an essential aspect of professional self-care is missing that will impact your health and effectiveness at work. I have been fortunate in my career to mostly have a robust support system of coworkers; however, I know many people who have not been as fortunate.

Included in setting up a professional greenhouse is supporting the development of others in the organization. Becoming a mentor to others helps those in caring professions—which leading is—develop through serving others.[65] Amarachi experienced this when, at the suggestion of her manager, she began to mentor young men and women in her organization who were beginning their software development careers. Becoming a mentor and sharing her experiences with others was a rewarding experience for her. She learned about the challenges that each person had faced transitioning into a technology career. Mentoring allows you to informally give back to others outside of formal organizational reporting relationships.

It is not uncommon to find yourself with an unhealthy balance between other-care and self-care. Because you are so focused on the well-being of those you

---

[63] Skovholt, Grier and, Hanson, "Career Counseling for Longevity," 174.
[64] Heemstra, "Self-Care is Not the Enemy," 2203.
[65] Skovholt, Grier, and Hanson, "Career Counseling for Longevity," 174.

serve, you ignore your well-being. A professional greenhouse requires a healthy balance between other-care and self-care.[66] You need to intentionally create boundaries so that you can pay attention to yourself. Have fun at work. As Joseph Campbell suggests, "Don't do anything that isn't play."[67] Play does not mean the absence of challenges, difficulty, or hardship while leading; instead, it means that you take on leadership challenges because you choose to. Acting from a position of autonomous choice leads to joy and satisfaction from work. If the job is not fun, you probably need to consider changing the conditions to make the work fun. As Maya Angelou said, "If you don't like something, change it. If you can't change it, change your attitude."[68]

Minimizing Ambiguous Professional Loss

A vital part of your role is team member development; however, and unfortunately, there are times when it does not work out with team members. Sometimes, the team member must separate from you (or you from the team). The team member may join another team in the organization or leave the organization entirely. Not understanding why the relationship did not work can leave you searching for answers and second-guessing your decisions. To minimize ambiguous professional loss, avoid loose ends when relationships do not work out. If you do not ensure that closure occurs when the relationship ends, you may experience ambiguous loss.

Do Not Neglect Self-Care

Facilitating the leadership process is not a profession for the faint of heart. It has been my experience that the more an individual's leadership responsibility increases, the more challenging the leadership process becomes. The larger the leadership system, the more volatile the context, or the more critical the adaptation, the more challenging it is to lead. As your scope of responsibility increases, the higher the stakes become for you and the people you lead and your decisions become more consequential in their impact. People hold you to a higher standard, and the organization expects a lot from you. I have challenged you to take on a leadership approach that puts people first—possibly in ways you had not previously considered. Adopting this approach might require significant changes to how you have led up to this point. Practicing these leadership approaches will most definitely challenge you. And yet, you need to avoid falling into the "rescuer" trap. Rescuers have a burning desire to help people even at their own expense because it makes them feel

---

[66] Ibid.
[67] Joseph Campell was an American mythologist, writer and lecturer.
[68] Maya Angelou was an American civil rights activist and poet.

good and appreciated.[69] To lead well, you will need to practice self-care. If you have not practiced self-care before now, start by developing a self-care plan. Taking care of yourself helps you become the best leader you can be.

Takeaways

- You must deal with the oft-overlooked caring demands of your organizations. You have the moral obligation of caring for the individuals your serve in the organization.

- Caring for others is hazardous. Sometimes caring does not work out as intended and can lead to distress, burnout, depression, and other ailments negatively impacting leader effectiveness.

- Before you can care well for others, you must first care for yourself. Self-care is a prerequisite for other care, and you need to practice personal self-care and professional self-care. Both types of self-care impact the other.

- Physical, emotional, social, and spiritual wellness are the various aspects of personal self-care that you attend to through exercise, maintaining a proper diet, having a social support system, and connecting to a larger purpose.

- Professional self-care requires that you take responsibility for your development in the workplace. You must create a "professional greenhouse" for yourself that makes work an enjoyable experience. Being part of the right organization is a critical aspect of professional self-care.

- If you practice personal and professional self-care, you will be able to give more of yourself in the service of their organizations. You will have more energy and a sharper mind, which helps you effectively cope with the demands of your leadership position.

- Develop a self-care plan today.

---

[69] Manfred F. R. Kets de Vries, "Are You a Mentor, a Helper or a Rescuer," *Organizational Dynamics* 42, no. 4 (2013): 239–247.

What Next?

Yesterday I was clever, so I wanted to change the world. Today I am wise, so I am changing myself.

—Rumi[1]

Leadership is not about you or me. It is about the group and how we move forward together. As such, I have tried to present a different way of understanding and facilitating leadership in the workplace. My goal has not been to tell you everything one could know about leadership because we continue to learn more about the leadership phenomenon. Instead, I am optimistic you have expanded your leadership philosophy with the essential leadership concepts, theories, and practices I have provided. Hopefully, you are now even more motivated to become a more effective leader who studies and practices leader behaviors that foster a workplace where people can thrive as they tackle organizational challenges. Choose behaviors that resonate with you, adapt them to your context, patiently practice them, resist the urge to abandon them when leading or following becomes difficult, and watch what happens to you, those you lead, and the organization at large.

I do not know where you are on your journey. Maybe you are just starting as a newly minted manager. Maybe you have led teams for a few years and have some experience. Or maybe you are a seasoned leader who has decades of experience leading all sorts of teams in all sorts of contexts. Regardless of

---

[1] Rumi was a 13th-century Persian poet and Islamic scholar.

© Ebenezer C. Ikonne 2021
E. C. Ikonne, *Becoming a Leader in Product Development,*
https://doi.org/10.1007/978-1-4842-7298-5_11

where you are on your journey, what I do know is that each one of us has room to improve as a leader, and so I hope that as you turned the pages, you discovered guidance that you have already put into practice. My desire for you is that you find the process of becoming a more effective leader fulfilling and rewarding. Effective leadership significantly benefits the people you lead, your organization, society, and you. It can be life-changing. Use your leadership position to do good. Let your legacy be that you made a positive difference in people's lives. Do not underestimate the positive impact you can have on the world around you.

I

Index

© Ebenezer C. Ikonne 2021

E. C. Ikonne, *Becoming a Leader in Product Development*,

https://doi.org/10.1007/978-1-4842-7298-5

GPSR Compliance
The European Union's (EU) General Product Safety Regulation (GPSR) is a set
of rules that requires consumer products to be safe and our obligations to
ensure this.

If you have any concerns about our products, you can contact us on

ProductSafety@springernature.com

In case Publisher is established outside the EU, the EU authorized
representative is:

Springer Nature Customer Service Center GmbH
Europaplatz 3
69115 Heidelberg, Germany